W9-BTM-306

SEWING MADE EASY

FOURTH REVISED EDITION

—◆—

SEWING MADE EASY

By Dorothy Sara

Revised by Irene Gora

—◆—

Doubleday & Company, Inc.
Garden City, New York

Acknowledgment with thanks
is made to Simplicity Patterns and McCall Patterns
for permission to use
the pattern information included in this book
and to Coats & Clark
for their assistance in supplying instructional material

Contents

Introduction   **1**

1   **Buying Your Pattern**   **3**

•Choosing a pattern according to your skills •Pattern sizing: understanding and determining your figure type •How to take your measurements •Pattern ease •Using design lines, fabric texture, and color to flatter the figure •How to analyze and use the information on the pattern envelope •What you should know about fabric: characteristics, care, and uses of fabrics made from natural and man-made fibers •Special fabric finishes •Understanding and using a pattern: identifying the pattern pieces; recognizing pattern symbols and markings

2   **Altering the Pattern to Suit the Figure**   **25**

•Techniques used to alter the paper pattern for a custom fit: lengthen bodice and skirt; shorten bodice and skirt; bust line dart adjustments; shoulder line adjustments; waistline adjustments; skirt adjustments; sleeve adjustments; neckline adjustments •Special problems of adjustments with pants

3   **Getting Ready to Sew**   **44**

•List of sewing supplies for cutting, sewing, measuring, marking, pressing •Use and care of your sewing machine: machine stitching; tension adjustments •Choos-

ing the correct needle and thread for machine and
hand sewing •Preparing the fabric for cutting: recognizing grain in fabric; straightening, shrinking, and pressing fabric •Following the cutting layout •Marking the
fabric •Stay stitching •Pressing techniques and aids

4   **How to Handle Special Fabrics**   67

•Cutting, sewing, and finishing techniques for: plaids;
striped fabrics; pile, nap, or one-way fabrics; border
prints; lace fabrics; sheer fabrics; wash-and-wear and
permanent-press fabrics; stretch fabrics; knit fabrics;
bonded fabrics; leather, suede, and leather-like fabrics; metallic and sequined fabrics; working with fur;
deep-pile and fur-like fabrics

5   **Interfacings, Underlinings, and Linings**   83

•Purpose and use of an interfacing, underlining, or lining in the garment •Interlining •Guide to choosing fabrics suitable for interfacings, underlinings, and linings

6   **Putting Your Dress Together**   90

•Factory method •Custom method •General procedure
for putting a dress together •Tips for a better fit •Tips
for a better fit in pants

7   **Simple Stitches, Seams, and Seam Finishes**   95

•How to tie a knot for hand sewing •Securing machine
stitching •Methods of basting: pin-basting; machine
basting; hand basting; even basting; uneven basting;
slip-basting or right-side basting; diagonal basting; basting an edge marked "Ease" •Basic sewing stitches:
running stitch; backstitch; combination stitch; overcasting; quick overcasting; overhanding •Types of seams:

plain seam; topstitched seam; lapped seam; flat felled seam; welt seam; strap seam; slot seam; French seam; mock French seam; machine-picoted seam; piped seam; corded seam; upholsterer's seam; taped seam •Ways of finishing seams: pinked seam; stitched and pinked seam; overcast seam; machine overcast seam; edge-stitched seam; rolled seam; bound seam; double-stitched seam; Hong Kong finish •Tricks with seams

8 Darts, Tucks, and Pleats   115

•Darts: how to make a smooth dart; finishing darts; decorative darts; where darts are used •Tucks: how to make a tuck; dart tucks; pin tucks; cross tucking; curved tucks; shell tucks; overhand tucks •Pleats: how to make a pleat; side pleats; box pleats; inverted pleats; fan or sunburst pleats; accordion pleats; kick pleats; double or set-in kick pleats

9 Neckline Finishes and Collars   131

•Bias-faced V neckline •Front slashed facing •Shaped neck facing •Shaped collar: to attach collar with bias binding; to attach collar with facing •Straight collar with slashed neckline •Convertible tailored collar •Detachable collar •Collar with edging

10 Sleeves and Sleeve Finishes   144

•Sleeve styles: cap sleeve; kimono sleeve; kimono sleeve with one-piece gusset; kimono sleeve with two-piece gusset; dolman or batwing sleeve; raglan sleeve; gathered sleeve; set-in sleeve •How to set in a sleeve •Finishing the sleeve: plain hem; turnback cuff cut with sleeve; turnback cuff cut separately; cuff applied with bias facing; tight sleeve opening faced with seam binding; band cuff

11   Facings and Hems   157

   •Types of facings: preparing the facing; stitching the
   facing; understitching; bias facings; facing for a
   corner; facing for a slashed opening; facing for a scalloped edge; facing for a saw-tooth edge •Bandings:
   applied band; extended band •Casings: elastic casing;
   applied casing •Waistline finishes: waistband; fitted
   facing; ribbon facing •Hems: marking a hem; finishing
   a hem; hem with seam binding; tailor's hem; catch-
   stitched hem; turned and stitched hem; faced hem;
   rolled hem; quick rolled hem; whipped hem; edgestitched hem; machine-stitched hem; damask hem;
   horsehair braid; hem in pleats

**12   Buttons, Buttonholes, Zipper Applications, and Other
       Fastenings**   181

   •Types of buttons •Making covered buttons •Making
   frogs •Sewing on buttons •Buttonholes: measuring for
   buttonholes; spacing •Bound buttonhole: patch method
   I; patch method II; two-piece bound buttonhole or
   piped buttonhole; corded bound buttonhole •Facing
   the bound buttonhole •Worked buttonhole •Tailored
   buttonhole •Machine buttonhole •Zipper applications:
   lapped application; center seam application; zipper
   in a slashed placket; hand application; invisible zipper
   application •Replacing a zipper •Care of zippers
   •Other fastenings: snaps; hammer-on snaps; nylon
   tape closure; hooks and eyes

13   Pockets   212

   •Patch pocket •Side seam pocket •Slot pocket; slot
   pocket for tailored garments •Welt pocket

14 Belts, Belt Loops, and Eyelets   222

•Belt without stiffening •Tie belt •Belt with interfacing
•Belt with backing •Belt loops •Eyelets

15 Gathering, Shirring, and Ruffles   227

•Gathers: gathering by hand; gathering by machine;
gathers to hold fullness •Shirring: using a stay under
shirring; shirring by machine; using elastic thread •Ruf-
fling: circular ruffle; double ruffle; ruffle with heading

16 Bias Binding and Cording Trim   234

•Bias binding: cutting; joining •Making a continuous
bias strip •How to stretch bias •Making a single bias
fold •Topstitching bias binding •Hand-hemming bias
binding •Double bias binding or French binding •To
bind scallops •To bind corners •Corded piping •Tub-
ing; corded tubing •Bias cord loops

17 Decorative Stitches and Techniques   242

•Satin stitch •Outline stitch •Cross-stitch •Catch stitch
or herringbone stitch •Chain stitch •Lazy daisy stitch
•French knots •Blanket stitch •Scallops •Feather stitch
•Seed stitch •Couching stitch •Bullion stitch •Saddle
stitch or cable stitch •Hemstitching or drawn work
•Fagoting •Smocking •Quilting •Appliqué •Machine
embroidery •Patchwork

18 Decorative Trimming Tricks   263

•Lace edging •Lace inserts or bands •Braid (passe-
menteries) •Arrowhead •Self-fringe •Knotted fringe
•Tassels •Embroidered edgings •Rickrack •Sequins
•Beading •Tailored bow

19 Tailoring 274

•How to choose your pattern and material •Tailoring supplies •Making a coat or jacket: cutting and fitting the pattern; interfacing and pad-stitching the front section; muslin reinforcement for the back unit; interfacing the undercollar; pad-stitching to shape the roll of the collar; stitching upper collar and facing; setting in the sleeves; hemming; finishing •Lining the coat or jacket; interlining a coat; underarm shields •Making the suit skirt or pants

20 Sewing for Children 293

•Choosing fabric •Pattern sizes •How to take measurements •Understanding your pattern •Sewing tips

21 Sewing for Men and Boys 301

•Pattern sizes •How to measure •Pattern adjustments: crotch depth; outseam; waist; width at hem; sleeve length on shirts; jackets •Suitable fabrics •Notions •Seams and seam finishes •Construction points for sewing the classic shirt: yoke; collar; collar on a band; collar and band in one; continuous lap placket; cuffs; stitching sleeve to shirt •Construction points for sewing men's pants: fly-front zipper opening; pockets; waistband; pressing pants

22 Accessories and Gifts to Make 322

•Bags •Belts •Hats •Shawls or stoles •Vests •Scarves •Straight collar; Peter Pan collar •Toys

23 Simple Mending and Altering Techniques 332

•How to avoid zipper trouble •Mending rips and tears; using mending tape •Reweaving problems •Darning •Reinforcing •Patching; elbow patches •Turning collar and cuffs •Repairing a trouser pocket •Making alterations in ready-to-wear clothing: buying for size; shortening a skirt; lengthening a skirt; taking in a skirt; letting out a skirt; pants

24 Taking Care of Your Clothes 340

•Pointers for daily care •Pressing •Mending, darning, and patching •Removing stains •Recycling clothes: what is worth making over?; selecting patterns; preparing material; piecing insufficient material; cutting; suggestions for make-overs

25 Sewing for the Home 347

•Fabric suggestions •Decorating the windows: window hardware; measuring for curtains and draperies •Construction techniques: preparing the fabric; seams; side hems; bottom hems; weights; top hems; plain casing with heading; pleated headings; scalloped headings •Shirred curtains •Café curtains •Ruffled curtains •Curtain with a ruffled valance •Tiebacks •Unlined draperies •Lined draperies: to join drapery to lining •Valances: gathered valance; pleated valance; swag •Fabric shades: Austrian shades; Roman shades •Bedspreads: throw spread; coverlet; dust ruffle •Slipcovers: suitable fabrics, color, and design; amount of material required; cutting fabric and pin-fitting to chair •Details for construction: seams; seam finishes; stitching the slipcover; joining the finished sections; skirts and skirt finishes; inserting the zipper; covering the cushions •To cover a couch; to sew the cover •Slipcovers for a new look to an old piece •Decorative pillows: knife-edge pillow; box-edge pillow •Bolsters: round, square, wedge-type

Index 407

SEWING MADE EASY

Introduction

Revised for the fourth time since 1950, SEWING MADE EASY has shown hundreds of thousands of women that the fine art of sewing is more valuable today than ever before. Ideas and techniques for things to make for herself, her home and family described in earlier editions, have been brought up to date in this new revised edition to include all the new fabrics, styles, and sewing ideas. Today's woman can now practice the ever-popular art of sewing with all the advantages of the materials and techniques of the present day.

To women in all walks of life, sewing is a source of lasting personal satisfaction. More than that, it is one of the most useful skills a woman can acquire. Few women can afford to buy the distinctive custom-made clothes they would like to wear, but the woman who sews can be well dressed for any occasion. She can make many of the basic and costly items in her wardrobe at a fraction of their retail cost and, with the money she has saved, buy the good-looking accessories which are so much a mark of the well-dressed woman.

Any woman can learn to sew if she has sufficient interest and is given the proper instruction. This book begins at the beginning with a discussion of the choice of pattern and material; then progresses, step by step, through all the procedures for making a dress—from the moment the idea is conceived through the necessary sewing equipment, down to sewing the last button in place. The improved sewing methods described and recommended in each section of the book insure a smooth, professional finish that clearly stamps the old "homemade" look as the result of careless workmanship. All of the material has been carefully arranged so that each procedure is explained at the time it is needed, and there is no necessity for turning to another part of the book for the information.

The art of sewing is more than the ability to cut and stitch. It is made up of many skills, each of which contributes its share to the perfect finished work. To help the home sewer achieve the smart, well-tailored look so much admired, there are chapters on such relevant subjects as the choosing of suitable accessories to frame her handiwork, ideas for remodeling, and tips on the care of clothes.

The many and varied aspects of sewing for the family and the home, as well as all other phases of sewing, have been given the same comprehensive treatment in separate chapters covering each subject.

The planning of this book was aimed to show the reader that learning to sew can be a pleasant experience and one in which each new project brings a growing sense of accomplishment. The instructions are clear and comprehensible. Hundreds of illustrations have been most carefully integrated with the text and have been used lavishly to insure the utmost clarity. In content and arrangement this book is useful to every woman who wants to learn to sew or to learn to sew better and more easily.

Acknowledgment of our deep appreciation is given to all those whose interest and industry helped make the book possible. Particular thanks are given to Loretta Stipe, Assistant Director of Product Development, The McCall Pattern Company; Janet Klaer, Educational Director, Coats & Clark; Linda Lombri, Editor of Educational Publications, Coats & Clark; and Janet DuBane, Editor of Educational Publications, Simplicity Pattern Company.

Ruth Schaub and Amelia Golfinos have contributed their considerable talents to the illustrative work in this present revision.

1 Buying Your Pattern

The success of any sewing venture depends in a large part upon the pattern you select. Unless you are an experienced sewer, you will want to buy the pattern before you buy the fabric. There are several reasons for this:

- The pattern indicates the amount of fabric you need to buy for the style you want, in your size, and according to the width of the fabric you choose.
- The pattern lists all the small things you need such as thread, buttons, and zipper, to give your garment the perfect finish.
- The pattern has a list of suggested fabrics that will look especially well for the style you have selected.

If you are making your first garment, look for a pattern that will be easy for you to make. These patterns are identified in the pattern catalogue by such designations as "Easy," "Quickie," "Jiffy," "Recommended for Beginners," "How-to-Sew." There are few pattern pieces and the construction techniques are simple, so that those with limited skills can cut and sew these garments successfully. As you become more proficient in your sewing ability, you can select patterns with intricate construction detail, which are found in the "Designer" patterns.

PATTERN SIZING

To buy the pattern size that is right for you, it is necessary that you understand the factors involved in pattern sizing. The first factor is *figure type,* and the second, the *correct* size within the figure type. Once you have determined the figure type that is suitable for you, buy patterns in this figure type only. This will eliminate unnecessary fitting problems and pattern adjustments and will result in a garment that fits properly and is satisfactory to you.

Patterns have been designed to suit seven different groups of figures with differences in height and contour: Misses, Miss Petite, Junior, Junior Petite, Young Junior/Teen, Women, Half-size.

Misses—Misses patterns are designed for a well-proportioned and well-developed figure, about 5'5" to 5'6" (1.65 to 1.68 m) without shoes.

Miss Petite—This size range is designed for the shorter Miss figure, about 5'2" to 5'4" (1.58 to 1.63 m) without shoes.

Junior—Junior patterns are designed for the well-proportioned, shorter-waisted figure, about 5'4" to 5'5" (1.63 to 1.65 m) without shoes.

Junior Petite—Junior Petite patterns are designed for a well-proportioned, petite figure, about 5'0" to 5'1" (1.53 to 1.55 m) without shoes.

Young Junior/Teen—This size range is designed for the developing pre-teen and teen figures, about 5'1" to 5'3" (1.55 to 1.60 m) without shoes.

Women—Women's patterns are designed for the larger, more mature figure, about 5'5" to 5'6" (1.65 to 1.68 m) without shoes.

Half-size—Half-size patterns are for a fully developed figure with a short back waist length, and waist and hip larger in proportion to bust than other figure types; about 5'2" to 5'3" (1.58 to 1.60 m) without shoes.

There are various sizes within each figure type. Pattern sizes are not comparable to ready-to-wear sizes, but figure types are. The type you wear in ready-to-wear will probably be the same for you in a pattern.

Do not estimate or guess at your pattern size; select your pattern size by your own measurements.

HOW TO TAKE YOUR MEASUREMENTS (Fig. 1)

Fig. 1

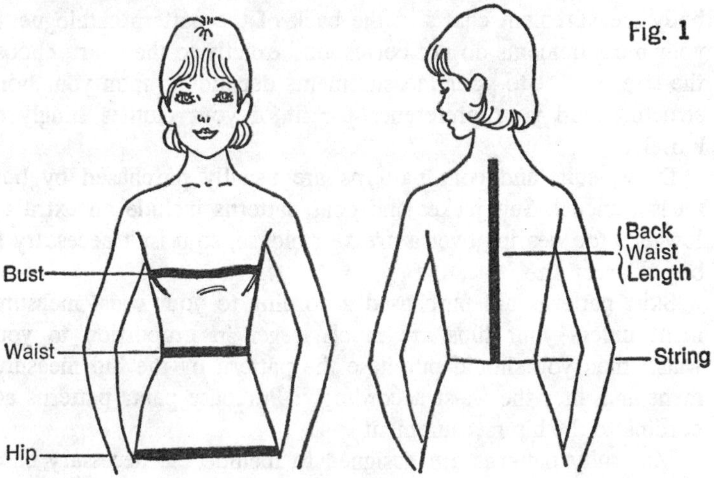

- If possible, have someone help you take your body measurements over whatever undergarments you will be wearing.
- Stand in your normal posture with your feet together.
- Place a string or ribbon around your waist.
- Height and back waist length are necessary to determine figure type.
- Bust, waist, and hip measurements are important to determine size.

To Measure Height—Stand against a wall in your stocking feet. Place a ruler on the top of the head; have position marked. Measure from floor to marked point.

To Measure Back Waist Length—From the prominent bone at the center back of your neck to your natural waistline, where you have placed the string or ribbon.

To Measure Bust—Place the tape over the fullest part of your bust, under the arms, and straight across your back.

To Measure Waist—Hold the tape snugly around your natural waistline.

To Measure Hips—At their fullest point, usually 7 inches (18 cm) below the waist for Miss Petite, Half-size, Junior Petite, and Young

Junior/Teen; 9 inches (23 cm) below the waist for Misses, Women, and Junior.

Compare your measurements to those listed on the standard body measurement charts in the back of the pattern catalogue. If your measurements do not correspond exactly to the chart, choose the size nearest to your measurements depending upon your bone structure and your preference for fit of your clothes snugly or loosely.

Dress, suit, and coat patterns are usually purchased by bust measurements. Suit jacket and coat patterns include an extra allowance for wearing over a dress or blouse, so it isn't necessary to buy a larger size.

Skirt patterns are purchased according to your waist measurement unless your hips are much larger in proportion to your waist; then you should purchase the pattern by the hip measurement and alter the waist accordingly. Purchase pants patterns according to the hip measurement.

Maternity patterns are designed to include the necessary ease; therefore buy your pattern according to the size you usually wear.

Never substitute an incorrect size when your size is not available—ask the store to order the pattern size you need.

Pattern Ease

Remember that the measurements given on the charts are body measurements, not actual measurements of the tissue pattern you will use. Ease in the garment is necessary to allow freedom of movement; the amount of ease will vary according to the type of pattern and the silhouette the pattern designer wishes to achieve. For example, patterns indicated "For Stretchable Knits Only" have less ease to allow the stretch or elasticity of the knit fabric to give a comfortable fit.

HOW TO SELECT THE MOST BECOMING DESIGN AND FABRIC FOR YOUR FIGURE

You will probably be faced with choosing a pattern from the counter catalogue, and one of the difficulties is choosing the design and fabric that will be suitable for your figure and adaptable to your sewing skills. Too often you are influenced by a pretty picture in the catalogue, and when you make the pattern up for yourself, you are disappointed. Sewing can and should be creative—learn to select your patterns and fabrics for the flattering effects you wish to achieve. With a little knowledge of the elements of design—line, color, and texture—you can create an illusion to make you look taller or shorter, larger or smaller, slimmer or more rounded.

The Design—Any line made by the construction or design details of the garment—the seam, dart, yoke, pleat, collar, or sleeve—can influence the way the eye will react.

Straight lines moving in a vertical direction usually create the effect of height, since it is necessary to carry the eye upward. (Fig. 2)

Horizontal lines will emphasize width. If you want to appear shorter, the eye must move in a horizontal direction rather than a vertical one. (Fig. 3)

A short diagonal line will create the impression of width, while a long diagonal line will draw the eye toward a longer, more lean look. (Fig. 4)

Curved lines are softer than straight vertical or horizontal lines, yet create a similar illusion in a more subtle way. (Fig. 5)

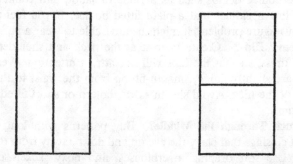

Fig. 2

Fig. 3

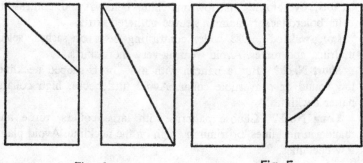

Fig. 4

Fig. 5

Are You Short?—You can add to your height by choosing patterns with vertical lines to give an illusion of height and a taller appearance. Long sleeves, V necklines, pleats, the one-piece dress with unbroken vertical seams, will aid in adding height to your appearance. Avoid wide belts and repeated horizontal lines, which will cut the figure.

Are You Tall?—Tall women are fortunate because they can wear the striking, unusual clothes shown in the fashion magazines. Wide belts, medium-long jackets, and horizontal stripes will help to keep the figure in balance and proportion. If you are extremely tall, choose horizontal lines, crosswise yokes, or wide colorful cummerbunds to make you appear shorter.

What Are Your Figure Faults?

Large Bust?   Wear clothes with soft draping, surplice closings, and simple necklines. Sleeves should end above or below the bust. Avoid low necklines, frilly collars, and dolman sleeves.

Small Bust?   Select patterns with a softly draped bodice, decorative bodice details such as a ruffle or jabot, and collars. Avoid very low necklines and a plain fitted bodice. If you feel this is a serious figure problem, it might be advisable to wear a padded bra.

Heavy Hips?   Create interest at the neck and shoulder line of your dress, so that the hips will not attract attention. Wear skirts that are slightly flared, smooth-fitting from the waist to the fullest part of the hips. Avoid sheath skirts, bolero or short fitted jackets, peplums.

Thick Through the Middle?   Buy patterns with long, slender front closings that carry the eye up and down, away from the waistline. Use soft draping, overblouses, and boxy jackets or vests. Avoid wide, fancy belts, or snugly fitted midriff styles.

Short-waisted?   Select patterns with low waistlines, hip-length jackets, overblouses, narrow matching belts. Avoid contrasting belts, bolero jackets, dolman sleeves, gathered skirts.

Long-waisted?   Use wide, contrasting belts or sashes, set-in midriffs, and tunics. Avoid wearing very short skirts.

Short Neck?   Buy a pattern with a V- or U-shaped neckline, low round or convertible collar. Avoid turtlenecks, high collars, halter necklines.

Long Neck?   Choose patterns with large collars, turtle and mandarin necklines, or trimming high on the neckline. Avoid plain, low necklines.

Broad Shoulders? Choose set-in, raglan, kimono, or dolman sleeves. Avoid empire line, square necklines, and yokes.

Narrow Shoulders? Choose set-in sleeves with a small amount of padding. Avoid asymmetric closings, dolman, kimono, or raglan sleeves.

The Fabric—The texture and color of a fabric will have an effect on how it appears on the figure. Shiny fabrics will reflect light, increasing the size of the figure, while a dull finish will have a minimizing effect.

Heavy, bulky textures will conceal the outline of the figure but appear to increase the size. Stiff fabrics will also conceal the silhouette but appear to increase the size of the figure. Clingy fabrics will reveal the figure.

Light- and medium-weight materials do not seem to affect the appearance of the figure.

Print designs should be chosen in proportion to the size of the wearer: small prints for the smaller figure, large prints for the larger figure. Remember, vertical designs in a print or stripe will add height, while horizontal designs add width and shorten the figure.

Use color to your advantage. Warm colors—the reds, yellows, and oranges—make the figure appear larger; cool colors—greens, blues, and violets—will make the figure appear smaller.

Light colors appear to increase the size of the figure, while dark colors have a slenderizing effect. To appear more slender, select solids in the medium to dark color values.

Bright colors tend to make the figure look larger; dull colors will give the figure a smaller appearance. Select bright colors with shiny or chunky textures to add roundness to the slim figure.

A monochromatic or one-color fashion scheme will give the illusion of height; a dress or separates in two colors will make the figure appear shorter. Contrasting separates can be worn well by the tall figure.

THE PATTERN ENVELOPE

Before you purchase fabric, take time out to study the pattern envelope—there is a wealth of information to be absorbed.

The Envelope Front—The illustrations tell a fashion story. They indicate the characteristics of the fabrics, such as the weight and texture, and designs that are suitable for the style of the garment.

Fig. 6. MISSES' DRESS OR TOP AND PANTS

BODY MEASUREMENTS

Size	8	10	12	14	16	18	20	
Bust	31½	32½	34	36	38	40	42	Ins.
Waist	24	25	26½	28	30	32	34	"
Hip	33½	34½	36	38	40	42	44	"
Back waist length	15¾	16	16¼	16½	16¾	17	17¼	"

FABRIC REQUIRED			MISSES' SIZES					
	8	10	12	14	16	18	20	

VIEW A – Dress

	8	10	12	14	16	18	20	
44/45" With Nap	4½	4⅝	4⅝	4⅝	4¾	4⅞	5	Yds.
44/45" Without Nap	4⅜	4⅜	4⅜	4½	4½	4⅝	4¾	"
58/60" With Nap	3½	3½	3⅝	3⅝	3¾	3¾	3¾	"

VIEW B – Dress

	8	10	12	14	16	18	20	
44/45" With Nap	4¾	4¾	4¾	5¼	5½	6⅜	6½	Yds.
44/45" Without Nap	4¾	4¾	4¾	5⅛	5⅜	5½	5½	"
58/60" With Nap	4⅜	4½	4½	4⅝	4⅝	4⅝	4¾	"
Width at lower edge	76½	78	80	82½	85	87½	90	Ins.

VIEW C – Top

	8	10	12	14	16	18	20	
44/45" With Nap	3⅛	3⅛	3⅛	3⅛	3¼	3¼	3¼	Yds.
44/45" Without Nap	3⅛	3⅛	3⅛	3⅛	3¼	3¼	3¼	"
58/60" With Nap	2½	2½	2⅝	2⅝	2⅝	2⅞	2⅞	"

VIEW C – Pants

	8	10	12	14	16	18	20	
44/45" With Nap	2¾	2¾	2¾	2¾	2¾	2¾	2¾	"
44/45" Without Nap	2¾	2¾	2¾	2¾	2¾	2¾	2¾	"
58/60" With Nap	1⅜	1⅜	1⅜	1⅜	1½	2⅜	2⅜	"
Width, each pants leg	21½	22	22½	23⅛	23¾	24⅜	24⅞	Ins.

Use with nap yardages and layouts for fabrics with one-way design.

Note: Additional fabric may be needed to match stripes, plaids, one way designs.

Adaptation of a McCall's fabric chart courtesy of the McCall Pattern Company.

BODY MEASUREMENTS							
....	8	10	12	14	16	18	20
....	80	83	87	92	97	102	107 cm
....	61	64	67	71	76	81	87 cm
....	85	88	92	97	102	107	112 cm
....	40	40.5	41.5	42	42.5	43	44 cm

FABRIC REQUIRED		MISSES' SIZES					
	8	10	12	14	16	18	20
VIEW A – Dress							
115cm	4.20	4.20	4.20	4.30	4.40	4.40	4.50 m
115cm	4.00	4.00	4.00	4.10	4.20	4.20	4.30 m
150cm	3.20	3.20	3.30	3.30	3.40	3.40	3.40 m
VIEW B – Dress							
115cm	4.30	4.40	4.40	4.80	5.00	5.80	5.90 m
115cm	4.30	4.30	4.40	4.70	4.90	5.00	5.00 m
150cm	4.00	4.10	4.10	4.20	4.20	4.30	4.30 m
....	194	198	203	210	216	222	229 cm
VIEW C – Top							
115cm	2.80	2.80	2.80	2.90	2.90	3.00	3.00 m
115cm	2.80	2.80	2.80	2.90	2.90	3.00	3.00 m
150cm	2.30	2.30	2.40	2.40	2.40	2.60	2.60 m
VIEW C – Pants							
115cm	2.50	2.50	2.50	2.50	2.50	2.50	2.50 m
115cm	2.50	2.50	2.50	2.50	2.50	2.50	2.50 m
150cm	1.30	1.30	1.30	1.30	1.40	2.20	2.20 m
....	55	56	57	59	60	62	63 cm

SUGGESTED FABRICS: Dress or Top and Pants – Soft Fabrics such as Lightweight Cotton, Cotton Blends, Challis, Surah, Wool or Synthetic Crepe, Wool or Synthetic Jersey, Crepe Back Satin.

If the views include plaid or striped fabrics, the pattern is suitable for that type of fabric; if it is not illustrated in a plaid or stripe, the pattern may not be suitable for fabrics that require matching.

Study the construction lines of the garment and decide if the design features will be flattering to the effect you wish to achieve for your figure.

Decide on the particular view you will make. If you are a novice at sewing, make the garment as illustrated; with experience you will learn how to combine various features of several views.

The Envelope Back—In addition to the chart of standard body measurements and corresponding pattern sizes, you will find:

- The yardage chart, which indicates the amount of fabric needed according to the view, pattern size, and fabric width.
- Back views, which are line drawings to indicate the construction lines and design details not easily recognized on the fashion sketches.
- A description of the garment, which will give you additional information about the construction details.
- A list of all the notions such as thread, zipper, buttons, in the size and quantity needed. Buy them when you buy the fabric so that the colors will match perfectly and you will have everything at hand when you are ready to sew.
- Suggested fabrics to help you with the selection of a fabric suitable for each view. Although you are not restricted to these fabrics, you should choose a fabric of similar "hand"—that is, weight, body, and drapability—to achieve the overall effect the designer intended.

The chart in Fig. 6 is taken from the back of a pattern envelope.

Most patterns have more than one view and can be made in more than one way, and the amount of fabric will vary according to the style you have selected. (Fig. 7a, b)

Fabrics come in different widths, so the yardage is given in the widths of the suggested fabrics for each view.

Home sewers also come in different sizes! Be sure to check your pattern size, in the view you intend to make, and the width of the fabric you plan to use. You must know these things in order to purchase the correct amount of fabric.

Fig. 7

Look at the chart once more. To be sure that you understand how to find the amount of fabric required for a dress, let us suppose you are making View A in a 44″/45″ (115 cm) fabric without nap; and you wear size 14:

1. Find the heading "View A—Dress."
2. Look down the list under "Fabric Required" until you see 44″/45″ (115 cm) fabric.
3. Follow along this line to the right until you find the yardage listed under size 14. For this pattern it is 4½ yards (4.10 cm). (Fig. 6)

The amount of fabric required for any garment differs:

- with the style,
- with the width of the fabric,
- with the size.

Buy exactly the yardage indicated, except when your fabric is plaid or striped or has a pile or one-way design, when the fabric is not preshrunk, and for extra seam allowance if the fabric is likely to ravel easily.

For a plaid or striped fabric you will need ⅛, ¼, or ½ yard (0.15, 0.25, or 0.5 m) of extra fabric, depending upon the size of the plaid or stripe.

Pile fabrics such as corduroy or velvet and fabrics with a one-way design will also require additional yardage, unless the pattern includes "With Nap" yardage on the chart.

The reason for the extra yardage is that there are cutting problems involved in the use of these fabrics. Plaids and stripes must be matched at all seam joinings. Fabrics with a pile, nap, or one-way design must be cut with the top of each pattern piece laid in the same direction, as shown in Fig. 8. If the pattern pieces are

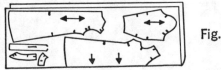

Fig. 8

laid with the tops in different directions, the garment will appear to have been cut from two different shades of the same fabric.

Unless you are liberally endowed with patience and are not easily discouraged, it would be better not to choose a stripe, plaid, one-way design, or pile fabric for your first attempt at sewing. (Fig. 9)

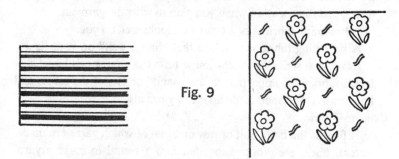

Fig. 9

Why try to make sewing seem like work? Do it the easy way!

From the viewpoint of fabric design, a small allover print is the easiest fabric for a beginner to cut and sew for a first garment. There is no need to worry about matching the design, and any little imperfections in your work will be hidden in the design itself. The allover print will also tend to conceal the simple lines of the dress and make it appear much trickier than it actually is.

Either of the two types of fabric designs shown in Fig. 10 is easy to use and will produce satisfactory results.

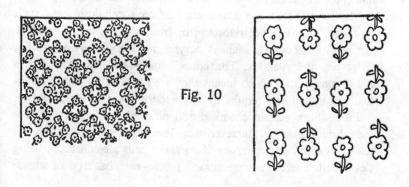

Fig. 10

WHAT YOU SHOULD KNOW ABOUT FABRIC

Now that you understand the information on your pattern envelope and why it is wise to choose fabric that will be easy to work with, you are ready to purchase your fabric. The important thing to remember is that you must choose the fabric. Don't let the fabric choose you! Keep in mind your pattern, your coloring, your figure, and the occasion when you plan to wear the garment.

A becoming fabric is of a color that looks well on you.

A becoming fabric is also one that "hangs well" on your figure.

Develop a sense of touch—know how the characteristics of different fabrics are important to the "hand" or feel of the fabric and how it will react when made up into a garment.

Fiber to Fabric

A fiber is the basic unit of raw material of which yarns are made. Several fibers are grouped together into a strand to make a yarn. Fabric is constructed from yarns through various processes:

Weaving, the interlacing of warp and weft yarns at right angles.

Knitting, an arrangement of interlocking loops of yarn.

Felting, the process of matting fibers together by heat, steam, and pressure to form a fabric.

Bonding, the process of pressing fibers into webs held together by heat and chemical adhesives. Non-woven fabrics are manufactured by this method.

A fiber is classified as natural or man-made.

Natural Fibers are derived from nature and are divided into two categories: vegetable (cellulosic), such as cotton and linen; or animal (protein), such as wool, silk, or specialty hair fibers.

Man-made Fibers are manufactured from a cellulosic base, such as rayon, acetate, and triacetate; or from a noncellulosic base or synthetic compounds, such as acrylic, modacrylic, nylon, olefin, polyester, and spandex. The noncellulosic-base man-made fibers are thermoplastic, which means they are softened by heat. Fabrics made of these fibers require low to moderate ironing temperatures.

Fibers have certain chemical and physical properties that give the fabric distinctive characteristics. These characteristics affect the use and care of a fabric. New fibers and blends are constantly being developed. There is no one miracle fabric—each has its own advantages and disadvantages—but understanding the major properties may help you in your fabric selection.

Natural Fibers

Cotton

Characteristics Strong, even when wet; durable; cool; absorbent; can be preshrunk; dyes easily in brilliant colors; wrinkles easily; susceptible to mildew unless specially treated.

Care Can withstand frequent hard laundering; easily ironed at high temperatures.

Uses Light- and medium-weight apparel; can be made into a variety of fabrics from sheers to heavy-duty; household textiles.

Linen

Characteristics Very strong; crisp; durable; absorbent; does not shed lint; wrinkles easily; susceptible to mildew unless specially treated.

Care Beauty and luster endure through frequent hard launderings; iron at high temperatures for smooth appearance; avoid pressing in sharp creases.

Uses Available in various weights and textures; blouses; dresses; summer suiting; table linens; household fabrics.

Silk

Characteristics Natural luster and strength; wrinkle-resistant; good absorbency; damaged by sunlight and perspiration; resistant to moths and mildew.

Care Should be dry-cleaned; washable silks should be washed by hand with a mild soap.

Uses Light- and medium-weight apparel; accessory items; summer suits.

Wool

Characteristics Warm, absorbent, naturally wrinkle- and mildew-resistant; springs back into shape after wearing; subject to moth damage.

Care Dry-clean most items; never wash wools in hot water; heat and agitation will shrink and felt wool.

Uses Outerwear; light-, medium-, and heavyweight apparel.

Man-made Fibers

Rayon

Characteristics Absorbent; inexpensive; good draping qualities; wrinkles easily; dyes easily in brilliant colors.

Care   Most fabrics should be dry-cleaned; if laundering is recommended, launder carefully to prevent shrinkage or stretching.

Uses   Can be made to imitate almost any fabric; used in blends with cotton, polyester, nylon, and wool; men's- and women's-wear fabrics; linings; home fashions.

Acetate

Characteristics   Soft; absorbent; silk-like; good draping qualities; moth- and mildew-resistant; subject to fume-fading; inexpensive; wrinkle-resistant.

Care   Very sensitive to heat, iron at low temperature; should be dry-cleaned; dissolves in acetone (nail polish remover).

Uses   Available in a range of fabrics; light- and medium-weight apparel; drapery and upholstery fabrics; ribbons; linings.

Triacetate

Characteristics   Excellent colorfastness to washing and sunlight; quick-drying; can be permanently pleated; comfortable to wear.

Care   Easily washable; if ironing is necessary, use steam iron or warm iron with press cloth.

Uses   Available in many fabrics, including knits; often used in blends with other fibers; apparel; pleated garments; fleece robes; drapery and upholstery fabrics.

Acrylic

Characteristics   Wool-like feel and warmth; lightweight bulk; wrinkle- and shrink-resistant; resistant to sunlight, moths, and mildew.

Care   Usually washable; remove oily stains before washing; static electricity may be reduced with the use of a fabric softener.

Uses   Pile fabrics; bulky knits; often used in blends with wool, rayon, and cotton; carpets; blankets.

Modacrylic

Characteristics   Similar to acrylic; resistant to chemicals, wrinkling; soft; resembles fur in appearance and warmth.

Care   Usually washable; static electricity may be reduced with the use of a fabric softener.

Uses   Fake-fur coats; pile lining for coats; often used in blends with other fibers; scatter rugs; carpets; wigs.

Nylon

Characteristics   Exceptional strength; high elasticity; retains permanent shape; quick to dry; extremely abrasion-resistant; not very absorbent; woven fabrics are often hot and uncomfortable to wear.

Care Washes easily but tends to attract dirt; use nylon whitener to maintain whiteness; remove oily stains before washing; static electricity may be reduced with the use of a fabric softener; iron, if necessary, at low temperature.

Uses Lingerie; hosiery; swimwear; ski pants and jackets; carpets; sheer curtains.

Olefin
Characteristics Lightweight; abrasion-resistant; highly stain-resistant.

Care Easily cleaned; blot stains with absorbent tissue.

Uses Pile fabrics; knitwear; indoor-outdoor carpeting; slip-covers; upholstery.

Polyester
Characteristics High strength and abrasion resistance for durability; able to resist wrinkling and spring back into shape; does not shrink or stretch out of shape; comfortable to wear because it absorbs body moisture; quick-drying.

Care Usually machine-washable; remove oily stains before washing; static electricity may be reduced with the use of a fabric softener; use commercial color removers to brighten grayed or yellowed polyesters.

Uses Wide range of knitted and woven fabrics; often blended with cotton, rayon, or linen to give strength to permament-press articles; wash-and-wear apparel; curtains; fiberfill.

Spandex
Characteristics Excellent stretch and recovery; resistant to damage from body oils and perspiration.

Care Wash by hand; drip-dry; do not use chlorine bleach.

Uses Swimwear; foundation garments; lingerie; ski pants.

Metallic
Characteristics Metallic fibers are usually aluminum filaments "sandwiched" between several layers of polyester or plastic materials.

Care Fibers protected with a covering of polyester or plastic will not tarnish and can be dry-cleaned or laundered. Use a low heat setting and press cloth to press.

Uses Provide a variety of decorative yarns in gold, silver, and bright glittery colors.

SPECIAL FABRIC FINISHES

Most fabrics have one or more chemical finishes applied during the final processing. Finishes contribute to the final character and appearance of the fabric; they can add to the comfort, ease of care, or aesthetic look. Some of the following finishes may be important for you to consider in your choice of fabric.

Anti-static Finish Prevents or reduces electrical charges that cause fabrics such as nylon and polyester to cling to the wearer or to other garments. These finishes are usually not permanent but can be restored by using a fabric softener.

Flame-resistant Finish Prevents the fabric from supporting a flame; it does not make the fabric fireproof. This finish may need to be renewed after dry cleaning or laundering.

Mercerization Primarily applied to cotton fabrics to add strength, luster, and a greater affinity for dyes.

Shrink-resistant Finish Processing the fabric by a mechanical or chemical treatment to control shrinkage.

Stain- and Spot-resistant Finish Protects the fabric and makes it easier to lift off or sponge away spills of food, water, and other substances.

Water-repellent Finish Makes a fabric shed water in normal wear, but does not make the fabric waterproof.

Waterproofing The application of chemicals to fill the pores of the fabric so that water can not pass through.

Wrinkle-resistant (Wash-and-wear; Durable-press; Permanent-press) Finish The application of resin to the fabric to improve resistance to wrinkling in wearing and laundering. The shape retention and wrinkle recovery of the fabric are improved.

Learn to read the label on the end of the bolt of fabric. It will give you the necessary information about fiber content, shrinkage, and colorfastness.

The technological advances made in the textile industry in the past years have led to the necessity of federal regulations being imposed on the manufacturers of ready-to-wear garments and fabrics sold by the yard. Permanent care labels must be supplied with fabrics sold for the purpose of making apparel, unless the fabrics are remnants. These labels must inform you of the necessary procedures to care for the particular fabric.

Ask for the permanent care fabric label when you purchase your fabric, and sew it to an inside seam so that you will have a handy reference on how to care for the garment.

UNDERSTANDING AND USING A PATTERN

Here you are with a pattern in your hand and a piece of fabric on the table. And you're trying to decide what you should do next in order to put the two together to make a dress!

Look at the pictures on the front of the pattern envelope. There are two or more of them, aren't there? You have already decided which one to use, because you bought exactly the amount of fabric needed for it, as listed on the yardage chart on the back of the pattern envelope.

Now take your pattern pieces and the printed instruction sheet from the envelope. The printed instruction sheet with your pattern is your guide for cutting and sewing. The purpose of this instruction sheet is to help you, step by step, in the making of your garment.

Each pattern piece is identified by name—for example, back, front, sleeve, collar—and a number or letter. To know which pattern pieces you need for the style you have selected, look for the diagram of the pattern pieces on the cut and sew guide under the heading SELECT PATTERN PIECES. (Fig. 11)

The pieces you will need will be indicated according to the style you have chosen, like this:

View A, B, C—Use pattern pieces 1 through 7
View D—Use pattern pieces 1 through 6, 8
View E—Use pattern pieces 1 through 4, 7, 9, 10, 11

Separate all the pattern pieces. Keep out the pieces you will need for the style you are making; fold the pattern pieces you will not need and put them back into the pattern envelope. This will eliminate confusion and you will always be sure that you have the right pieces.

Small pieces such as facings, collars, and belts are usually printed on one large sheet of tissue. Cut out only the pieces you

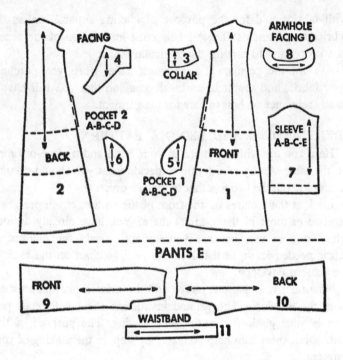

FACING

4

3
COLLAR

ARMHOLE
FACING D

8

POCKET 2
A-B-C-D

BACK

2

6

5

POCKET 1
A-B-C-D

FRONT

1

SLEEVE
A-B-C-E

7

PANTS E

FRONT

9

BACK

10

WAISTBAND

11

Fig. 11

will need, leaving extra tissue beyond the cutting line on each one.

The "Cutting Layouts" are also found on the instruction sheet. Circle or mark with a colored pencil the diagram showing the layout plan for the style you have chosen, in your pattern size and fabric width. (Fig. 12)

5   6   FOLD

4 3

7   1   2

SELVAGES

Fig. 12

Pattern pieces are given for only half the section when both sides are exactly alike. The pattern piece must be placed on the fold of the fabric in the layout, as indicated on the pattern piece. Do *not* cut through the fold of the fabric.

If the pattern is an asymmetric design, you are given two separate pieces, one for the right side and one for the left side. The pieces could look something like those in Fig. 13.

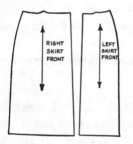

Fig. 13

Analyze each of the pattern pieces—you will see various markings printed on the tissue. This is the language of patterns, and each marking has a definite meaning that is important to you when you cut out and sew your garment. You will find the meaning explained in detail on each piece, but because you may have some questions about these markings, we can review them together.

Small circle, large circle, square, triangle (Fig. 14) are symbols used to match seams and other construction details.

Fig. 14

Notches (Fig. 15) are V-shaped markings on the cutting line that indicate where pattern pieces are to be joined together. Cut notches outward, never into the seam allowance. When there is a group of two or more notches, cut them as a single unit.

Fig. 15

Cutting Line (Fig. 16) is printed around each pattern piece to show you exactly where to cut. It is not necessary to trim the excess tissue beyond the cutting lines (margin) before cutting, just overlap the margin when you lay the pattern pieces on the fabric, and cut the margins away as you cut the garment.

━━━━━━━━━━━━━━━━━━━━━━━━━━━━━▶ Fig. 16

Seam Line (Fig. 17) The standard seam allowance of all pattern companies is ⅝ inch (1.5 cm), which is indicated by a broken line inside the cutting line. Some pattern companies will indicate the direction of stitching with small arrows on the seam line. If for purposes of a design feature the seam allowance is less than ⅝ inch (1.5 cm), this will be clearly marked on the pattern piece.

━━━━━━━━━━━   ━━━━━━━━━ Fig. 17

Alteration Lines (Fig. 18) indicate where to lengthen or shorten the pattern.

═══════════════════════════ Fig. 18

Grain Line (Fig. 19) indicates how to place the pattern on the fabric parallel to the lengthwise or crosswise threads of the fabric.

◀━━━━━━━━━━━━━━━━━━━━━━━━━▶ Fig. 19

Fold Line (Fig. 20) Used to indicate that the pattern piece is to be placed on the fold of the fabric, such as the center front or center back.

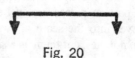

Fig. 20

2 Altering the Pattern to Suit the Figure

The purpose of alterations is to make the garment fit well. Almost every person needs to make some small change, since no two of us have exactly the same body contours. But it stands to reason that a pattern that requires a great many changes is not the right size pattern. You can avoid unnecessary alterations by taking your measurements carefully and by buying your pattern in the size and figure type that most nearly matches them.

If your measurements fall between two sizes, take the pattern in a smaller size if you have a small body frame, in the larger size if your bone structure is large. Remember that the standard set of measurements you find on the pattern envelope has been designed to fit the average figure. You can expect some slight variations—at the waistline, the hipline, or in some cases at the shoulder line—but if the pattern is the right size, no major alterations should be necessary. However, it could be advantageous to make a trial garment in muslin or an inexpensive fabric using a basic pattern. This is a good method to check the alterations required for an individual fit, particularly if you have a figure problem.

There are two kinds of pattern adjustments: pattern alterations, which are made in the tissue pattern before the garment is cut out, and fitting alterations, which are made during the construction of the garment.

TECHNIQUES USED TO ALTER THE PAPER PATTERN FOR A CUSTOM FIT

It seems unnecessary to point out that all pattern alterations should be made carefully. Yet we have seen women who seem to run wild as soon as they pick up a pair of scissors, slashing the pattern here, adding or whacking off there. The result was exactly what you would expect—a badly fitting, unattractive garment that clearly reflected the careless and haphazard way in which it had been handled.

Whenever you add width to a pattern, remember that ¼ inch (6 mm) added to each of the four sides—front and back—means an increase of 1 inch (2.5 cm) in the width of the garment.

Terms Used in Pattern Alterations—Pattern pieces can be altered in any of the following ways:

By Spreading   Slash or cut the pattern, and then spread it until it fits your measurements. The spread is retained by pinning or taping the two slashed edges to another piece of paper, which holds them apart. A slash can be used to make a pattern longer or wider. (Fig. 21)

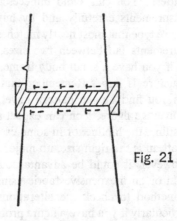

Fig. 21

By Making a Tuck   Fold a piece of pattern horizontally and then crease it again so it can be pinned flat. This is used to make a pattern piece shorter. (Fig. 22)

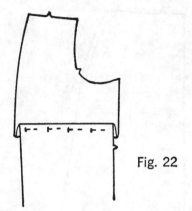

Fig. 22

By Making a Pleat   Make a lengthwise fold in the same way as a tuck. This is used to make a pattern piece narrower. (Fig. 23)

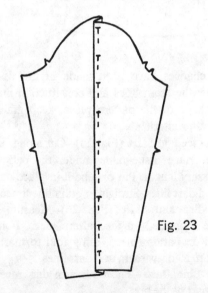

Fig. 23

By Tapering   Take away fullness from the side of a garment by increasing the seam allowance. The new seam line is begun at the depth needed, and slanted outward gradually, until the new line joins the original seam line. (Fig. 24)

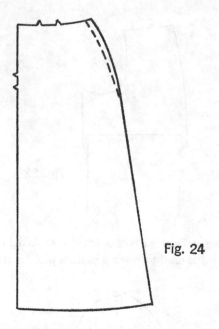

Fig. 24

After the changes have been made in the tissue pattern, be sure to redraw the seam lines and construction markings to keep the original shape of the pattern piece; keep grain lines straight, or straighten after altering.

To Lengthen Bodice and Skirt (Fig. 25)–Cut along line indicated on pattern piece. Place tissue paper under the pattern. Spread pattern the necessary length. Pin or tape it in place on the paper. Redraw seam and dart lines. Straighten grain line if necessary.

To Shorten Bodice and Skirt (Fig. 26)–Measure and mark the amount to be shortened on the pattern piece. Fold pattern along line indicated on pattern piece, bring fold to marked line, pin or tape in position. Redraw seam and dart lines.

To Adjust Bust Line Darts–The underarm dart must point directly to the fullest part of the bust.

High Bust If your bust is higher than average, the dart will be low and will need to be raised. For an adjustment of less than 1 inch (2.5 cm), measure and mark up from the point of the dart the amount to be raised. Redraw stitching lines of the underarm

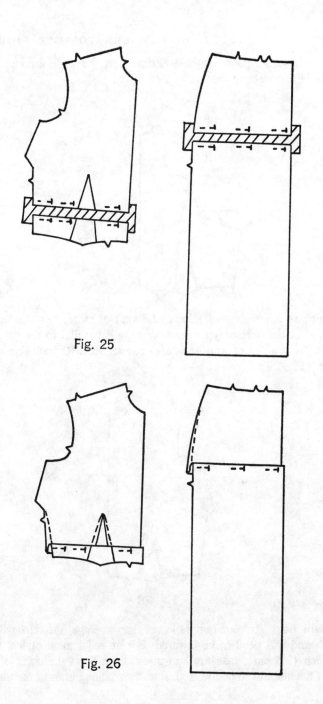

Fig. 25

Fig. 26

dart. Raise the point of the waistline dart the same amount you raised the underarm dart. (Fig. 27)

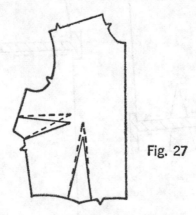

Fig. 27

For an adjustment of 1 inch (2.5 cm) or more, raise the entire side dart the necessary amount, keeping it parallel to the original dart. Raise point of waistline dart same amount. Redraw side seam line. (Fig. 28)

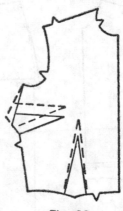

Fig. 28

Low Bust If your bust is lower than average, the dart will be high and will need to be lowered. For an adjustment of less than 1 inch (2.5 cm), measure and mark down from the point of the dart the amount to be lowered. Redraw stitching lines of the underarm dart. Lower the point of the waistline dart the same amount as you lowered the underarm dart. (Fig. 29)

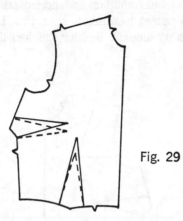

Fig. 29

For an adjustment of 1 inch (2.5 cm) or more, lower the entire side dart the necessary amount, keeping it parallel to the original dart. Lower point of waistline dart same amount. Redraw side seam line. (Fig. 30)

Fig. 30

To Adjust Shoulder Line—Make the same adjustment on bodice front and bodice back.

Narrow Shoulders (Fig. 31) On pattern piece, draw a line down from the middle of the shoulder seam to a point even with the armhole notch and another line horizontal to the armhole seam line. Slash pattern to armhole seam line. Lap cut edges of pattern the necessary amount. Redraw shoulder line from neck to armhole edge.

Fig. 31

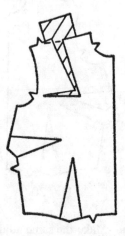

Fig. 32

Broad Shoulders (Fig. 32)   On pattern piece, draw a line down from the middle of the shoulder seam to a point even with the armhole notch and another line horizontal to the armhole seam line. Slash pattern to armhole seam line. Spread pattern the required amount over paper. Pin or tape in place. Redraw shoulder line from neck to armhole edge.

Sloping Shoulders (Fig. 33)   Measure and mark amount to be decreased at the armhole edge. Redraw shoulder line from neck to armhole edge. Lower the underarm seam the same amount and redraw armhole.

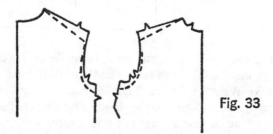

Fig. 33

Square Shoulders (Fig. 34)   Place paper under pattern piece and pin or tape it in position. On armhole edge of shoulder line, mark amount to be raised and draw a new shoulder line to neck edge. Adjust underarm the corresponding amount.

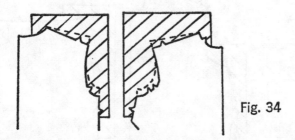

Fig. 34

Round Shoulders (Fig. 35)   Make adjustment in bodice back only. Slash into pattern from the center back to the armhole seam at the part where your shoulders are the heaviest. Spread the slash the required amount; pin or tape to paper. Redraw center back line from slash to neckline. Use pattern as a guide to restore neckline and shoulder seam to the original lines.

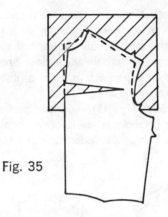

Fig. 35

To Adjust Waistline—Adjustments must be made in the front and back of garment and in both bodice and skirt of a dress.

To Make Waistline Larger (Fig. 36, bodice, skirt) You can add up to 2 inches (5 cm) to the waistline by dividing the amount needed by four and increasing each side seam this amount. Place paper under pattern piece (or use margin on pattern). Increase waistline of bodice and skirt one-quarter the amount needed. Redraw side seam lines on bodice and skirt.

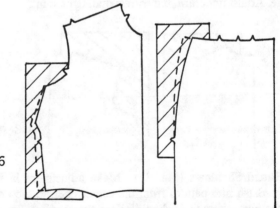

Fig. 36

NOTE: If more than 2 inches (5 cm) is needed in the waistline, you can decrease the width of the waist darts by up to ¼ inch (6 mm) each; taper to the point of the dart.

To Make Waistline Smaller (Fig. 37, bodice, skirt)   You can decrease up to 2 inches (5 cm) at the waistline by dividing the amount to be decreased by four and altering each side seam by this amount. Redraw side seam lines on bodice and skirt.

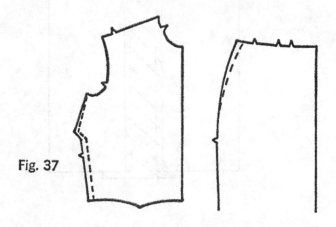

Fig. 37

NOTE: Additional fullness can be removed from the waistline by increasing the width of the waist darts up to ¼ inch (6 mm) each; taper to the point of the dart.

To Adjust the Skirt—Maintain an ease allowance of at least 2½ inches (6.5 cm) in the hip measurement of the skirt.

For Large Hips (Fig. 38)   Add one-quarter the amount needed to each side seam allowance at hipline, 7 to 9 inches (18 to 23 cm) below waistline. Place paper under pattern piece (or use margin on pattern). Draw new line extending from hipline to lower edge. Taper from hipline to waistline.

For Small Hips (Fig. 39)   Decrease one-quarter the amount from each side seam at hipline, 7 to 9 inches (18 to 23 cm) below waistline. Draw new line extending from hipline to lower edge. Taper from hipline to waistline.

To Adjust the Sleeve

For a Large Arm (Fig. 40)   Draw a straight line from top of sleeve cap to wrist; slash pattern. Place paper under the pattern piece and spread the necessary amount; pin or tape in place. Increase front and back bodice sections one-half the amount added to the sleeve; taper to nothing at waist.

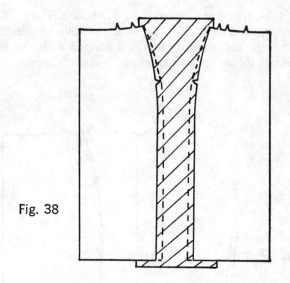

Fig. 38

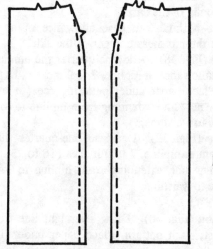

Fig. 39

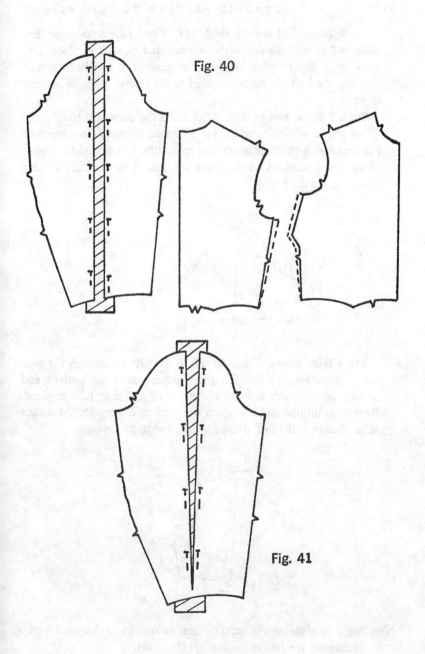

Fig. 40

Fig. 41

For a Large Upper Arm (Fig. 41)   Place paper under pattern piece and spread the necessary amount; pin or tape in place. Redraw grain line on pattern piece. Increase front and back bodice sections one-half the amount added to the sleeve; taper to nothing at waist.

For a Narrow Sleeve (Fig. 42)   Slash the pattern through center of sleeve to dot; overlap slashed edges the necessary amount. Pin or tape in place. Redraw the grain line and straighten sleeve along lower edge. Make the same adjustment to the cuff, if there is one, and to the facing.

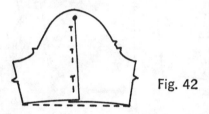

Fig. 42

For a Wide Sleeve (Fig. 43)   Slash the pattern through the center of the sleeve to the dot. Place paper under the pattern and spread the necessary amount at bottom edge. Pin or tape in place. Redraw grain line and straighten sleeve along lower edge. Make the same change to the cuff, if there is one, and to the facing.

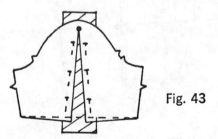

Fig. 43

Neckline Adjustments—A neckline can be raised or lowered easily by redrawing the line as necessary. (Fig. 44)

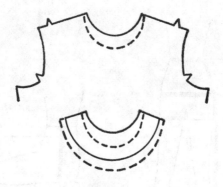

Fig. 44

Any adjustments in the shape of the neckline must include the same change to the facing and collar, if there is one.

SPECIAL PROBLEMS OF ADJUSTMENTS WITH PANTS

Be particular about purchasing the correct pattern size for pants, since they should fit very well and are tricky to adjust. Take all your measurements carefully and adjust the pattern before cutting into the fabric.

May we suggest that you make the necessary adjustments on the paper pattern and cut the pants in muslin or an inexpensive fabric to check the fit.

Measurements Needed (Fig. 45)

Waist Measure snugly at your natural waistline. (a)

Hip measurement 7 inches (18 cm) below waist for Miss Petite, Half-size, Junior Petite, and Young Junior/Teen; 9 inches (23 cm) below waist for Misses, Women, and Junior; maintain 2 inches (5 cm) for ease. (b)

Length Measure from waistline to ankle (or desired length) along side of leg. (c)

Thigh Measure at fullest part; maintain 2 inches (5 cm) for ease. (d)

Crotch depth Measure from your waist to the chair while seated; add ¾ inch (2 cm) for ease. (e)

Over instep and around heel To determine necessary width at lower edge. (f)

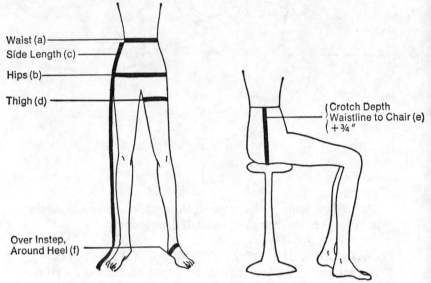

Waist (a)
Side Length (c)
Hips (b)
Thigh (d)
Over Instep, Around Heel (f)

Crotch Depth
Waistline to Chair (e)
+ ¾"

Fig. 45

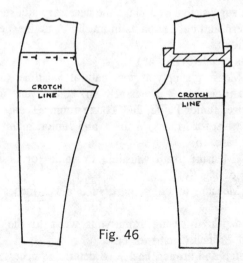

CROTCH LINE

CROTCH LINE

Fig. 46

Adjust if Necessary

Crotch (Fig. 46) Draw a line across pattern back at right angles to the grain line, from the side seam to the point of the crotch. Check the measurement from the waistline to the drawn line at the side seam. This should equal your crotch measurement. (Fig. 45e)

If there is a difference in the two measurements, that is the amount to be shortened or lengthened. Adjust as indicated to correspond with your measurement. Make same adjustment to pattern back and front.

Length (Fig. 47) Measure the side seam of the pattern from waistline seam to hemline at lower edge. Compare to your measurement. (Fig. 45c) If there is a difference in the two measurements, that is the amount to be shortened or lengthened.

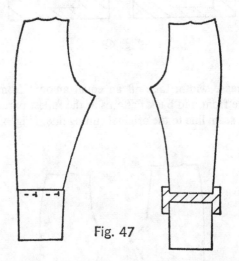

Fig. 47

Waist or Hips Follow instructions for the skirt in Chapter 2. Additional adjustments can be made in the first fitting depending upon your personal taste.

Make same adjustments to facing and waistband pattern pieces as necessary.

Width in Thigh Area Maintain 2 inches (5 cm) ease in thigh area. For additional width, add one-quarter of the needed amount to each seam edge on the front and back patterns at the fullest part of the thigh. Taper new seam line to the original cutting line. (Fig. 48)

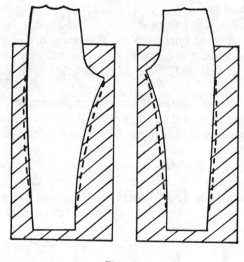

Fig. 48

To decrease width, take off an equal amount from each seam edge on the front and back patterns at the fullest part of the thigh. Taper new seam line to the original cutting line. (Fig. 49)

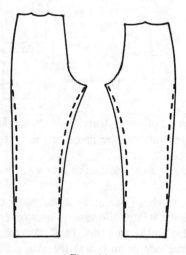

Fig. 49

Width at Lower Edge The lower edge of your pants should measure 1 inch (2.5 cm) more than your body measurement. (Fig. 45f) The width will vary with the fashion silhouette and style of your pants. However, if you wish additional width, add one-quarter of the needed amount to each seam edge. Taper from lower edge to hipline as shown. (Fig. 50)

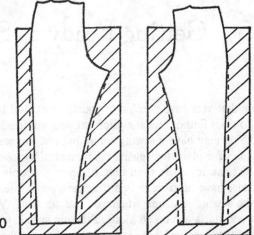

Fig. 50

To decrease the width, take off an equal amount from each of the four seams, and taper from the lower edge to the hipline as shown. (Fig. 51)

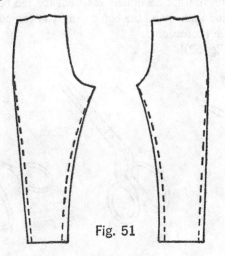

Fig. 51

3 Getting Ready to Sew

Now that you have purchased your pattern and fabric, the next thing to do is find out what equipment you will need to create your dress. You may have a sewing room, but not too many women do. Our idea of a place for sewing equipment is a closet with shelves. We don't ask for more than that, and you probably feel the same. You must have an ironing board somewhere in the house; keep it near the sewing machine when you are stitching. Why? To press seams and darts as you go along. Pressing speeds your sewing and is one of the secrets of that made-to-order look in clothes.

SEWING SUPPLIES

Let us list your sewing supplies in an orderly fashion. All of these supplies are not absolutely essential for the beginner, but if you know and understand the equipment, you can collect it as you become more professional.

For Cutting (Fig. 52)

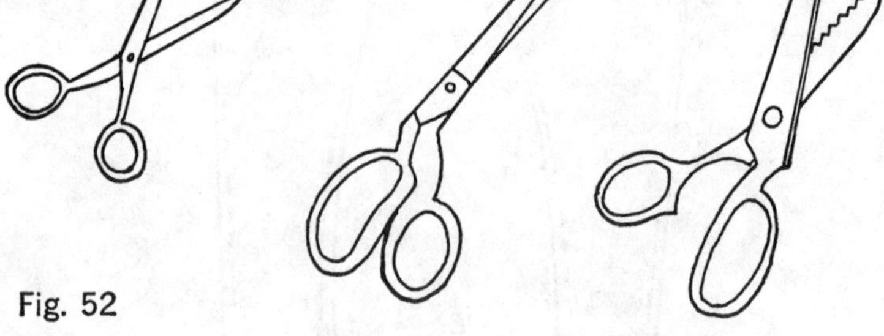

Fig. 52

Scissors A 4-inch (10 cm) or 5-inch (12.5 cm) size is convenient for cutting threads and buttonholes.

Dressmaker Shears A 7-inch (18 cm) or 8-inch (20.5 cm) length is a good size. Those with the bent handle make cutting more accurate because the fabric is not lifted from the table; if you are left-handed, left-handed shears are available.

Pinking Shears have saw-toothed edges to finish seams and prevent fraying. Do not cut out a garment with pinking shears.

For Sewing (Fig. 53)

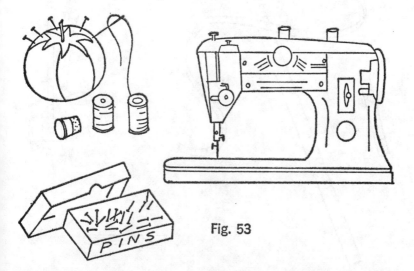

Fig. 53

Fabric, Thread, and Needles For the best sewing results, match the thread and needles to the fabric each time. Check the thread and needle chart that appears later in this chapter.

Thimble Wear it on the middle finger of the hand holding the needle. You'll find it handy to give a push to the needle as you stitch.

Pins Buy fine-quality silk or dressmaker pins with fine points; ball-point pins should be used with knits.

Pincushion To keep pins and needles near at hand while you are working.

Sewing Machine An indispensable tool for sewing. Learn how to use and care for your machine and its attachments.

For Measuring (Fig. 54)

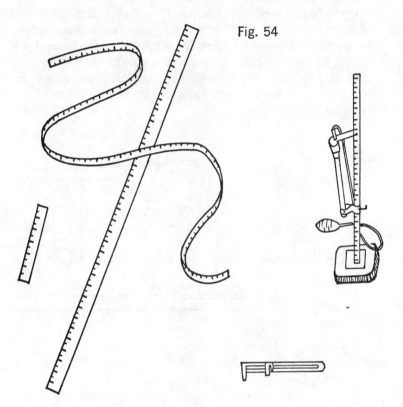

Fig. 54

Tape Measure   Choose one of linen or fiberglass with metal tips. Tape measures are available with inches on one side and metric measurements on the other side.

Yardstick   A good wooden one with clear markings and smooth edges is handy for drawing lines on patterns or marking hems.

Ruler   A 6-inch (15 cm) or 12-inch (30.5 cm) one to mark buttonholes, pockets, depths of hems; a plastic ruler is excellent. A 4-inch (10 cm) hem gauge with a movable indicator for measuring hems and spacing buttons is a handy gadget.

Skirt Marker   An extra that can make measuring hemlines an easy task.

For Marking (Fig. 55)

Fig. 55

Tailor's Chalk   Used to transfer markings to the fabric. Buy the non-wax variety. Chalk pencils that can be sharpened to a point are also available.

Dressmaker's Carbon Paper comes in a variety of colors; white or yellow is preferred. Always test the fabric first to be sure markings will not show through to the right side.

Tracing Wheel   Used with dressmaker's carbon paper.

For Pressing (Fig. 56)

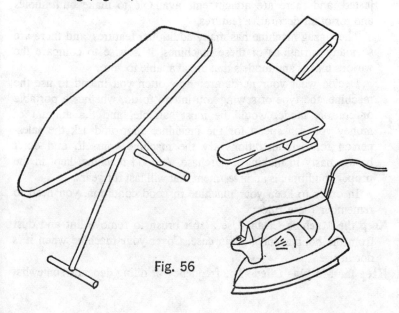

Fig. 56

Iron A combination steam-dry iron with an adjustable and clearly indicated thermostat control will be adaptable to all fabrics.

Ironing Board of a convenient height, with a firm, well-padded surface. Keep the ironing board cover clean.

Press Cloth of firm cotton or cheesecloth washed to remove lint or sizing. The cloth is placed between the iron and the fabric to be pressed, to prevent shine. Treated press cloths have chemicals to do a professional pressing job.

Sleeve Board Excellent for pressing sleeve seams, darts, and curved edges. It is shaped like a small ironing board.

Additional pressing equipment that will give you the most professional results includes a tailor's ham or cushion, seam roll, pounding block or clapper, needle board, and point presser. We will discuss the use of this equipment in detail later in this chapter.

USE AND CARE OF YOUR SEWING MACHINE

If you are buying a sewing machine, select one that is made by a well-known, reliable manufacturer. Then you will be able to buy attachments or replacement parts to fit your machine, and repairs can be made easily. Consider the sewing machines at your disposal. The straight-stitch machine will stitch forward in a straight line, and reverse- or backstitch. The length of the stitch can be adjusted, and there are attachments available to make buttonholes and for other decorative features.

The zigzag machine has many additional features, and there are so many variations of these machines, it is wise to compare the various makes and models that are available to you.

Decide what your needs are: how often you intend to use the machine, the type of sewing you intend to do, whether a portable or console model would be most suitable, and the amount of money you can spend for the machine. Shop and ask the salesperson for demonstrations—try the machine yourself, and don't be too hasty in making a purchase. A good machine, kept in the proper condition, is an investment that will last for years.

In order to keep your machine in good condition, you need to remember these rules:

Keep the Machine Clean—Use a soft brush to remove lint and dust from the bobbin and bobbin case. Cover your machine when it is not in use.

Keep the Machine Oiled—The frequency of oiling depends somewhat on the use you give your sewing machine. It is best to follow the instruction book on this, until you learn from experience how often to oil it. Use a high-grade machine oil and apply one drop to each point indicated for your machine. After you have oiled it, wipe off the excess oil and stitch away on a piece of flannel or other absorbent material to soak up any extra oil before you start to sew on a good piece of fabric.

Know the Possibilities of Your Machine—When you buy your machine, ask for demonstrations of threading the machine, putting in the needle, winding and inserting the bobbin, regulating the size of the stitch, and using the attachments that accompany it. Practice all these operations on the machine before you buy it. Then do the same thing at home until you become adept with them.

Some sewing centers include a mini-course of instructions on how to use the sewing machine. Take advantage of this if it is included in your purchase.

Learn the most important parts of your sewing machine so you can identify them. They are shown on a diagram in the instruction book.

Practice stitching on a double thickness of fabric before you start your first sewing project. You can draw straight lines on the sample piece with pencil or tailor's chalk. After you have threaded the machine, check to be certain the needle and bobbin threads are pushed away from you, toward the back, and are under the presser foot of the machine. If you are careful to do this with every line of sewing you start, your threads will not snarl and tangle. Allow about 6 inches (15 cm) of thread to extend through the needle and under the presser foot when you start to sew.

Start on the straight line that you marked as a guide. The presser foot must be down when you sew, to hold the fabric firmly in place. When you come to the end of a line and want to turn a square corner in your stitching, leave the needle in the fabric, raise the presser foot, and pivot the fabric at right angles to the line. Lower the presser foot and continue to sew as before. To end your sewing, stop with the needle raised to its highest point, raise the presser foot, and push the fabric away, under the presser foot and toward the back of the machine. Pull the needle and bobbin threads and cut them off, leaving about 2 inches (5 cm) of thread, which will be sufficient to tie; or reverse-stitch. Also allow about a 6-inch (15 cm) length of thread through the needle and bobbin hole, so that you won't have to rethread the needle with every new line of stitching.

If your machine is stitching correctly, the upper side and the underside of the stitching will be balanced. The upper and lower threads will look alike and will pull evenly when you draw them under the presser foot and away from you. (Fig. 57)

Fig. 57

If the tension or pull on the needle thread is too tight, or if that on the bobbin thread is too loose, the needle thread will lie straight along the upper side of the fabric. (Fig. 58)

Fig. 58

If the tension on the bobbin thread is too tight, or if that on the needle thread is too loose, the bobbin thread will lie straight along the underside of the fabric. (Fig. 59)

Fig. 59

The instruction book will tell you how to adjust the tension properly. The pressure regulator will control the amount of pressure on the presser foot so that the fabric is held firmly while stitching, yet feeds through smoothly. The amount of pressure varies with finish, fiber, and weight or bulk of fabric.

For some types of fabrics you may want to use a short machine stitch and for others you may prefer a long stitch. The average is usually 12 to 14 stitches to the inch (2.5 cm). The chart on pages 52–53 indicates the proper machine stitch length for various weights of fabric.

For basting, easing, or gathering, use the longest stitch on your machine. To reinforce stitching at points of strain such as corners, points of collars, or bound buttonholes, use a short stitch. The instruction book will show you how the length of the stitch can be adjusted.

Make it a habit to do a test seam before you start any project. Cut two pieces of the fabric you will be using and make a seam to check the pressure, tension, and stitch length for that particular fabric.

Do a little practice stitching using the attachments, too, so that you will understand their operation. The attachments that came along with the machine were made to be used. They are simple to operate and will help you to save time and to produce finer and more professional-looking results. Our favorite attachments are the buttonhole maker and the zipper-cording foot. The buttonhole maker can produce buttonholes in various sizes from about ¼ inch (6 mm) to 1 inch (2.5 cm) long in practically no time at all. The combination zipper-cording foot is used to cover cording, to stitch cording into a seam, or to sew a zipper in place.

The zigzag attachment can produce many kinds of decorative stitches, which can be used as edgings and borders for playclothes, children's clothes, curtains, and other household articles.

The zigzag machine has many more adjustments, which must be studied and learned before this machine can be used to its greatest value. Here too, as with plain stitching, you should practice until you have perfected your skills.

CHOOSING THE CORRECT NEEDLE AND THREAD

For satisfactory results in sewing, needle, thread, and fabric must be suited to each other.

Sewing Machine Needles—are bought according to type and size.

Type is determined by the make and model of your sewing machine.

Size of needle must conform to the weight of the fabric being used. The needles can be categorized as fine (size 11), medium (size 14), or coarse (size 16 to 18). There are special needles for special purposes—the ball-point needle for stitching on knit fabrics, the wedge-shaped needle for stitching leathers. Be sure your needle is inserted correctly—check the diagram in your instruction book.

Hand Sewing Needles—come in ten sizes, from very coarse (size 1) to very fine (size 10). Use a good needle; an inferior needle may fray the thread or have a blunt point. Packaged assortments of needles, sizes 3 to 9 and 5 to 10, are practical. Sharps, betweens, embroidery, and milliner's needles are most commonly used for hand sewing. Other needles are made for many special purposes and include beading, quilting, upholstery, tapestry, chenille, and glovers' needles for leatherwork.

Fig. 60

How to Choose the Right Thread and Needle

The chart to the right will help in selecting the correct thread, needle, and stitch length for the fabric. Keep in mind the thread should be compatible with the fiber content, construction, weight, and care requirements of the fabric.

When buying thread, remember the following:

• For the best color match, buy thread at the same time fabric is purchased.

• Select thread one shade darker, because it will appear lighter when it is sewn into fabric.

• For plaids, tweeds, and prints, select thread to match the main color.

• Check yardage on the spool to be sure there is enough for your project. Approximately one small size spool of DUAL DUTY PLUS® makes a simple A-line dress, or a blouse, or a skirt. Additional thread is needed for topstitching, zigzag stitching, or overcasting seams.

FABRICS	
The fabrics listed below may be made of any fiber or combination of fibers; they are listed only as an example of weight.	
LIGHT WEIGHT	nylon tricot for lingerie batiste, chiffon, dress-weight tricot, dotted Swiss, net, organdy, sheer crepe, voile
MEDIUM LIGHT WEIGHT	challis, crepe, gingham, jersey, percale, taffeta, wool crepe
MEDIUM WEIGHT	broadcloth, corduroy, double knit, flannel, linen, piqué, polished cotton, poplin, satin, shantung, suiting, velvet, velveteen
MEDIUM HEAVY WEIGHT	bonded fabrics, coating, denim, double knit, drapery fabric, felt, fleece, gabardine, leather, leather-look, quilted fabric, sweater knits, terry cloth
HEAVY WEIGHT	awning cloth, canvas, duck, fake fur, sail-cloth, ticking, upholstery fabric

Courtesy of the Consumers and Educational Affairs Department of Coats & Clark, Inc.

PREPARING THE FABRIC FOR CUTTING

Grain—Look at a piece of woven fabric. You will see that the lengthwise threads are parallel to the selvages, or finished edges. These lengthwise threads are the warp threads and are placed on the loom first in the weaving process. This is the lengthwise grain or the straight grain of the goods. The crosswise threads (filling, weft,

J. & P. COATS THREAD			J. & P. COATS NEEDLES	
For all fabrics including knits	For all fabrics except knits	Cottons and linens in white and black	Hand sewing	Machine sewing UNIVERSAL BALLPOINT
DUAL DUTY PLUS® EXTRA FINE FOR LIGHTWEIGHT FABRICS			sizes 9, 10	size 11 10-12 sts per inch (2.5 mm long) for tricots 12-14 sts per inch (2 mm long) for wovens
DUAL DUTY PLUS® POLYESTER thread with cotton covering; mercerized	SUPER SHEEN® MERCERIZED SEWING thread use thread one shade darker than fabric	MERCER-IZED BEST CORD® thread size 60	sizes 8, 9	size 11 12-14 sts per inch (2 mm long)
		sizes 50, 60	sizes 7, 8	size 11 or 14 12-14 sts per inch (2 mm long)
use thread one shade darker than fabric		size 40	size 6	size 14 or finest needle fabric will take 10-12 sts per inch (2.5 mm long)
	MERCERIZED BEST CORD® thread sizes 8, 20, 30	sizes 8, 20, 30	sizes 1-5	size 14 or 16 6-8 sts per inch (4 mm long)

For topstitching, use DUAL DUTY PLUS® Topstitching & Buttonhole Twist. For buttons and hand-sewing on heavy fabrics, use DUAL DUTY PLUS® EXTRA STRONG, BUTTON & CARPET thread.

woof) are woven over and under the lengthwise threads from selvage to selvage, and this is known as the crosswise grain. (Fig. 61)

When you fold the fabric so that a lengthwise thread (or the selvage) is lying along a crosswise thread, the line formed by the fold is the true bias. (Fig. 62) The true bias gives the greatest elasticity or stretch and the most graceful drape to the fabric.

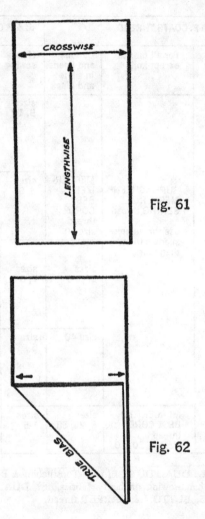

Fig. 61

Fig. 62

In cutting and fitting a garment, the lengthwise and crosswise grain lines must be placed so that the fabric is balanced on the figure. The lengthwise grain runs parallel to the perpendicular line of the body, the crosswise grain is kept in a horizontal position around the figure. For design purposes, the true bias can be substituted for the lengthwise grain. If you follow the instructions on your pattern, your garment will have correct balance and will hang properly.

To Straighten Fabric—Although the fabric is woven so that the length-wise and crosswise threads are at right angles to each other, it is possible that the fabric is pulled off grain in the finishing process. Look at the ends of your fabric. Are they straight? If the ends are uneven, pull a crosswise thread and cut along the puckered line. (Fig. 63) Some fabrics can be torn easily; make a cut into the

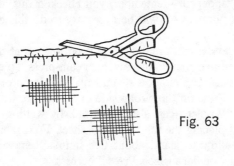

Fig. 63

selvage and tear across. A stripe, plaid, or rib can be cut along a prominent thread of the fabric from selvage to selvage. Fold the fabric in half lengthwise with selvages matching; the crosswise ends should be at right angles with the selvage. If the ends do not match, the fabric grain must be straightened by pulling the fabric firmly on the true bias, in the direction opposite to the off-grain threads. Start at one end and continue along the length of the fabric, until ends are even. (Fig. 64) You may need an assistant for wide fab-

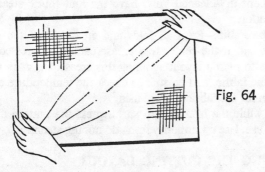

Fig. 64

ric or extra-long lengths. Fabric that is only slightly off grain can usually be straightened by steam pressing. Fold fabric in half lengthwise, with right sides together. Press with the lengthwise (straight) grain, using a steam iron.

Some fabrics, such as those treated to resist wrinkles and stains, and bonded fabrics, cannot be straightened. With fabrics of this type, cut the ends and be sure they are square with the selvage.

To Shrink Fabric—If the fabric you plan to use has not been pre-shrunk or "sponged"—remember, you checked this information at the time of purchase—it will be necessary to do this before cutting the pattern.

Woolen fabrics can usually be sponged for you at the dry cleaners for a nominal charge, or you can steam-press a piece of woolen fabric at home. Use either a steam iron or a damp press cloth and warm iron. Press on the wrong side of the fabric, with the lengthwise grain. Woolens can also be shrunk by wetting a sheet thoroughly and placing the fabric on the sheet. Fold fabric within the sheet and allow to stand about five hours. Remove fabric from sheet and dry on flat surface. Press if necessary.

Cotton and washable fabrics should be folded lengthwise with ends and selvage edges pinned. Fold fabric several times and soak thoroughly in hot water for about one hour. Remove from water, unfold fabric but do not remove the pins, and allow to dry on a shower rod. Press if necessary. Synthetic fabrics usually require no shrinking; however, we have found it necessary to shrink polyester knits before using. If you plan to wash the garment, pre-shrink the length of fabric in the washing machine. This will also remove the sizing used in the finishing process. If you plan to have the garment dry-cleaned only, have the knit fabric steam-pressed by the tailor.

To Press the Fabric—Press all folds and creases from the fabric before it is cut. If the center fold crease cannot be pressed out, you will have to plan a layout avoiding this crease. Press on the wrong side of the fabric, and be sure to check the temperature control on your iron for the fabric you are using.

And, while the iron is still warm, press the pattern pieces that you will use. Use a warm, dry iron—do not use steam!

FOLLOWING THE CUTTING LAYOUT

Now you are ready to cut out your garment. To do this you will need a flat cutting surface. Preferably this should be a large table, since it is the most convenient space on which to work. If there is no table available, use the floor, or, in a pinch, the bed, but it is advisable to place a large piece of plywood or a cutting board of heavyweight cardboard (available at notion counters for this purpose) over the bed to keep the fabric even and to avoid cutting the bedspread.

Collect all the things you will need—straight pins, shears, a yardstick or tape measure, tailor's chalk, and so on—and put them in a convenient spot near where you plan to cut out the fabric.

Don't forget to circle the cutting layout (Fig. 65) on the pat-

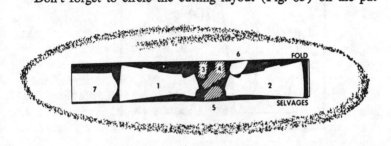

Fig. 65

tern instruction sheet that you will use according to the style you are making, the size of your pattern, the width of the fabric, and the type of fabric you are using (remember nap fabrics or those with a one-way design have a special layout). These layouts indicate how to place the pattern pieces so that the straight grain of the fabric is in the correct position on each piece.

If the fabric is to be cut double, fold with the right sides inside and pin selvages together if necessary to prevent slipping. If the pattern is to be cut on a single thickness of fabric, place the fabric with the right side up.

Lay the pattern piece in position on the fabric, carefully measuring the distance from each end of the straight grain arrow to the selvage. (Fig. 66) Place a pin at each end of the grain line. Pin remainder of pattern, smoothing from grain line to point of pin-

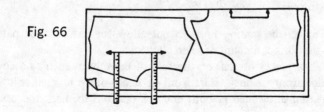

Fig. 66

ning. When you are working with a single thickness of fabric and must cut two identical pieces, such as sleeves or cuffs, be sure the pattern piece is turned face down before cutting the second piece. (Fig. 67)

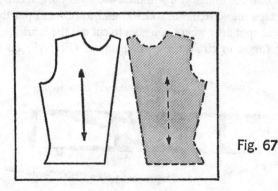

Fig. 67

Cut your fabric with long, clean strokes of your shears; do not use pinking shears. Do not lift the fabric from the table, and don't bypass those notches along the edges. Cut the notches outward, as shown, not in, so that there will be no danger of cutting into the seam allowance—you may want to let out on the seam line in a fitting later. It is also easier to see the notch when you pick up the piece to work on it. Cut every notch as you come to it —if there is a group of two or more notches, cut them as one rather than individually. (Fig. 68)

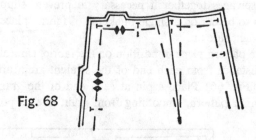

Fig. 68

Cut on the cutting line—do not allow for seams, your pattern has the correct amount of seam allowance.

When pieces are cut on the fold of the fabric—such as a collar, bodice front or back, skirt front or back—make a small snip into the seam allowance at both ends of the fold to mark the center.

(Fig. 69) This makes it easier for you to match it to the piece to which it will be joined.

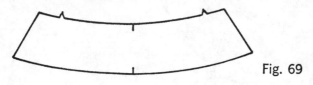

Fig. 69

MARKING THE FABRIC

Never remove a pattern piece from the fabric until you are absolutely certain that you have marked every construction symbol that you will need to help you put the garment together correctly. Marking is done in several ways—tailor's tacks, tailor's chalk, dressmaker's carbon paper and tracing wheel. The method you choose will be determined in part by the fabric you are using; therefore, you should familiarize yourself with more than one technique.

Tailor's Tacks—Use double thread, unknotted, in a color that will contrast with your fabric. A soft thread, such as darning cotton, will stay in the fabric more easily. Take a stitch through the pattern and fabric, leaving a 1-inch (2.5 cm) thread end. Take a backstitch, making a 1-inch (2.5 cm) loop of thread as shown. (Fig. 70) Cut thread, leaving a 1-inch (2.5 cm) end. When all

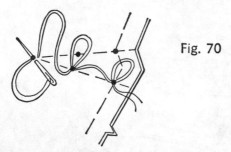

Fig. 70

the symbols have been marked, cut through loop to remove pattern. Separate fabric layers carefully and clip the tailor's tacks between the thicknesses of fabric as shown. (Fig. 71) The marking threads will remain in both pieces.

Tailor's Chalk—This is a quick and practical method for most fabrics. Pin through pattern and fabric layers at construction symbols. Turn the piece over with points of pins facing upward. Use a ruler and

Fig. 71

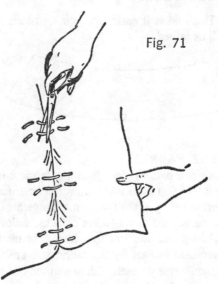

sharpened tailor's chalk or chalk pencil to connect the markings between pins. Complete all markings on the underside, then turn piece over to the other side. Carefully pull pattern tissue over the heads of the pins and draw the connecting lines from pin to pin. Remove marking pins. For a single thickness of fabric, mark only the wrong side. (Fig. 72)

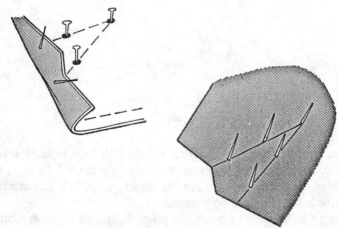

Fig. 72

Dressmaker's Carbon Paper and Tracing Wheel—Dressmaker's carbon paper is specially treated waxed tracing paper to be used with a tracing wheel to transfer markings from pattern to fabric. Use a contrasting color, but one that will not show through the fabric —test it on a scrap of fabric before using it on the garment. Protect the surface of the table or work area you are using with a magazine or newspaper. For easy use, cut the dressmaker's carbon paper into strips about 2 inches (5 cm) wide. Fold the strip with the carbon side in. For marking double thickness of fabric, insert the folded strip so that one end is under the fabric. (Fig. 73) Use a ruler

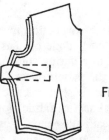

Fig. 73

to guide marking dart lines. (Fig. 74) For a single thickness of fabric, place carbon paper to wrong side of fabric.

Fig. 74

To Mark on the Right Side of Fabric—The location of pockets, buttonholes, and some decorative detail work is necessary on the right side of the fabric. Mark the fabric on the wrong side first and then machine-baste, or hand-baste fabrics that mark easily, over these markings. The basting is visible on the right side. (Fig. 75)

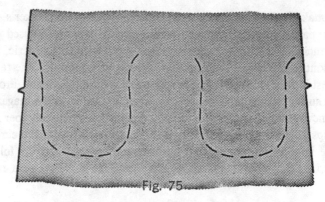

Fig. 75

Stay Stitching—This is a line of regulation machine stitching, 12 to 15 stitches per inch (2.5 cm), done on bias and curved edges to protect the grain of the fabric during construction. Stay-stitch immediately after removing the pattern piece from each section with the grain as indicated on the illustrations, use matching thread, and stay-stitch on a single thickness of fabric ⅛ inch (3 mm) beyond the seam line within the seam allowance. (Fig. 76) With a ⅝-inch (1.5 cm) seam allowance, you would stay-stitch ½ inch (1.3 cm) from the cut edge.

Fig. 76

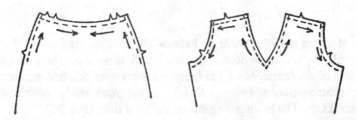

PRESSING TECHNIQUES AND AIDS

Learning to press goes hand in hand with learning to sew. The proper pressing gives shape to the garment; each seam, or dart, should be pressed before it is crossed by another seam. To press is not to iron a garment. In *ironing,* the iron is pushed along the fabric; in *pressing,* the iron is placed on the section to be pressed, then lifted and moved to the next section. Always press with the grain, in the same direction as the stitching.

- Press *skirt seams* from the bottom to the top.
- Press *shoulder seams* from the neckline to the armhole.
- Press *bodice side seams* from armhole to waist.
- Press *sleeve seams* from underarm to wrist.
- Press *darts* toward point; horizontal darts at bust line or elbow are pressed down, waistline and shoulder darts are pressed toward the center of the garment. (Fig. 77)

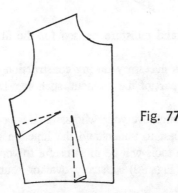

Fig. 77

NOTE: With heavyweight fabrics, slash dart along fold line to ½ inch (1.3 cm) from point, and press seam open over tailor's cushion. (Fig. 78)

- Press *waistline seam* and *armhole* in one direction.

If the fabric you are using has a tendency to show an impression on the right side, slip a strip of paper under the seam allowance or dart. (Fig. 79)

Most fabrics will require dampness in pressing. You could use a steam iron or a damp (not wet) press cloth. Make it a habit to test a scrap of the fabric you are working on to determine

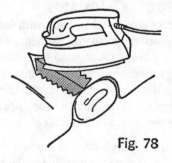

Fig. 78

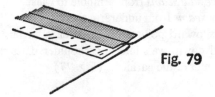

Fig. 79

the correct heat and moisture needed for the fiber and finish of the fabric.

It is sometimes necessary during construction to *shrink* excess fullness out of a part of the garment, such as a hem or the sleeve cap.

Pressing Aids—Although everyone who sews does not need all of this equipment, it is best to understand the function of each in order to evaluate which tools will be most useful to you.

Tailor's Ham (Fig. 80)   Usually oval or round in shape and

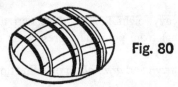

Fig. 80

can vary in size. A ham provides shape for darts and curved areas during pressing. It can be filled with sawdust or scraps of wool; the covering is usually of wool or cotton drill cloth.

Sleeve Board (Fig. 81)   One that is well padded provides the form for shaping and steaming the fullness of set-in sleeves, and for pressing seams.

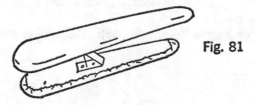

Fig. 81

Seam Roll (Fig. 82) Used for pressing seams open. It helps

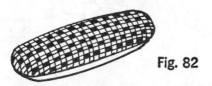

Fig. 82

to eliminate seam edges showing on the right side of the fabric. A tightly rolled magazine covered with smooth cloth can be substituted.

Pounding Block (Fig. 83) Used to flatten seams and sharpen

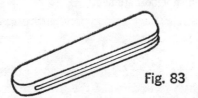

Fig. 83

edges of woolen garments when tailoring; often referred to as a clapper. It is held in the left hand while the iron and steam are applied to the garment's edge with the right hand. Then, when the iron is removed, the block should be "pounded" onto the edge with force and held there a few moments.

Point Presser (Fig. 84) Used for pressing seams of pointed

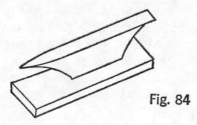

Fig. 84

edges in collars. The point is shaped to fit in this collar area so that pressing is possible.

Velvet or Needle Board (Fig. 85)   Used for pressing napped

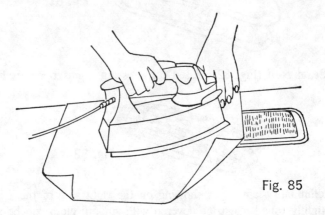

Fig. 85

and pile fabrics such as velvet, corduroy, and wool broadcloth. It provides the depth of surface to hold the pile during pressing, so that the pile will not be flattened.

4 How to Handle Special Fabrics

SEWING WITH PLAIDS

Always in fashion, plaids can add interest to a simple style. In choosing a plaid, consider your own coloring and figure type—there are bold clan plaids, miniature plaids, vivid plaids, and muted plaids. Small-scale plaids are best for the petite, while large-scale designs are flattering to the tall woman. To add height, choose a fabric with a dominant vertical design; to add width, pick a horizontal design.

To make cutting and sewing easier for you, the pattern should be simple, with few pieces. The design of your fabric will show to best advantage with a minimum number of seams. Check the suggested fabrics on the pattern envelope to be sure that plaid fabrics are recommended. Allow extra yardage for matching—for small-scale plaids and checks, buy an extra ⅛ yard (0.15 m); for medium-scale plaids or checks, buy an extra ¼ to ½ yard (0.25 to 0.50 m); and for large-scale patterns, 1 extra yard (0.95 m) is best.

Types of Plaids (Fig. 86)—Study the design of the plaid you choose. An *even or balanced* plaid repeats the pattern, color, and spacing of each block throughout the fabric, making it easier to match and sew.

An *uneven or unbalanced* plaid varies in pattern and spacing, which makes the layout of the pattern more difficult.

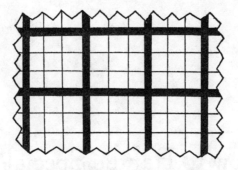

Fig. 86

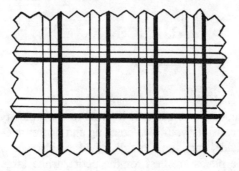

Fig. 87

If you are not sure of the type of plaid you have, fold the fabric in half across a dominant block of the plaid to see if the design is repeated. Then fold the fabric in half vertically. If the design and coloring is repeated exactly in both directions, the plaid is balanced.

Matching a Plaid (Fig. 87)—Careful planning and preparation of the design in fabric and pattern pay dividends with plaids. The dominant lengthwise line of the plaid should be up and down the center front. If there is a dominant crosswise line in the fabric design, plan this to run across the bodice front just below the shoulder line. Once you have established a dominant line as the center line, each piece of the pattern must be placed and cut in relation to it. The design should match at the stitching lines of the pattern pieces, not the cutting line. Also try to avoid placing darts on the most noticeable bars of the plaid, where they tend to distort the design.

Even Plaids (Fig. 88)—Because the design is balanced in spacing and

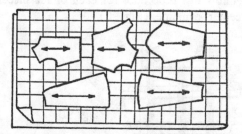

Fig. 88

color, the fabric can be folded lengthwise or crosswise. Pin the layers of fabric together along the plaid lines crosswise and lengthwise, so that the plaids in both layers match exactly. To lay out the pattern, use the cutting layout given for fabrics without nap. Be sure that the corresponding notches are matched on identical portions of the plaid design. (The numbers on the notches can be helpful here.)

Uneven Plaids (Fig. 89)—Because of the unbalanced design in pattern and spacing, this type of plaid can help you create some interesting effects. Lay the pattern pieces on the fabric so that the tops of the pattern pieces point in the same direction—use the cutting layout for a fabric with nap. Be sure the notches to be matched fall on identical portions of the plaid design.

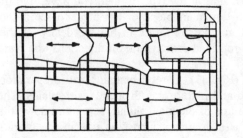

Fig. 89

To "balance" an uneven plaid, you must use a pattern with a
center seam and the fabric must be reversible (that is, the same
on right and wrong sides). Lay the pattern pieces on one thickness
of fabric, matching the center seam line to the center of a lengthwise bar of the plaid design. Be sure you have allowed ⅝ inch
(1.5 cm) for seams. Cut out the pattern piece, place it on a second
area of the fabric, match exactly, and cut. To stitch, reverse the
second piece. Follow this procedure for each of the pieces to be
matched at the center seam line. (Fig. 90)

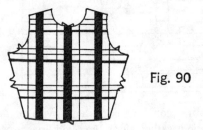

Fig. 90

Basting Plaids—For perfection in matching plaids at the seams, it is
necessary to slip-baste the garment (see Chapter 7). This stitching will give you a plain seam with even basting on the wrong
side. Machine-stitch seams on wrong side, matching your thread
to the background color of the plaid.

STRIPED FABRICS

A striped fabric can be balanced or unbalanced in design.
Striped fabrics are handled much like plaids in the preparation of
the fabric for cutting—pin the layers of fabric together along the
stripe lines, plan for the placement of darts, match the stripes at

corresponding notches and seams. For balanced stripes, follow the layout without nap; for unbalanced stripes, cut as a fabric with nap, having the tops of pattern pieces in one direction.

Slip-baste seams for perfect matching of stripes (see Chapter 7).

PILE, NAP, OR ONE-WAY FABRICS

A pile or nap fabric, such as velvet, corduroy, or wool broadcloth, has small fibers on the surface of the fabric. A one-way fabric has the design going in one direction. These materials must be cut with the top of each pattern piece laid in the same direction, as shown. (Fig. 91) Check the pattern envelope to be sure

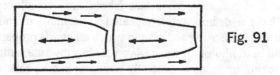

Fig. 91

yardage is given for "Fabric with nap"; if not, buy an extra ½ to ¾ yard (0.50 to 0.70 m) of fabric.

When the nap runs up, the fabric will appear darker; when the nap runs down, the fabric will look lighter and shinier. To determine the direction of the nap, move your hand lightly down over the fabric. If it is smooth, the nap is running down; if it feels rough, the nap is running up. Long-napped fabrics such as wool broadcloth and fleece will usually be cut with the nap running down toward the hem of the garment; with short-napped fabrics such as velvet, corduroy, and velveteen, the nap will usually run up toward the top of the garment.

A pattern that suggests these types of fabrics will include a special layout—follow it carefully.

If you are topstitching on these fabrics, use mercerized sewing thread, and test your fabric for stitch length and pressure to prevent marking of the pile.

For best results in pressing seams and darts in pile and napped fabrics, use a velvet board. Place the right side of the fabric against the needles and steam-press.

BORDER PRINTS

Choose a pattern that is suitable for this type of fabric—one with a skirt having a straight lower edge. Lay the pattern pieces on the crosswise fold of the fabric, so that the border can be used as a decoration along the hemline of the skirt.

LACE FABRICS

Lace fabrics are made in cotton, rayon, silk, synthetics, and blends. The fabric can be made with finished lengthwise edges similar to the selvage, or one edge may have a decorative finish such as a scallop design. Choose a pattern that is simple in design, with few seams or other construction details. The fabric is dressy and will make the simplest of patterns look like an elegant fashion if it is handled properly. Some lace fabrics have an allover design; others have a definite motif repeated at regular intervals. Study the fabric you are using and plan to match all motifs properly.

Avoid buttonholes if possible—you could substitute button loops.

A backing or lining is generally required; choose this according to the weight of the lace and the pattern design. If you are backing a lace garment, you could use net, organza, organdy, marquisette for a sheer transparent effect; taffeta, peau de soie, cotton sateen for opaqueness. Washable linings or backings for washable laces! If interfacings are necessary, use net, marquisette, or organza.

Test your fabric for stitch length, tension, and pressure.

Darts should be stitched in the regular manner; then make another row of stitching ⅛ inch (3 mm) from the first row (Fig. 92) and trim close to the second row of stitching. (Fig. 93) Press.

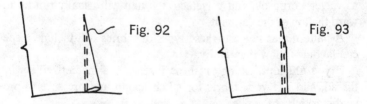

Fig. 92   Fig. 93

For seams, stitch seams in regular manner, then make another row of stitching ⅛ inch (3 mm) from stitched seam through both seam allowances and trim close to second row of stitching.

To finish edges that are to be faced or hemmed, use a strip of tulle or net. Cut the strip 2½ inches (6.5 cm) wide on the straight grain and fold in half lengthwise. With raw edges together, stitch along seam line, then make another row of stitching ⅛ inch (3 mm) from first row, within seam allowance. Trim close to second row of stitching. Press tulle to wrong side and slip-stitch folded edge in place.

If you want your hem to stand out, use horsehair braid (which comes in several widths) along the edge of the hem. (See Chapter 11, Fig. 287)

Your zipper will look neater and be less conspicuous if the final topstitching is done by hand. (See Chapter 12, Fig. 339)

SHEER FABRICS

Sheer fabrics can be soft and filmy as chiffon, or crisp as organdy. They are available in various fibers. Your choice of a pattern design can vary from one with soft, fluid lines to a more slender silhouette.

Crisp sheers are easier to cut and sew than the softer sheers. If your fabric slips or shifts as you cut, pin it to tissue paper first, and then cut through fabric and tissue paper. Place a strip of tissue paper, about 1½ inches (3.8 cm) wide, between the fabric and machine when stitching. Tear tissue away from seam after stitching.

Darts should be double-stitched and trimmed, as with lace fabrics. (See Figs. 92 and 93)

To make seams as inconspicuous as possible, choose a French seam, mock French seam, or the double-stitched seam.

Double bias binding, also called French binding, in self fabric makes an elegant finish for necklines and sleeveless armholes; use facings only on sheers that have been backed with an opaque fabric.

Deep hems, 3 to 8 inches (7.5 to 20.5 cm), can be used on a gathered skirt. Remember to allow extra fabric at the hem edge when cutting if this is your choice. Circular hems can be finished with a narrow rolled hem.

WASH-AND-WEAR AND PERMANENT-PRESS FABRICS

This fabric group includes a variety of fabrics, woven or knitted of synthetic yarns or in blends with other fibers such as cotton, rayon, wool, and silk. Various finishes are applied to these fabrics to give them characteristics that will require a minimum amount of care—quick drying with little or no ironing, and crease resistance. Check the label or hang tag on the bolt for washing or cleaning instructions when you purchase your fabric.

The finishes used in the various processes to make these fabrics trouble-free present certain problems to the home sewer.

The surface is harder and smoother, which makes the fabric less pliable and resistant to pins, needles, and scissors. Choose a simple pattern, avoid set-in sleeves or seams on the straight grain—these pucker more than seams on the bias. All notions such as interfacings, shoulder pads, seam tape, and linings should have the same wash-and-wear characteristics as the fabric.

Because of the finish on these fabrics, it is almost impossible to straighten an off-grain fabric. However, the finish holds the shape, so it is permissible to disregard the crosswise grain. Lay the straight grain of the pattern pieces on the lengthwise grain, parallel to the selvage—this will give the garment the best hang.

For cutting, use sharp pins and shears; mercerized cotton or dual-duty thread, and fine needles for sewing. Test a scrap of your fabric for stitch length, pressure, and tension—a looser tension will help to eliminate puckers; use a medium to long stitch length and the throat plate with a small round hole.

Understitch faced edges for a crisp, sharp edge. (See Chapter 11, Fig. 246) Be sure of the final seam lines before you press, since the pressed creases will remain in the fabric.

STRETCH FABRICS

Stretch is a feature that has been added to various types of fabric; it allows the fabric to give while being worn and return to shape when the garment is removed.

Choose a pattern with simple lines and in the same size you regularly use, since stretch is a comfort factor only.

Check the label or hang tag for fiber content and care requirements.

Allow the fabric to relax about twenty-four hours before cutting to release any stretch created while the fabric was rolled on the bolt. Follow pattern layout—place pattern pieces in direction in which stretch is desired.

Do not underline the garment, since this will interfere with the stretch of the fabric. If a lining is necessary, use a tricot or other fabric with similar qualities. Interfacing should be planned carefully, since it will stabilize the stretch in the area it is used.

To cut, use sharp shears; avoid stretching fabric unnecessarily.

To sew, use dual-duty thread, which will give greater elasticity; test the fabric for stitch length, pressure, and tension. Do not stretch the fabric as you stitch.

Use a tailor's ham. (See Chapter 3, Fig. 80) If buttonholes are made, stabilize the area with a piece of iron-on interfacing. Press lightly to avoid stretching.

KNIT FABRICS

There are a variety of knit fabrics available to the home sewer today, made of natural and synthetic fibers or blends. A great advantage of knit fabrics is their easy care and wrinkle resistance. Check the information on the bolt or hang tag for fiber content and suggested fabric care when purchasing your fabric.

The construction of a knit fabric is different from a woven fabric. Knits are made by a series of interlocking loops that give the fabric its stretch quality. There is no grain line in a knit, but there is a noticeable lengthwise rib that must be used as the straight grain when placing the pattern pieces. Some knits are made in a tubular form. Tubular knits must be cut along one rib before they can be used; press out the lengthwise fold.

Knits will vary in the amount of stretch. Stable knits are fairly firm and have a limited degree of stretch. They can be used for patterns recommended for knits. Stretchable knits can vary from moderate to very stretchy. There is a special group of patterns available "for stretchable knits only" that cannot be used for stable knits. These patterns have less allowance and are not for the person who wants to avoid a snug fit. Stretchable knits are meant to reveal the figure—remember this in choosing the fabric and pattern. The pattern companies have a special knit gauge printed on the pattern envelope as a guide for determining the degree of stretch, so if you are anticipating making a knit garment it is wise to use this gauge when purchasing your fabric.

Jersey adapts well to designs with draped and soft ease detail; double knits are particularly good for tailored dresses or suits. Avoid circular skirts and bias cuts. Tricot knits are used for lingerie and sleepwear. Other stretchable knits are used for a variety of garments from dresses to tank tops and bathing suits.

Preshrink washable knits to remove sizing and prevent shrinkage of the garment. Preshrink all notions to be used.

To cut, use a long, flat surface; do not allow fabrics to hang. Make a line of basting along a rib as a guide for the straight grain. Knits should be cut following the with-nap layout to prevent a variance in the shading of the garment. Use sharp shears (shears are available with serrated edges that are particularly good for lingerie or tricot knits) and sharp or ball-point pins.

To sew, use ball-point needles for the sewing machine; this type of needle does not cut the fibers of the knit but separates them, making it easier to stitch. Stay-stitch shoulders, neckline, and armhole edges. Shoulders and waistline seams may be stabilized by sewing seam tape into the seam. Fusible or nonwoven interfacing should be used to reinforce areas where needed.

Seams should be able to "give" with the fabric; use dual-duty thread for extra stretch. Some zigzag machines have special stretch stitches and seam finishes that are particularly beneficial with knits. If you are using a straight-stitch machine, stretch the fabric *slightly* as you sew the seam; make a double-stitched seam to eliminate the bulk of seam allowances. Always make a test seam in the fabric you are using to determine the correct pressure, tension, and stitch length or special stretch stitch before sewing on your garment.

Allow garment to hang twenty-four hours before hemming. You can use stretch lace to finish the raw edge of the hem or make a tailor's hem (see Chapter 11, Fig. 277) or a catch-stitched hem (see Chapter 11, Fig. 278).

BONDED FABRICS

A bonded fabric is made of two fabrics that have been fused together by a special process and are handled as one fabric in construction. There are a great variety of bonded fabrics—from bonded lace to bonded knits—available today. These fabrics avoid the need for backing, since this is already done as part of the manufacturing technique. The backing fabric is tricot or acetate. Check the label or hang tag for fiber content and laundering or dry-cleaning instructions.

Choose a pattern according to weight and hand of fabric. Do not purchase a bonded fabric that is considerably off grain since it will be impossible to straighten. To cut, follow the grain of the face fabric by measuring from the selvage. You could eliminate unnecessary bulk by cutting facings of a lining fabric of the same color.

To sew, test your fabric for pressure, tension, and stitch length. With heavy fabrics, stitch darts, slash, and press open. *Understitch* all faced edges for a sharp edge. (See Chapter 11, Fig. 246)

To press, set iron to the fiber of the face fabric.

LEATHER, SUEDE, AND LEATHER-LIKE FABRICS

Leather and suede are sold by the skin. Select skins as uniform as possible in color and weight. Choose a pattern with simple, straight lines. Avoid eased seams; raglan sleeves are easier to handle than set-in sleeves. If you choose a set-in sleeve, remove some of the ease from the sleeve cap pattern. The yardage recommendations on the pattern envelope do not apply to leather, so bring your pattern with you when buying the skins to determine how many you need. Leather-like fabrics are sold by the yard. If the pattern you have selected suggests the use of a leather-like fabric, the amount required will be listed on the yardage chart.

There is no special preparation of the skins; however, lay all the pattern pieces in the same direction on the skins as you would for a pile or napped fabric. With suede the nap should run down. Alterations should be made on the pattern before cutting since marks from ripped-out stitching cannot be removed from the skins. If you have any doubt as to fit, it would be worth your while to make the garment in muslin first. Since these fabrics should be cut on a single thickness, it is also helpful to cut a complete paper pattern for pattern pieces to be placed on a fold.

To cut, pin pattern to skins *in seam allowance only,* or fasten with tape. Make all construction markings on the wrong side. Test a scrap of the skin for the best method to use.

To sew, test for pressure, tension, and stitch length on a scrap of the skin. There is a special wedge-shaped needle for leathers that makes stitching smoother. Use paper clips or tape to hold seams in place while stitching. Tie thread ends at darts and seams; backstitching could cut into the leather. Seams should be topstitched an equal distance either side of the seam line; topstitched to one side of the seam line, in a similar way to a welt seam; or stitched with a piece of seam tape included in the seam, pressed open, and the seam allowances glued to the garment. Use rubber cement or fabric glue. Pressing should be done on the wrong side with a warm iron—no steam. Follow the manufacturer's instructions for pressing leather-like fabrics, since most of these are synthetic and can be harmed by heat. Finger-pressing may be sufficient.

Most leather and leather-like fabrics should be lined; use nonwoven interfacings to stabilize the areas where needed.

Hems can be turned and topstitched, or glued in place for an invisible finish. The hem allowance should not be more than 2 inches (5 cm) wide.

Leather and suede will have to be dry-cleaned by a cleaner specializing in this work. Make your dry cleaner aware of the leather-like fabrics—these, too, may require special handling. Some of the suede-like and imitation suede fabrics are machine-washable. Information on the care and maintenance of these fabrics will be included in the manufacturer's instructions.

METALLIC AND SEQUINED FABRICS

These fabrics are ideally suited to special occasions. Choose a fabric with very simple lines and few seams and darts—the fabrics are elaborate in themselves. The weight of these fabrics will vary with the amount of trim on the surface. You may have to cut heavily textured fabrics on a single thickness; otherwise you can follow the with-nap layout, having the pattern pieces all going in one direction.

To sew, test a piece of the fabric for pressure, tension, and stitch length. Use a backing of a sheer fabric, such as net or organza; or you may want to line the garment for a more finished look inside. Do not use moisture or steam. Press on the wrong side along the seam line, using a dry iron and low heat setting. Sew the zipper in by hand. (See Chapter 12, Fig. 339)

WORKING WITH FUR

Whether you have a new fur, or want to use a piece of fur you have salvaged, the procedure is the same.

Cut a whole paper pattern of the collar or band you want to make—do not cut a half pattern, since fur is never cut on the fold. No seam allowances are necessary. Determine how the fur runs—its direction should be straight up and down or toward the center back. You will want to know this if you have to piece the collar or band. It is a good idea to mark matching arrows on the skin, or back of the fur, and then on the pattern, to enable you to lay the fur properly before cutting. If you have to piece the fur, lay the pieces side by side—do not overlap—and place the pattern on the skin side. With tailor's chalk or pencil, draw the outline of your pattern. (Fig. 94)

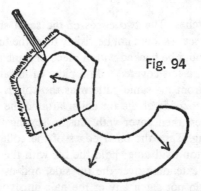

Fig. 94

Cut the fur on this outline, using a single-edged razor blade or a very sharp knife. (Fig. 95) Cut only through the skin—do not

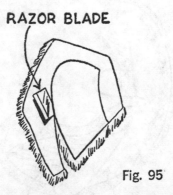

RAZOR BLADE

Fig. 95

cut the hairs on the other side. If piecing, cut the pieces to meet evenly with no jagged edges.

To join seams, put the fur sides together. Hold tight, and with a strong needle and waxed thread, sew the two edges together with overhand stitches. (Fig. 96) Be careful not to catch any of the

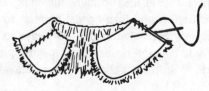

Fig. 96

fur in the stitches. The two edges of the seam should meet each other and the seam should not be visible from the fur side.

The fur should be backed with a piece of lamb's wool or flannel for padding and this covered with a piece of muslin. Cut the backing material from the same pattern as the collar. Attach the padding to the underside of the fur collar around the edges with loose basting stitches, then cover with muslin, sewing the muslin collar to the padding. Tape the outer edges of the collar with a ½-inch (1.3 cm) cotton twill tape: hold the fur with the skin toward you and the tape extending over the fur side, and use small overcasting stitches—do not catch any of the hair into your stitches. Turn tape over padding and catch-stitch to muslin. (Fig. 97)

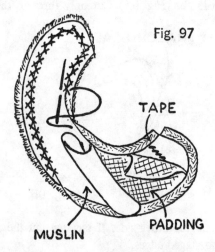

Fig. 97

TAPE

PADDING

MUSLIN

If you are going to attach the fur collar to a coat, turn in the seam allowance on the undercollar and place the wrong side of the fur collar to the wrong side of the undercollar. (Fig. 98)

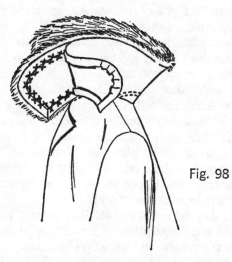

Fig. 98

Slip-stitch collar in place, catching the stitches in the tape. To hold the undercollar in place, make a line or two of running stitches at the roll line in the back, catching the interlining of the fur.

DEEP PILE AND FUR-LIKE FABRICS

With the variety of fake furs on the market today, everyone can have that little fur jacket or coat. It is frequently almost impossible to distinguish the fake from the real. The fake furs have a pile of synthetic yarn and a backing or foundation of woven or knitted fabric in cotton or synthetic. Some fake furs are washable, others can be dry-cleaned only. Read the label or hang tag for fiber content and care instructions.

The fabric is 54 to 60 inches (140 to 150 cm) wide and, because of the pile, you must purchase the yardage for with-nap layout. Choose simple patterns with few seams. To eliminate bulk, cut facings in one with the garment, if possible, or substitute a facing of lighter-weight fabric for a self facing. Plan for decorative closures such as frogs, metal hooks, or toggle bolts in place of buttonholes.

Deep-pile fabrics must be cut on a single thickness; do not fold the fabric. Cut a whole paper pattern, and place pattern pieces on the backing side of the fabric with all the pieces facing in the same direction. The pile or hair should run down. Pattern pieces may be taped in place rather than pinned.

To cut, you might find it easier to use a razor blade, particularly with long-haired furs, and cut only the backing—the pile will separate itself. Do not cut notches out; place a mark inside the seam line. Mark other construction details as necessary on the wrong side with chalk or ball-point pen.

To sew, use dual-duty thread and a needle compatible with the weight of the fabric, and stitch in the direction of the pile.

Use a long needle to lift pile out of the seam on the right side. Shear pile from seam allowances of deep-pile fabrics to remove bulk. Finger-press seams open and sew seam allowances to backing fabric with a loose hemming stitch.

Reinforce shoulder seams by stitching a piece of preshrunk seam tape into the seam. Slash through center fold of dart, shear pile as on seam allowances, and sew edges of dart to backing fabric.

Slip-stitch raw edge of hems and facings to backing fabric.

5 Interfacings, Underlinings, and Linings

There is more to the construction of a garment than meets the eye. It's "what's underneath" that shapes and forms the fashion silhouette. Women's clothes have been shaped from within by such understructures as crinoline, hoops, panniers, whalebone, bustle—all planned to exaggerate and emphasize the silhouette.

Fashion lines today can be achieved and maintained by such hidden assets as interfacings, underlinings, and linings.

INTERFACING

An interfacing is a reinforcement between the facing and outer fabric of a garment that gives body and shape. Jacket and coat fronts, collars and cuffs, are interfaced to achieve the correct roll of the lapel or stand of the collar.

Your pattern will indicate where to use interfacings, what pattern pieces are to be interfaced, and how much interfacing to purchase. The use of interfacing may be listed on the pattern as "optional." You can then use your own discretion as to the effect you wish to achieve; if you prefer a soft look to the garment, eliminate the interfacing.

Fabrics for interfacing are categorized into two groups—woven and non-woven fabrics. Woven fabrics are made with a lengthwise and crosswise grain, and the interfacing must be cut on the true grain of the fabric. There are some woven fabrics made specifically for interfacings, and other fabrics you might have on hand that are suitable to use as an interfacing.

Non-woven fabrics are made by a felting process that bonds the fibers together. There is no grain to this type of interfacing and the edges of the fabric do not ravel. A "bias" non-woven interfacing stretches in any direction and reacts much like the bias grain of a woven fabric.

Iron-on interfacing can be woven or non-woven; a fusible webbing is also available and can be used as an interfacing where reinforcement without bulk is needed. This type of interfacing is ironed on to the wrong side of the outer fabric and so fused to the fabric by heat and pressure. Make a test on a sample swatch of the fabric being used before applying this to the garment, following the manufacturer's instructions. Fusible interfacings are not recommended for certain heat-sensitive fabrics.

Hair canvas is a special interfacing containing goat's hair that is used to shape and reinforce tailored garments. It is available in light-, medium-, and heavyweights.

In selecting an interfacing, be careful to choose one according to the weight of the outer fabric, the design of the garment, and the final effect you wish to achieve, and one with the same cleaning or laundering characteristics as the outer fabric. Before you make the final decision on the type of interfacing you will use in your garment, put the outer fabric and interfacing together to see how they drape and feel in the hand. Always check the label on the interfacing; if the fabric is not preshrunk, be sure to do this properly before cutting.

UNDERLINING

An underlining is the fabric used as a backing to give shape and silhouette to the garment. The underlining is cut according to the pattern piece, then pinned and hand-basted to the wrong side of the outer fabric about ¼ inch (6 mm) from the edges; baste through the center markings, and through the center of each dart. The two pieces of fabric are then handled as one in "double fabric construction." (Fig. 99)

The design of the garment and the fabric used will determine the need for an underlining. It may be necessary to underline the entire garment, such as the front and back sections of a straight or bell-

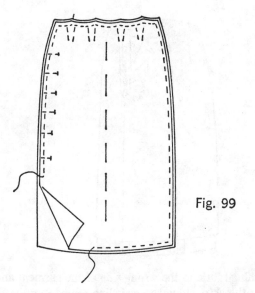

Fig. 99

shaped skirt. Sometimes a partial underlining to mid-thigh length is sufficient as a stay to prevent a "baggy" seat.

Loosely woven fabrics, tweeds, and fine silks benefit most from underlinings.

The fabrics used for underlinings are similar to those used for interfacings; remember to choose the underlining according to the weight and texture of the outer fabric as well as the finished silhouette of the fashion.

A jacket or coat that has been completely underlined with hair canvas usually will not require additional interfacing at the front edges.

LINING

A lining is meant to finish the garment on the inside and cover all the seams.

A completely lined skirt is best when the skirt and the lining are two separate units, joined only at the waist and zipper. Cut the lining according to the pattern pieces; stitch and press all darts and seams in the lining fabric and in the skirt (with bulky fabrics, press darts in lining in opposite direction to those of skirt)—leave the zipper placket open in the lining. (Fig. 100) Place the wrong side

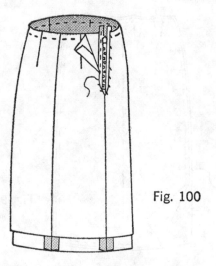

Fig. 100

of the lining fabric to the wrong side of the garment and attach the lining to the skirt along the waistline seam. Sew the lining to the zipper tape by hand. (Fig. 100) Hem the skirt and lining separately, making the hem on the lining at least 1 inch (2.5 cm) shorter than the garment. (Fig. 101)

Fig. 101

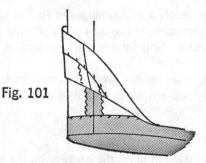

The side seam allowance of the skirt and lining may be attached by basting stitches in matching thread. Baste to about 6 to 8 inches (15 to 20.5 cm) above the hem.

If the skirt is partially lined, attach the lining to the garment at the seams and waist edge. Stitch and pink the bottom edge of the lining; a narrow hem might form a ridge on the right side. (Fig. 102) Finish the skirt according to pattern instructions.

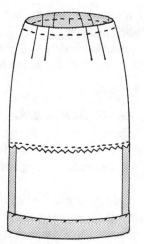

Fig. 102

When lining or partially lining a skirt with a center back pleat, it is wise to eliminate the pleat in the lining fabric to reduce bulk.

Bodice linings are cut according to the pattern pieces for the bodice. Stitch and press all darts and seams in the lining fabric and in the bodice. (With bulky fabrics, press darts in lining in opposite direction to those of bodice.) Place the lining and bodice together with wrong sides facing. Finish the neckline edge. Baste lining and bodice together around armhole edge. Attach lining at waist of dress. If sleeves are lined, attach lining as above and stitch to armhole of bodice.

If you are making a jacket or coat, separate pattern pieces are given for the lining as well as detailed instructions for sewing it in.

For linings, choose fabrics of silk, rayon, acetate, polyester crepe, or fine cotton. Patterned linings of narrow stripes or small allover prints have a particular fashion flair, and fleece-type linings are popular for outerwear since an interlining can then often be eliminated. Developments in the lining and interlining combination include a twill fabric chemically treated for warmth and a satin face fabric with a fleece backing.

INTERLINING

An interlining is the fabric used between the outer garment and the lining to give additional warmth. Your pattern will indicate the procedure for interlining a coat or jacket. Use fabrics such as flannel, lamb's wool, or quilted padding.

The interlining can be applied separately to the inside of the garment, or it can be stitched as one with the lining before the lining is sewn to the garment.

GUIDE TO INTERFACINGS, UNDERLININGS, LININGS

Your prime purpose in choosing an interfacing, underlining, or lining is to achieve the effect *you* want. Consider the weight of the fabric you are using, the texture, and the design of the garment in the over-all picture.

There are many woven and non-woven fabrics made specifically for interfacing and underlining. These are usually found in a special section of the fabric department; ask the salesperson for assistance if you cannot find them.

Woven Fabrics Suitable for Interfacings and Underlinings—include:

batiste	nylon net
muslin (bleached or unbleached)	nylon organdy
durable-press cotton broadcloth	acetate sheath lining
acetate taffeta	cotton sheath lining
organdy	China silk
organza	

Guide to Choosing an Interfacing and Underlining

Fabric	Fiber Content	Suggested Interfacing or Underlining
sheers	cottons	organdy
	blends	batiste
	nylons	organza
	rayons	nylon organdy
	silks	nylon net
	laces	acetate sheath lining
		acetate taffeta
lightweight	cottons	batiste
	blends	organdy
	rayons	nylon net
	wools	sheath lining
	linens	non-woven, lightweight or
	synthetics	bias

medium-weight	cottons	bleached muslin
	blends	cotton broadcloth
	rayons	acetate taffeta
	wools	sheath lining
	linens	non-woven, medium-weight
	synthetics	or bias
heavyweight	wools	bleached or unbleached
	pile fabrics	muslin
	blends	hair canvas
	linens	acetate taffeta
		sheath lining
		non-woven, medium-weight
		or bias

6 Putting Your Dress Together

If you are a novice at sewing, you will be wise to eliminate experimenting when putting the pieces of your garment together. It is much better for you to follow exactly the step-by-step directions given in the pattern instruction sheet (cut and sew guide). When you have become entirely familiar with pattern directions, you can begin to try your own shortcuts in sewing.

METHODS OF PUTTING A GARMENT TOGETHER

There are two distinct ways of putting a garment together after it has been cut from the paper pattern. One is the method usually followed in factories, where there are no fitting problems and where the most important factor is speed of production on a large scale. The other way of putting a dress together is known as the custom method and is followed by the fine shops where clothes are made to the exact measurements of the women who order them. In the custom method the clothes may be fitted several times before the actual sewing and finishing are completed.

Factory Method—Every dress factory has its own methods and each differs somewhat from the others. In general, however, the steps are as follows:

- The entire front of the dress is put together; the blouse front and skirt front are assembled separately and then joined together at the waistline.
- The entire back of the dress is put together, first the skirt back,

then the blouse back; the two sections are then joined at the waistline.

- The front and back of the dress are joined at the shoulder seams.
- The neck is finished completely.
- The sleeves are sewn flat into the armhole; that is, before the underarm seams have been stitched.
- The dress is pinned or basted together, and the sleeve and side seams are stitched in one continuous operation.
- The zipper is stitched in.
- The bottom of the sleeve is finished.
- The hem is turned up and finished, and the dress is complete by the quick factory method.

Custom Method—Dressmaking houses, too, differ in their methods and procedure. The following sequence of steps is most frequently used:

- Construction is done on flat pieces, such as a yoke.
- The blouse front and blouse back are completed separately and then basted together at the shoulder and underarm seams, and the final stitching done after proper fitting.
- The skirt front and the skirt back are each completed separately, and then basted together at the side seams, and the final stitching done after proper fitting.
- The bodice and skirt are basted together for a fitting on the person who is to wear the dress; the correct position of the waistline seam is marked at this fitting.
- The armhole is checked to see that its position is right for the figure.
- The sleeves are fitted into the armhole, pinned, then basted.
- All basted parts get their final stitching.
- The length of the hem is marked at the last fitting; this is best done when the entire dress has been stitched and is ready for the hemline.

Since speed is the single advantage of the factory method of putting a dress together, it should be used only in making children's clothes or other garments that do not require fitting. For all other purposes, and especially for dresses, where emphasis is on good fitting and fine sewing, the custom method is much to be preferred.

GENERAL PROCEDURE FOR PUTTING A DRESS TOGETHER

Your cut and sew guide combines factory and custom techniques. It uses the unit method of construction, which simply means that the instructions for each individual garment are written in such a way that you will be working on one section of the garment, completing it before going on to the next section. The purpose is to be organized in your work and to handle the garment as little as possible. As you complete a unit, place it on a hanger to keep it fresh and wrinkle-free.

Usually the guide sheet will advise you to follow this order of construction:

1. Mark all construction markings on the wrong side of fabric before removing the pattern pieces. (See Chapter 3 for instructions on various techniques.)
2. Baste guidelines at center front and center back. If the garment is to hang well, these lines must be perfectly straight on the figure when the garment is fitted.
3. For the first fitting, prepare the bodice section—pin and baste darts and seams in bodice front and back; prepare the skirt section—pin and baste darts and seams in skirt front and back. Do not do the final machine stitching. Do not press. You may need to make some slight change before stitching, and it is easier to take out a basting stitch than to rip a machine-stitched seam.
4. Baste bodice and skirt together for first fitting. If you are using shoulder pads, put them in place. Tie a string around your normal waistline. The seam should come beneath the string. Make any needed corrections.
5. Stitch and press darts and seams of bodice.
6. Complete neckline with facing. If the garment has a collar, prepare collar and attach it to the neck edge.
7. Stitch and press darts and seams in skirt. Leave opening as indicated on the pattern piece for a zipper or other type of closing.
8. Prepare sleeves—stitch underarm seam; pin and baste the sleeves to the armholes. If there is a cuff, make the cuff but do not attach it until after the sleeve fitting has been checked.

9. For the second fitting, pin and baste bodice to skirt. Check sleeve fitting.
10. Complete sleeves, finish bottom edge with hem or cuff; stitch to armhole. Stitch waistline seam.
11. Complete the openings in the garment.
12. Allow the garment to hang at least twenty-four hours before marking the hemline. Wear the belt, if the dress is to have one, and the shoes you plan to wear with this garment. Mark the hemline. (See Chapter 11.)
13. Complete the hem; sew on hooks and eyes or buttons if necessary; give the garment a final pressing even though you have been pressing as you go.

FITTING

Few figures are perfect. If you have chosen your pattern in the correct figure type, size, and style for your figure as suggested in Chapter 1, and if you have made alterations in your paper pattern, as described in Chapter 2, your fitting will be a smooth one.

Rules for Fitting

- Wear the undergarments you intend to wear with the garment.
- Wear the shoes you intend to wear with the garment.
- Always put the garment on right side out for a fitting, with shoulder pads in place if they are to be used, and a belt if the design requires one.
- Be sure the guidelines at center front and center back are marked; keep guidelines in position during fitting.
- Do all fitting in front of a full-length mirror if possible.
- Try to have someone help you with the fitting.
- Follow the lines of the pattern to maintain the design and style of the garment; allow for ease—remember, *do not overfit.*
- Hang your finished garment on a good hanger.

Tips for a Better Fit

If the center front and center back guidelines of bodice slant to one side—one shoulder may be slightly lower than the other. Both shoulders can be made to appear alike by using a shoulder pad for the lower shoulder.

If there are slight wrinkles from the neck to the underarm—these can be corrected by the use of a shoulder pad.

If the neckline is too high or too tight—be sure to slash neckline seam to the stay-stitching line; wrinkles or pulls at the neckline will often disappear with proper slashing. To cut a new neckline, mark one side with pins; fold the neckline in half and cut both sides at the same time. Make a neckline larger by deepening it; to make a neckline smaller, try taking up only a ½-inch (1.3 cm) seam instead of the usual ⅝ inch (1.5 cm).

If there is gaping at the back of the neck—take several small darts in the bodice before finishing the neckline. This alteration can also be used when the back is slightly wide at the shoulders. Make the necessary corrections to the neckline facings.

If center front and center back guidelines of skirt slant to one side—this is caused by a slight difference in the size of the hips, a common figure fault. Let out the side seam at the larger hip or pin the seam deeper on the opposite side until the guideline hangs straight. Re-baste along the pinned line for stitching. Alteration will usually be needed on one side only.

If the skirt side seams swing forward—raise the skirt slightly at the back waistline until the side seams hang straight. This "take-up" will be widest at the center back and taper to nothing at the sides.

If the skirt side seams swing toward the back—raise the skirt slightly at the front waistline until the side seams hang straight. When this adjustment is made, the raised part will be widest at the center front and will taper to nothing at the sides.

Tips for a Better Fit in Pants

The waist, hip, and crotch are the most crucial areas of fit for your pants. The waist and hips can be fitted as you would a skirt. The crotch should fit smoothly, without wrinkles, yet you must have room to sit and bend.

Pants that reveal bulges in the thigh area are not becoming; maintain a minimum of 2 inches (5 cm) ease through the thigh.

7 Simple Stitches, Seams, and Seam Finishes

In this chapter you are going to learn the basic sewing stitches, and the different types of seams—how they are made and where they are used. This information will guide you in putting your garment together in a careful manner and give you a finished article that you will be proud to wear.

Before you begin, however, you must learn how to knot a thread for hand sewing and how to finish the ends of machine stitching, for without these basics your sewing will be wasted effort.

HOW TO TIE A KNOT FOR HAND SEWING
1. Hold the end of the thread between the thumb and first finger of the left hand. (Fig. 103)

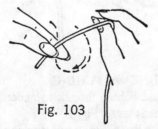

Fig. 103

2. Use the right hand to bring the long end of the thread completely around the first finger. Continue to hold down the other

end of the thread with the thumb and first finger of the left hand. (Fig. 104)

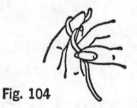

Fig. 104

3. Roll the short end of the thread away from you, pushing the loop off the end of the first finger. (Fig. 105)

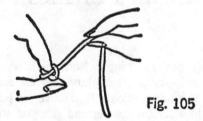

Fig. 105

4. Pull the loop between the thumb and the finger to form the knot. (Fig. 106) Practice until you achieve a smooth, small knot each time.

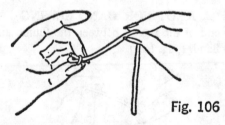

Fig. 106

SECURING MACHINE STITCHING
By Hand—Pull top and bobbin threads to underside of fabric.
1. Draw both threads taut. (Fig. 107)
2. Form a loop with threads at end of stitching. (Fig. 108)
3. Pull threads through loop, making a tight knot at end of stitching. (Fig. 109)

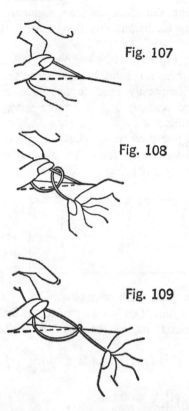

Fig. 107

Fig. 108

Fig. 109

By Machine—When you have completed stitching, raise the presser foot with your right hand, hold the fabric in position with your left hand, and take several stitches in the same position. This will secure the stitching. Remove fabric and clip thread ends.

You could also secure machine stitching by taking a few stitches in reverse.

METHODS OF BASTING

Basting is used to hold the fabric together before the final stitching. It is best to use a thread of contrasting color to make removal easy.

Must you baste? The answer is up to you! After you have been sewing for a time, you will find that you can pin straight seams together and stitch them by machine without basting first. This is called pin-basting. But when you are a beginner at sewing, you will be wise to follow the pattern directions exactly. If they say "baste," you baste!

Every sewer, experienced or beginner, is wise to baste the side seams of a garment for fitting because these are the places where changes most frequently need to be made—and ripping out a machine-stitched seam is certainly more work than removing a temporary basting.

Pin Basting—Use fine dressmaker pins and place the pins at right angles to the edges of the fabric, close enough so that the fabric does not slip. (Fig. 110)

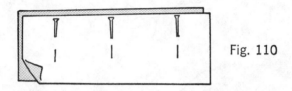

Fig. 110

Although you can stitch over pins by using a movable presser foot on the machine, this has a tendency to dull the point of the needle. It is wiser to remove the pins from the fabric as you come to them.

Machine Basting (Fig. 111)—This is a quick technique for basting

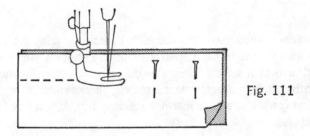

Fig. 111

and can be used on all fabrics that will not mark easily. Use the longest stitch on the machine and a slightly looser top tension to make it easier to remove the bobbin thread. Machine basting is also used to mark buttonhole and pocket locations on the right side of the fabric. The construction markings should be transferred from the pattern piece to the fabric on the wrong side. Then, in a contrasting thread, machine-baste along these markings so that the location is clearly visible on the right side for stitching. Some sewing machines feature a special basting stitch—a chain stitch—which is removed with one pull of the thread.

Hand Basting—Cut a length of thread from the spool about 24 inches (61 cm) long. Thread a long, slender needle and knot the opposite end of the thread. Use your thimble when hand-basting.

Keep the stitches going forward. Fasten the thread with two backstitches close together. The backstitches can be picked out with the point of the needle and the basting thread removed with one pull from the knotted end. When basting long seams, work on a flat surface, such as a table, to keep the seams straight. When pulling out the basting thread on long seams, clip the thread at intervals to avoid wrinkling the fabric.

Even Basting—Holds two pieces of fabric together and is used as a guide for fitting and stitching. Work the needle in and out of the fabric, making each stitch about ¼ inch (6 mm) long. (Fig. 112)

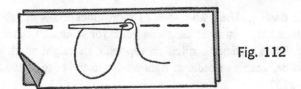

Fig. 112

Uneven Basting—A quickly made marking line through one thickness of fabric, also known as a guideline. Take a long stitch on top and a short stitch through the fabric on the underside. (Fig. 113)

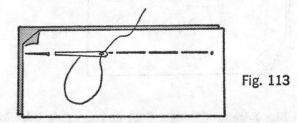

Fig. 113

Slip Basting or Right-side Basting—Used to match the seams with striped, plaid, or patterned fabrics. Turn under the seam allowance on one piece of the fabric; crease. Pin on top of the other piece of fabric, matching the design perfectly. Run the threaded needle through the fold in the upper piece. Bring the needle out, then take a small stitch in the under piece of the fabric. This makes a plain seam on the wrong side, with even basting.

Slip basting is also used to mark any changes in seam lines after the clothes have been fitted. (Fig. 114)

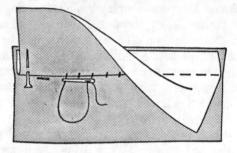

Fig. 114

Diagonal Basting—Used when two or more thicknesses of fabric are held together, it is never used as a guide for seam allowance or for fitting. Take a slanting stitch on top with a straight stitch on the underside, keeping needle at right angles to the edge of the fabric. (Fig. 115)

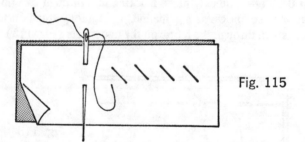

Fig. 115

Basting a Bias Edge to a Straight Edge or Basting an Edge Marked "Ease"—Keep the bias edge, or the edge to be "eased," on top, facing you. Place pins close together so they can be used to adjust fullness evenly. This technique is used when sleeves are basted into the armhole or if a yoke or collar has to be eased in. (Fig. 116)

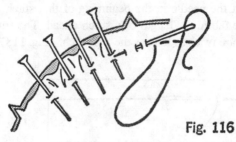

Fig. 116

BASIC SEWING STITCHES

You can sew a seam by hand or by machine. Hand stitching is used for finishing hems, necklines, and sleeve edges, and for decorative touches on well-made clothes. Hand stitching is not as strong as machine stitching, so it is not often used for seams in garments. However, hand stitching may be used for seams in baby clothes and fine lingerie.

If you are left-handed, your needle will probably be going in the opposite direction from that shown in the drawing—that is, if you find it easier to sew from left to right and not from right to left.

Running Stitch—This is the first, the basic sewing stitch. It is the stitch you used when you made your first doll's dress and is called running stitch because the sewer can fill the entire needle with stitched fabric before removing the needle from the fabric. Use thread not more than 24 inches (61 cm) long, since a longer thread may tangle or knot. Sew with a single thread, and fasten end of thread with two small backstitches. Work the needle in and out of the fabric, taking straight, even stitches. End stitching with several small backstitches one on top of the other. (Fig. 117)

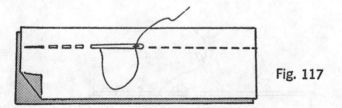

Fig. 117

Backstitch—This stitch is taken just the way it sounds—backward. Fasten the thread and take one running stitch forward. Then insert the point of the needle in the beginning of that stitch and bring it through the fabric the length of a stitch ahead. The stitches on the wrong side are twice as long as the top stitch. (Fig. 118)

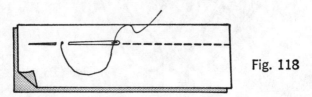

Fig. 118

Combination Stitch—This stitch combines the running stitch and the backstitch and is used for strong hand-sewn seams. Take three or four running stitches and then a backstitch. Repeat for length of the seam. (Fig. 119)

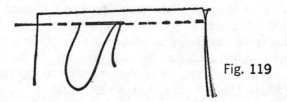

Fig. 119

Overcasting—This is most often used to finish the raw edges to prevent them from raveling. It is a slanted stitch ⅛ to ¼ inch (3 to 6 mm) deep, made by bringing the needle through the fabric from the underside and continuing to work the thread over and under the edge. Each stitch is taken from the underside and at an equal distance from the preceding one. The stitch may be worked from right to left or from left to right. (Fig. 120)

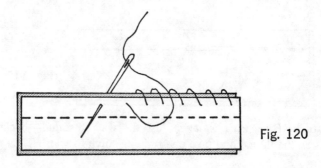

Fig. 120

Quick Overcasting—The needle is worked over and under the fabric and two or three stitches are taken at one time before the thread is drawn through the fabric. The thread should be kept loose. (Fig. 121)

Fig. 121

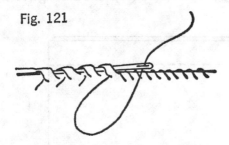

Overhanding—This is an over and under stitch that is taken with the needle at right angles to the fabric. The stitches are taken very close to the edge of the fabric and as close together as possible. The overhand stitch is used for joining two flat pieces of fabric or for hemming table linens. The thread should be kept rather loose to avoid making a ridge when the seam is pressed. (Fig. 122)

Fig. 122

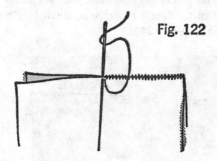

TYPES OF SEAMS

Too often the home sewer will spend time and effort in selecting the proper pattern, the right fabric, and the most suitable trimmings, and then ruin the finished appearance of the garment by crooked or unfinished seams. It is true, of course, that careful seaming takes more time than hastily "running up" a dress, but it is essential in turning out an attractive, well-fitted, and long-wearing garment. More than that, by giving careful attention to the small details and finishing touches you will increase your own pleasure in sewing and the sense of accomplishment that it can give you.

Plain Seam—The stitching of two pieces of fabric together on the wrong side after they have been basted or pinned. Press seam open and finish raw edges. (See "Ways of Finishing Seams," page 109.) (Fig. 123)

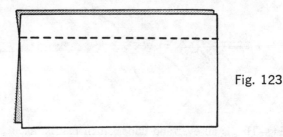

Fig. 123

Topstitched Seam—This seam can be used as a decoration or to join a straight edge to a gathered or shaped edge, such as skirt and bodice or yoke to blouse. A topstitched seam is made by turning under the seam allowance along the straight edge. Baste or press down this seam allowance. Place the folded edge along the seam line of the other piece; pin and baste the two pieces together. With the right side of the fabric facing you, stitch as close to the folded edge as possible. (Fig. 124)

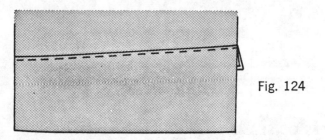

Fig. 124

If additional seam strength is desirable, make a plain seam first, press both seam allowances to one side, and then topstitch through both seam allowances, close to the seam line on the right side.

For a decorative finish, topstitch with buttonhole twist and a slightly longer stitch on a seam or finished edge. Use the edge of the presser foot as a guide, a seam guide attached to the machine, or a line of hand basting, to maintain an even width.

Lapped Seam—Used for decoration when one piece of fabric is to be stitched on top of another. Turn the edge under on the seam allowance of the top piece, and press. Pin and baste in position on bottom piece, matching seam lines. Stitch about ¼ inch (6 mm) from folded edge, unless the pattern specifies otherwise. (Fig. 125)

Fig. 125

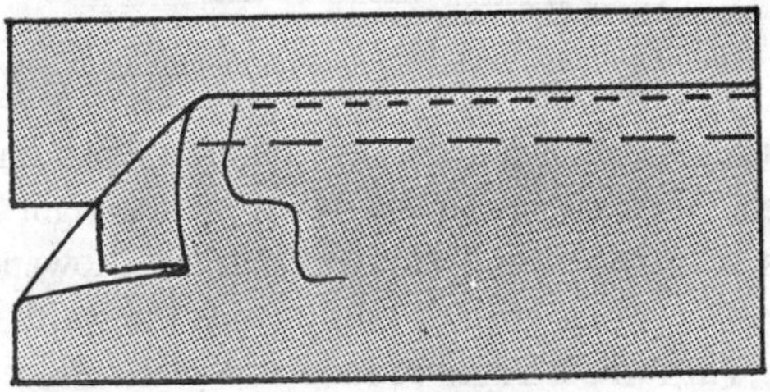

Flat Felled Seam—Used on men's shirts, women's tailored blouses and shirtwaist dresses, and pajamas. Place right sides of fabric together; pin and stitch along seam line. Press both seam allowances in one direction. Trim the seam allowance of the underside to ⅛ inch (3 mm). Trim the top seam allowance to twice the width of the finished seam. Turn under the raw edge and topstitch along fold, stitching the seam flat to the garment. (Fig. 126)

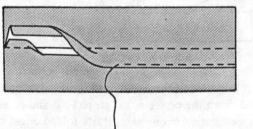

Fig. 126

A flat felled seam can also be stitched to the inside of the garment, in which case the wrong sides of the fabric are placed together.

Welt Seam—Used for women's tailored shirtwaist dresses or blouses and on tailored coats or jackets. Stitch a plain seam on the wrong side of the fabric. Press the seam to one side and trim the seam allowance of the underside to ⅛ inch (3 mm). On the right side, make a second row of stitching ¼ inch (6 mm) from the seam line to hold the seam allowance flat. (Fig. 127)

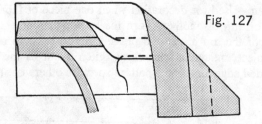

Fig. 127

Strap Seam—Used as a decorative tailored finish on unlined coats and
jackets. First stitch a plain seam on the right side of the fabric.
Press seam open and trim both seam allowances to ¼ inch (6
mm). Cut a bias strip of fabric twice the width of the seam allowance. Turn under edges of strip and press. Place the bias strip over
the seam and baste. Topstitch along both edges on the right side
of the garment. (Fig. 128)

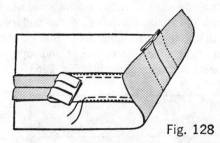

Fig. 128

Slot Seam—Another decorative seam for tailored garments. Cut a
straight strip of fabric twice the width of the seam allowance. Run
a basting thread down the center of the strip. Fold and press seam
allowances on garment to wrong side. Baste folded edges of garment sections to center line of strip. Then, working from the right
side, stitch carefully along each edge about ¼ inch (6 mm) from
the center line. Remove bastings and press. (Fig. 129)

This seam is particularly interesting if a contrasting color is used
for the strip.

French Seam—Used for children's clothes, sheer garments, and lingerie. Stitch a plain seam on the right side of the fabric ½ inch
(1.3 cm) from the edge. Trim the seam to ⅛ inch (3 mm) from
the stitching line and turn the fabric to the wrong side, creasing

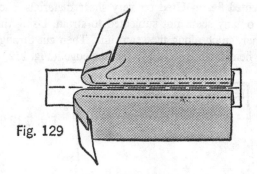

Fig. 129

sharply along the seam line. Stitch ⅛ inch (3 mm) from the fold, encasing the raw edges of the seam allowance. (Fig. 130)

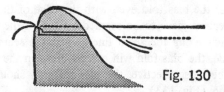

Fig. 130

Mock French Seam—A quick version of the French seam, though not as strong. Make a plain seam on the wrong side of the fabric. Then turn the raw edges in and stitch by hand or machine, as shown in the illustration. (Fig. 131) This technique is particularly useful for finishing the armhole or other shaped seams when French seams are used on the garment.

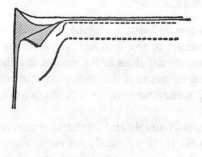

Fig. 131

Machine-picoted Seam—Used on very sheer materials, such as marquisette, or any seam not subjected to strain. Using the machine
hemstitcher, stitch along the seam line. Then cut through the center of the hemstitching to form a picoted edge. (Fig. 132)

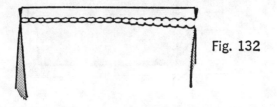

Fig. 132

Piped Seam—Used for decoration. Baste a folded piece of bias material to the right side of one of the pieces to be seamed. This bias
fold should extend ⅛ inch (3 mm) beyond the seam line, with the
raw edges of the bias fold even with the edge of the fabric piece.
Place the second piece to be seamed on top of the bias fold and
machine-stitch along the seam line. When the seam is turned to
the right side, the bias fold will extend between the two pieces of
fabric. To be most effective, the bias material should be of contrasting color. (Fig. 133)

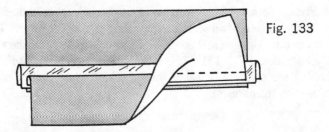

Fig. 133

Corded Seam—A corded seam is a piped seam with a piece of cotton
cable cord inserted in the fold of the bias material before it is
stitched in place. Stitch close to the cord, using the zipper-cording
foot. Corded seams are used for slipcovers and bedspreads as well
as for clothing. Ready-made covered cordings are available for use.
(Fig. 134)

Upholsterer's Seam—A simple and attractive seam and finish for slipcovers and cushions. It is actually a French seam in reverse. The
seam is stitched first on the wrong side and then turned without

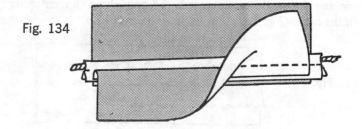

Fig. 134

trimming and stitched a second time on the right side. The second stitching should be done about ¼ inch (6 mm) from the turned-in seam. With this type of seam, no additional trimming or cording is necessary. (Fig. 135)

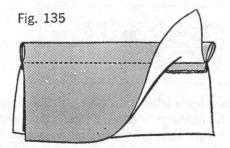

Fig. 135

Taped Seam—Used in areas where there is a possibility of seam stretching or with loosely woven fabrics and knits. Tape should be preshrunk. Pin or baste tape along seam line on the wrong side and stitch tape and seam in one operation. (Fig. 136)

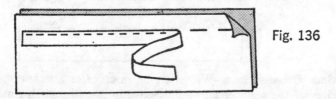

Fig. 136

WAYS OF FINISHING SEAMS

Pinked Seam—This is actually a plain seam with pinked edges. Pinked edges are the quickest finish for any firmly woven fabric. Press the seam open and pink the edge of each seam allowance with the pinking shears. Be careful to take off only about ⅛ inch (3 mm) of the edge. (Fig. 137)

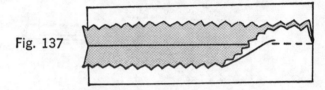

Fig. 137

Stitched and Pinked Seam—When the fabric is firm but may ravel slightly, press the seam open, stitch along the edge of each seam allowance about ¼ inch (6 mm) from edge, and then pink the edges beyond the stitching. (Fig. 138)

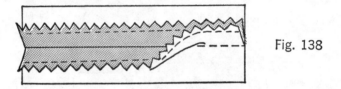

Fig. 138

Overcast Seam—This is a finish used by fine dressmakers. It is especially good for finishing the edges of fabrics that ravel easily. Overcast all raw edges after the seams have been pressed open. (Fig. 139)

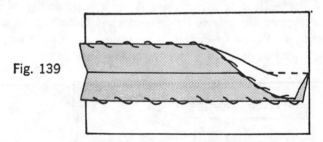

Fig. 139

Machine Overcast Seam—With a zigzag machine or attachment, the edges of the seam could be finished with a zigzag stitch close to the edge of a single seam allowance. (Fig. 140)

Edgestitched Seam—A good way to finish long, straight seams on fabrics such as rayon, cotton, silk, or lightweight woolens is to turn under the raw edges of the seam allowance and machine-stitch close to the folded edge. (Fig. 141)

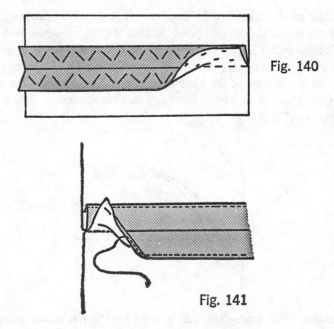

Fig. 140

Fig. 141

Rolled Seam—A finish for very sheer materials such as organdy or batiste. Stitch a plain seam by hand or machine. Trim the seam allowance to within ¼ inch (6 mm) of the stitching. Roll the edges of the fabric toward you with the raw edge under and finish. (Fig. 142)

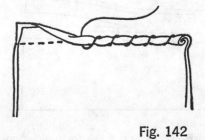

Fig. 142

Bound Seam—Used for finishing unlined coats or jackets. Press the seams open. For a firm binding, use bias tape to cover the raw edges of the seam. To be sure the binding will be fastened in a single stitching, fold and press the tape slightly off center with one side ⅛ inch (3 mm) wider than the other, and baste or pin to seam edge with narrow side of tape uppermost. Machine-stitch close to the edge of the binding on the upper side. Press the seam again. Flat silk or ribbon binding can also be used on lightweight fabrics. (Fig. 143)

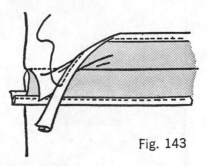

Fig. 143

Double-stitched Seam—This can be used for sheer fabrics if the seam is to be pressed to one side, at the armhole seam, and at the waistline. Make a plain seam and then make a second row of stitching ⅛ to ¼ inch (3 to 6 mm) from the first stitching through both seam allowances. Trim seam allowance close to the stitching line. (Fig. 144)

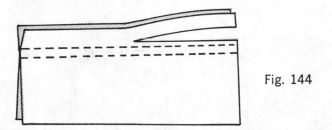

Fig. 144

Hong Kong Finish—An elegant finish for unlined coats or jackets and hems. Cut bias strips of lining fabric 1 inch (2.5 cm) wide. Stitch the bias strip to the right side of the seam ¼ inch (6 mm) from the raw edge. Turn bias to wrong side over raw edge of seam.

Machine-stitch close to the edge of the binding on the right side, encasing the raw edge. (Fig. 145)

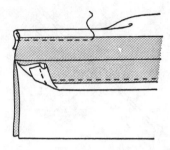

Fig. 145

The same effect can be achieved with the use of packaged bias tape, by opening out one folded edge and stitching this to the raw edge of the seam allowance.

TRICKS WITH SEAMS

Clip curved seams from the outer edge toward the stitching, so they will be smooth. Be careful not to clip the stitching. Inside curves should be slashed (Fig. 146); outside curves should be notched. (Fig. 147)

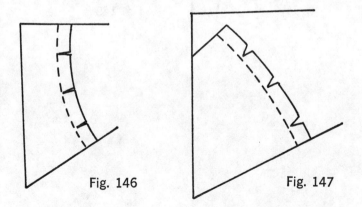

Fig. 146   Fig. 147

Press seam open before it is crossed by another seam in stitching. (Fig. 148)

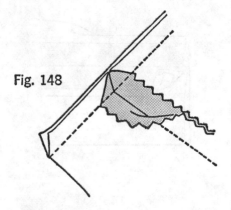

Fig. 148

With soft, thin materials such as chiffon and slippery nylons, pin or baste narrow strips of tissue paper under the seam, and stitch over the tissue paper. Tear the paper away carefully when the seam is completed. (Fig. 149)

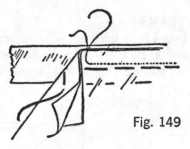

Fig. 149

8   Darts, Tucks, and Pleats

DARTS

A dart is a triangular fold of material stitched wide at one end and tapering to a point. (Fig. 150) A double dart (most often

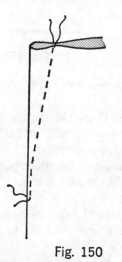

Fig. 150

used at the waistline) is a diamond-shaped piece of material folded and stitched as shown in the illustration, with one long point at each end of the fold. (Fig. 151)

Darts are used to shape clothes by controlling fullness or removing it where it is not needed. They are easy to make, but it is best

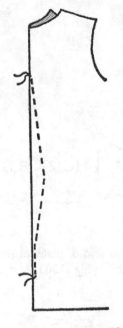

Fig. 151

to practice one or two sample darts before trying them on your garment.

How to Make a Smooth Dart—The trick is this:

- Match the construction markings outlining the dart and pin or baste along the line indicated.
- Then stitch, beginning at the wider part of the dart, and taper the stitching toward the fold at a point ½ inch (1.3 cm) from the end of the dart.
- Stitch this final ½ inch (1.3 cm) along the fold of the dart.
- Leave thread ends at least 3 inches (7.5 cm) long, cut, and tie a knot. (Fig. 152)
- Press the dart over the curved surface of a tailor's ham; when a dart is stitched and pressed in this manner, it will not have the unsightly pucker seen in a dart that has too rounded a point.

Finishing Darts—Careful attention should be given to finishing darts so that they will be as inconspicuous as possible.

- Darts in the skirt or blouse are pressed toward the center line.

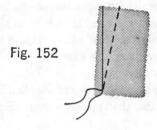

Fig. 152

- Underarm darts are pressed down.
- A group of small darts at the cap of the sleeve are pressed toward the back; elbow darts are pressed toward the bottom of the sleeve.
- Darts in heavy, bulky fabrics are slit open along the fold line of the dart toward the point and pressed open; the edges of the dart may be pinked (Fig. 153) or overcast (Fig. 154), depending upon the fabric.

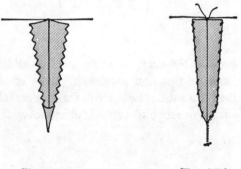

Fig. 153   Fig. 154

Decorative Darts—Although darts are used primarily for fitting purposes, they may also be used for decoration. These darts are stitched on the right side of the garment; make a bobbin-stitched dart so there will be no unnecessary thread ends. To do this, have machine set up for stitching, but remove spool thread from needle. Draw up about 20 inches (51 cm) of bobbin thread. Thread the bobbin thread through the needle in the opposite direction. Tie bobbin thread to spool thread and draw the bobbin thread back through the various thread guides and on the spool. Be sure that the thread take-up lever is at its highest point to avoid snapping the thread at the first stitch. Start to stitch from the point of the dart. Press over a tailor's ham.

Darts are most frequently used:

- *At the shoulder,* to give fullness to the bust. Sometimes two small darts are used rather than one large dart. (Fig. 155)

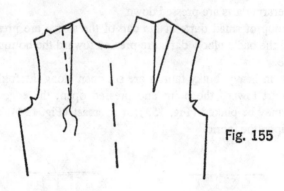

Fig. 155

- *At the back of the neck, or at the back shoulder,* to provide freedom and ease of arm movement. These darts are usually smaller than those used elsewhere in the garment. (Fig. 156a, b)
- *At the underarm seam,* to control fullness over the bust. (Fig. 157)

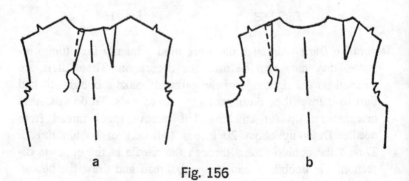

a   b

Fig. 156

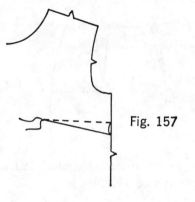

Fig. 157

• *At the elbow of long fitted sleeves,* darts are used to give elbow room. (Fig. 158)

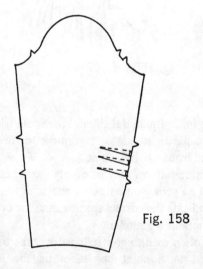

Fig. 158

• *At either side of a skirt back,* to allow for ease and fullness over the hips, and for a smoothly fitted back waistline. A gored skirt can be fitted smoothly without darts. (Fig. 159)

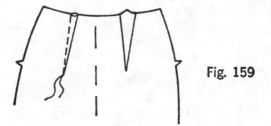

Fig. 159

• *At the side front of a skirt,* a slashed dart with gathered fullness is sometimes used. (Fig. 160)

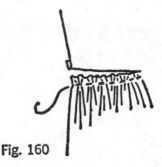

Fig. 160

TUCKS

A tuck is a fold of material usually the same width throughout, often made on the right side of a garment for decoration. Tucks may be stitched by hand or machine.

Tucks directing fullness may be evenly spaced in groups. If they are to be used on your garment, the pattern piece will have special markings to indicate the correct spacing, and the cut and sew guide will give instructions for stitching.

Dart Tucks—are often used to give fullness over the bust. A dart tuck is not stitched to a point but takes up the fullness for the entire length of the dart. (Fig. 161) Rows of dart tucks should always be ended on an even line. (Fig. 162) If the tucks are made on the right side of the garment, rethread the machine with the bobbin thread as directed for a bobbin-stitched dart, or pull thread ends to wrong side and tie.

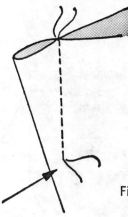

Fig. 161

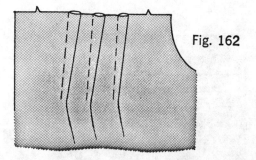

Fig. 162

Pin Tucks—are the tiny tucks used on baby clothes and on blouses. For specially fine work, the tucks should be made by hand. Use short running stitches; the depth of the tuck should take up only a few threads of material. (Fig. 163)

For a different finish on dresses of firm fabric, cording can be stitched into rows of decorative tucks so they will stand out. This can be done by hand or machine. Use the zipper-cording foot for machine stitching and turn the ends of the cord to the wrong side of the fabric, fastening each end securely. (Fig. 164)

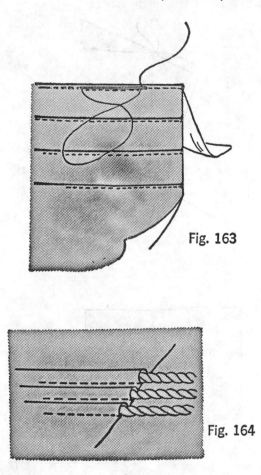

Fig. 163

Fig. 164

Cross Tucking—is a decorative arrangement of rows of tucks made crosswise and lengthwise on the fabric. Stitch and press all the lengthwise tucks in one direction. Then mark, stitch, and press the crosswise tucks. (Fig. 165)

Curved Tucks—are used on circular skirts. To make such tucks requires easing in the fullness on the underside. Baste the outside edges of the tuck first, then adjust the fullness evenly and baste the tuck before stitching. (Fig. 166)

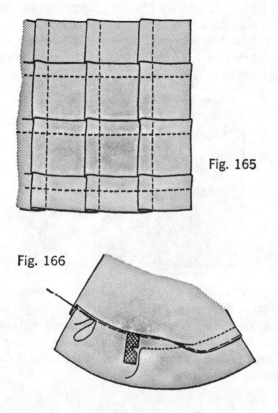

Fig. 165

Fig. 166

Shell Tucks—are used both for shortening and for decoration. The shells are first marked with pencil dots—usually ¼ inch (6 mm) deep and about ½ inch (1.3 cm) apart. Crease the tuck between the dots and take two overcast stitches through each set of dots, drawing them tight. If the tucks are being used for decoration, contrasting thread is effective. (Fig. 167)

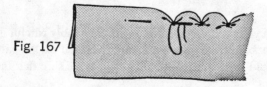

Fig. 167

Overhand Tucks—are another type of decoration used on curved lines. As with the pin tuck, only a few threads of material are taken up. The tuck is creased and overhand stitch⌐s taken over the edge of the fold. Marking the width of the stitches will help to keep the tucks even. (Fig. 168)

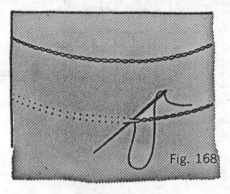

Fig. 168

Many mothers of growing girls run handmade tucks in the skirt or the hem of dresses for a practical reason—as the girl grows, the tucks can be released and the dress lengthened without redoing the hem. "Practical tucks" are also made in the hems of curtains on the wrong side, so they can be lengthened easily if they shrink in laundering. (Fig. 169)

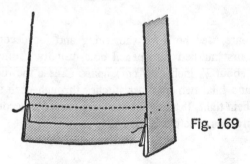

Fig. 169

PLEATS

When your pattern calls for pleats, be doubly careful in marking your fabric. Markings for pleats are indicated on the pattern piece and should be marked with tailor's tacks. Be sure that these markings fall on the straight grain of the fabric, otherwise the pleats will not hang correctly.

Lay the fabric flat on an ironing board to pin and baste the pleats. Do not press pleats at the bottom until after the skirt is hemmed. When rows of pleats are stitched, the stitching should end in an even line. (Fig. 170)

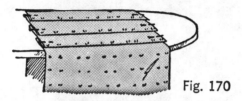

Fig. 170

There are six main types of pleats:

Side Pleats—in which the fold of the fabric is turned to one side. If there is a seam beneath a side pleat, do not press the seam open but press to one side. Side pleats are often graduated in size, so that they are deeper at the top of an all-pleated skirt to make it fit smoothly at the hips and waistline. (Fig. 171)

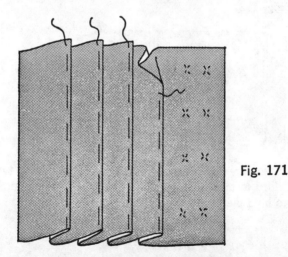

Fig. 171

Pleated skirts will hold a razor-sharp line without frequent pressing if you edgestitch each pleat on the fold. The edgestitching will appear to be a continuation of the stitching that holds the pleats to the upper part of the skirt. Hem the skirt before you edgestitch and continue the stitching to the top of the hem. Fasten the ends of the machine threads on the wrong side of the skirt. (Fig. 172)

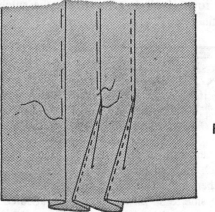

Fig. 172

Box Pleats—are two side pleats, side by side, turned away from each other. (Fig. 173)

Fig. 173

Inverted Pleats—are the reverse side of box pleats, with two side pleats folded to meet each other on the right side and stitched as shown to hold the pleat in place. (Fig. 174)

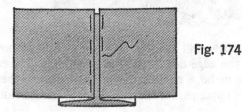

Fig. 174

These first three types of pleats may be used singly or in combination. Box pleats and side pleats are often used together in a skirt. A wide box pleat will come to the center front and center back, with side pleats over the hips. Rows of small side pleats close together are called knife pleats.

Fan or Sunburst Pleats—are a series of narrow side pleats that are wider at the bottom than at the top, since they are made on a perfect circle of material. They are most often used in the skirt of a crepe or chiffon evening dress. You can prepare the material for this type of pleating, but it is really a job for the professional pleater. (Fig. 175)

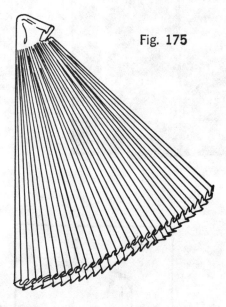

Fig. 175

Accordion Pleats—are made the same way but may be done on the straight grain of the material.

Kick Pleats—are used to give fullness to a skirt at the knee while retaining a smooth, unpleated hipline. Some skirts have kick pleats in either the front or back; others have them in the front and back; and there are skirts with kick pleats at the side seams.

A **single kick pleat** is a wide side pleat, and allowance is made for it in the skirt pattern by adding to the width of the seam at the bottom. Machine-stitch the seam of the pleat; adjust the pleat, pinning it so that the fold of the pleat lies along the seam line. Machine-stitch across the top of the pleat to keep it securely in place. (Fig. 176) Pull thread ends to the wrong side of the skirt and tie the ends.

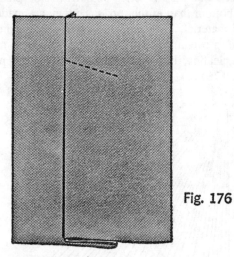

Fig. 176

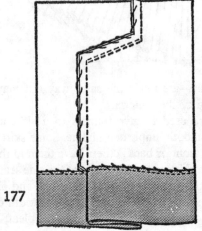

Fig. 177

After the pleat is stitched down at the top, turn under the hem, snipping the seam allowance of the pleat where it meets the hem, so that the seam allowance of the pleat may be pressed open and lie flat within the hem. Overcast the seam edges of the pleat. (Fig. 177)

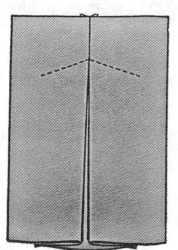

Fig. 178

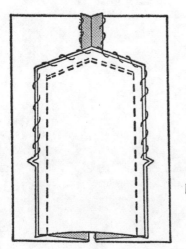

Fig. 179

Double or Set-in Kick Pleats look like inverted pleats at the bottom. A separate piece or underlay is cut for the back of the pleat. To make the pleat, stitch down the seam of the skirt as far as the seam extensions. Baste the underlay to the seam extensions and machine-stitch in place.

Make an inverted pleat, meeting in the center of the underlay. Machine-stitch on the right side as shown in the illustration, bringing the thread ends to the wrong side and tying them. (Figs. 178–179) Finish the pleat at the hemline in the same manner as described for a single kick pleat.

9   Neckline Finishes and Collars

The neckline of a garment may be finished with a collar or with a facing. The shape of the collar or neckline may vary with the design, and the technique for applying the collar or facing may vary as well. A neckline should fit perfectly before the collar or facing is attached, and any alterations made to the neckline of the garment must be made to the collar or fitted facing.

Stay-stitch the neckline of a garment to maintain its shape, ½ inch (1.3 cm) from the edge. Clip the seam allowance of the neck edge to the stay stitching before the collar is applied.

Attach the collar or facing to the neckline as soon as possible, following the pattern markings carefully.

Use interfacing at the neckline and in the collar for additional body and shape, and to keep a crisp, firm edge.

Bias-faced V Neckline—Pin or baste a bias strip about 1½ inches (3.8 cm) wide to the neckline with right sides together.

Stitch the bias to form a point at the V of the neckline, as shown. (Fig. 180) Turn the bias facing to the wrong side. Turn under the raw edge and slip-stitch invisibly to the neckline. (Fig. 181)

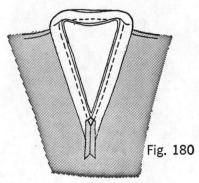

Fig. 180

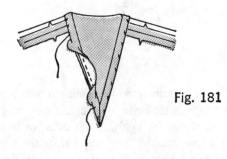

Fig. 181

Front Slashed Facing—Cut the facing pieces on the straight grain of the fabric. Join the front and back facing pieces at the shoulder seams. Stitch along the outer edges of the facing, ¼ inch (6 mm) from the edge. Turn facing under on stitched line and machine-stitch close to edge. Mark center front on facing to indicate the depth of the opening. Pin or baste the facing to the neckline, with right sides together; match notches and shoulder seams.

Stitch around neckline and ¼ inch (6 mm) either side of center front marking. Taper stitching to the point of the V, take one stitch across end of marking, continue stitching other side of opening. (Fig. 182)

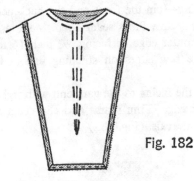

Fig. 182

Slash to the very point, trim seam allowance, and clip neckline seam; turn facing to the inside. (Fig. 183)

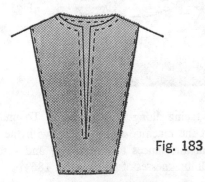

Fig. 183

Press and tack the facing to the garment at the shoulder seams. (Fig. 184)

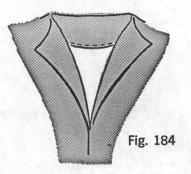

Fig. 184

Shaped Neck Facing—Join the front and the back neck facing pieces at the shoulder seams. Press seam open. Make a line of machine stitching along outer edge of facing, ¼ inch (6 mm) from edge. Turn under the raw edges on stitching line and machine-stitch along edge.

Pin or baste the facing to the garment, with right sides together, and stitch neck edge. Trim seams and clip seam allowance at ½ inch (1.3 cm) intervals. (Fig. 185)

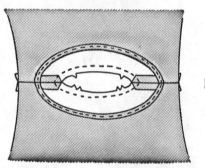

Fig. 185

Understitch facing along neckline seam. To understitch, place the garment at the machine right side up with the facing opened out. Turn seam allowances toward facing and stitch along seam line, through all thicknesses of fabric. (Fig. 186)

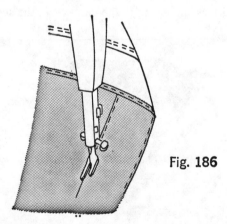

Fig. 186

Turn facing to the inside of the garment; press. Tack facing to shoulder seams.

To Cut a Shaped Facing Without a Pattern Make your own paper pattern by tracing the exact shape of the neck opening with the garment folded at the center front and center back. Add seam allowances and desired depth of facing. Cut the facing with center front and center back on the fold of the fabric.

Shaped Collar—Faced and Interfaced—Cut upper collar, facing, and interfacing from the same pattern piece.

Clip into the seam allowance at the neck edge to indicate the center back on all pieces.

Mark the seam line on the interfacing and cut off corners to eliminate bulk unless the interfacing is lightweight. (Fig. 187)

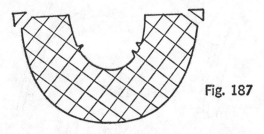

Fig. 187

Pin interfacing to wrong side of facing and stay-stitch. (Fig. 188)

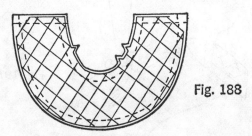

Fig. 188

Pin upper collar to facing, right sides together. With interfacing side up, stitch along seam line of outer edge only. (Fig. 189)

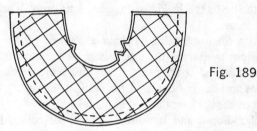

Fig. 189

Trim and grade (layer) seam allowances: upper collar to about ¼ inch (6 mm), facing to about ⅛ inch (3 mm), and interfacing close to the stitching line. Clip the seam allowances around the curve. (Fig. 190)

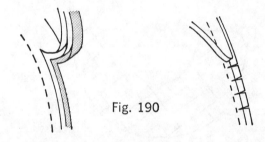

Fig. 190

Press seam allowances toward facing and understitch to hold the seam allowances in position; start and end understitching 1 inch (2.5 cm) from ends. (Fig. 191)

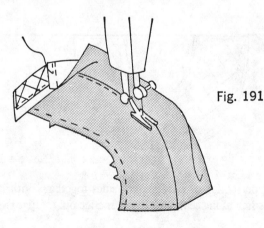

Fig. 191

Fold the collar with right sides together and stitch across the ends. Trim corners and seam to ¼ inch (6 mm); press seam open. (Fig. 192)

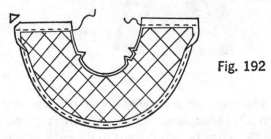

Fig. 192

Turn collar to right side, keep corners pointed, and press entire collar. Before applying collar to neckline, check both ends to be sure they are the same shape and length.

To Attach Collar with Bias Binding Pin or baste the collar in place, with the under side of the collar to the right side of the dress, matching the center back of the finished collar to the center back of the neckline, and matching all notches. (Fig. 193)

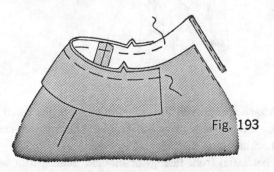

Fig. 193

Turn the facing extension back over the collar. Baste a 1½-inch (3.8 cm) bias strip on top of the collar, extending the strip over the facing turnback about ½ inch (1.3 cm). Ease the bias strip slightly. Stitch by machine. (Fig. 194)

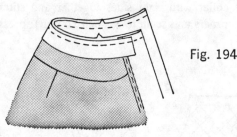

Fig. 194

Trim and grade the seam close to the stitching; clip neckline curve. Press the seam down and understitch through the bias strip and seam. Turn the facing extension to the inside. Turn under the raw edge of the bias strip and slip-stitch it to the neckline. (Fig. 195)

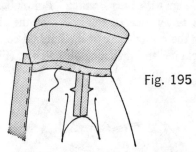

Fig. 195

To Attach Collar with Facing   Pin or baste the collar in place, matching the center back of the finished collar to the center back of the neckline, and matching all notches.

Join back and front facings at shoulder seams, trim seam to ¼ inch (6 mm), and press open. Make a line of machine stitching along outer edge of facing, ¼ inch (6 mm) from edge. Turn under the raw edge on the stitched line and machine-stitch along edge. This is called a "clean finish" for the outer edge of a facing. (Fig. 196)

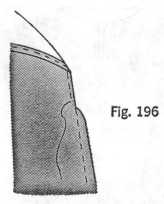

Fig. 196

With right sides together, pin facing to neck edge over collar; match centers, notches, and shoulder seams. Stitch, trim, grade, and clip the seam. Understitch the facing. (See Fig. 186)

Turn facing to inside; press and secure to shoulder seam allowance by hand.

Straight Collar with Slashed Neckline—This collar can be worn turned back or fastened high, Chinese style. To interface this type of collar, cut the interfacing half the size of the collar piece; pin and baste interfacing to wrong side of collar. (Fig. 197)

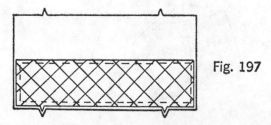

Fig. 197

Fold the collar in half with right sides together; stitch the ends along the seam line. Turn to right side and press.

Make the facing as directed for front slashed facing, but stitch only around the front opening. Slash, turn, and press. (Fig. 198)

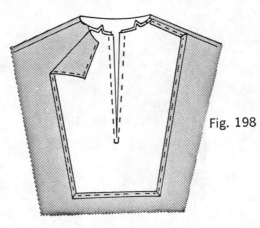

Fig. 198

Pin the underside of collar to neckline with right sides together; match notches, center back markings, and ends of collar to faced opening.

Clip the upper side of the collar ½ inch (1.3 cm) deep into seam allowance at shoulder seams. Pin upper collar to facing.

Stitch the collar and facing in one continuous row of stitching around the neckline. (Fig. 199)

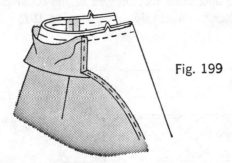

Fig. 199

Trim and clip seam allowances. Press the seam up.

Turn the facing to the inside of the garment.

Turn upper side of collar under from shoulder seam to shoulder seam across back of neckline. (The ½-inch [1.3 cm] clip into the seam allowance will enable you to do this.) Slip-stitch along the seam line. (Fig. 200)

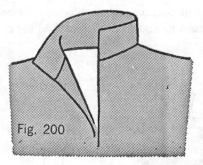

Fig. 200

Convertible Tailored Collar—The collar is prepared, placed, and stitched as the straight collar with slashed neckline.

Match the center back of the collar to the center back of the neckline; match all notches. (Fig. 201)

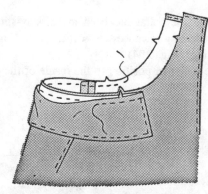

Fig. 201

A separate facing is not necessary since the front facing is turned back over the collar. (Fig. 202)

Fig. 202

The collar will not come to the edge of the front facing and the lapels will extend an equal distance beyond the ends of the collar. (Fig. 203)

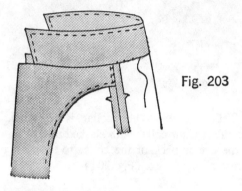

Fig. 203

Detachable Collar—After the collar has been made, stay-stitch along the neck edge. Trim seam allowances to ⅜ inch (1 cm), and finish edge with bias binding. (Fig. 204)

Baste or snap the collar in position to the inside of the garment. (Fig. 205)

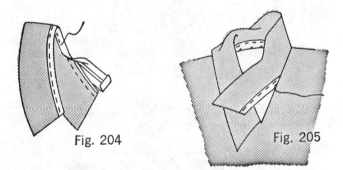

Fig. 204   Fig. 205

Collar with Edging—If you plan to add lace or ruffling to your collar, be certain that you make allowance for the extra length it will add. This allowance will be twice the width of the trimming.

Baste the edging along the outer edge of the collar, matching raw edges. Then pin and stitch facing in place. (Fig. 206)

Turn and press collar. (Fig. 207)

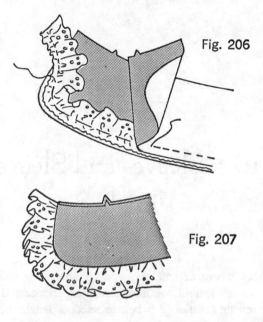

Fig. 206

Fig. 207

10 Sleeves and Sleeve Finishes

A tricky sleeve or cuff may add an interesting touch to your clothes; however, until you have gained experience and confidence in your sewing abilities, it is best to select a pattern with a simple type of sleeve.

SLEEVE STYLES

Cap Sleeve—is simplest to make. It is merely an extension of the armhole. It should not be fitted too closely or it may pull under the armhole. (Fig. 208)

Fig. 208

Kimono Sleeve—is a longer version of the cap sleeve, extending farther on the arm. It is usually rather loose under the arm. (Fig. 209)

Fig. 209

Reinforce the underarm seam with a piece of seam tape stitched into the seam. Clip the seam allowance at the curve to prevent puckering and press the seam open. (Fig. 210)

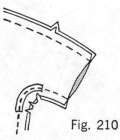

Fig. 210

Kimono Sleeve with One-piece Gusset requires that the garment be slashed. Before making a slash, stay-stitch along markings indicated on the pattern. Cut to the point of stitching. Stitch sleeve and side seam to point of gusset. Pin gusset to slashed edges and stitch. Press seam allowance toward garment and topstitch. (Fig. 211a, b)

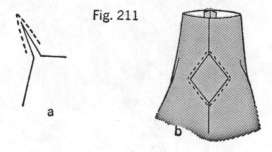

Fig. 211

Kimono Sleeve with Two-piece Gusset requires that the garment be slashed. Before making a slash, stay-stitch along markings indicated on the pattern. Cut to the point of stitching. Pin and stitch gusset into front slash and back slash. Press seam toward garment and topstitch. Stitch underarm seam. (Fig. 212a–c)

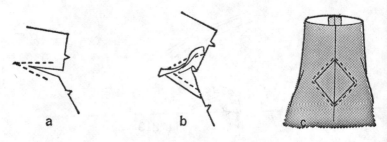

Fig. 212

Dolman or Batwing Sleeve–is an exaggerated sleeve style, popular every few years, but not flattering to the very short figure or the heavy bust line. It is a wide, loose sleeve that tapers to the wrist. (Fig. 213)

Fig. 213

Raglan Sleeve—is used frequently in sports clothes. It is not a good style for the figure with a heavy bust line since it adds width to the figure. The sleeve and the shoulder are cut in one piece. Clip the seams at the curve so they will lie flat, and press seams open. The underarm seam of sleeve and blouse is stitched in one operation. (Fig. 214)

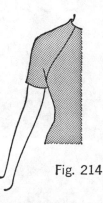

Fig. 214

Gathered Sleeve or Short, Puffed Sleeve—can also be cut in a long full version with a tight band cuff at the wrist. Gather top of sleeve between notches, using two rows of long machine stitches ¼ inch (6 mm) apart. Pin and baste into armhole, distributing fullness evenly. Stitch and press seam toward sleeve. (Fig. 215)

Fig. 215

Set-in Sleeve—is the most commonly used and most generally becoming to all figure types. It can be short, long, or three-quarter length. (Fig. 216)

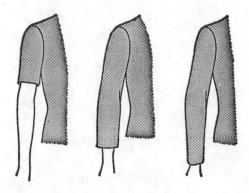

Fig. 216

A two-piece set-in sleeve is often used in tailored coats and suits. (Fig. 217)

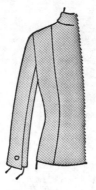

Fig. 217

How to Set In a Sleeve Make a continuous line of machine stitching around cap of the sleeve, just inside the seam line; use a regulation stitch from the underarm to the notch, then a long stitch to the other notch, and a regulation stitch to the underarm seam. (Fig. 218)

Fig. 218

Stitch underarm seam of sleeve; press open. Carefully pull up the bobbin thread at the large dot to form cap. Adjust ease evenly, so that the distance from notch to shoulder point is the same on sleeve and garment. (The sleeve is about 1 inch [2.5 cm] larger than the armhole.) Turn sleeve to the right side. With the wrong side of the garment toward you, slip the sleeve into the armhole. Check to see that the notches correspond, so you will be sure to have each sleeve in the correct armhole. Pin the sleeve into the armhole, matching underarm seams, notches, and shoulder seam to large dot. Place pins at a right angle to the edges of the fabric. (Fig. 219)

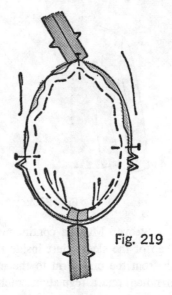

Fig. 219

Pin around the armhole, always working with the armhole toward you. (Fig. 220)

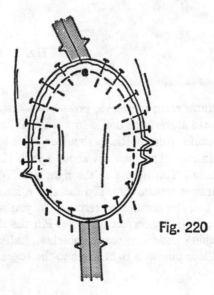

Fig. 220

The sleeve should look perfectly smooth in the armhole—there should be no little pleats or puckers.

Stitch on seam line with sleeve side up, starting and ending at underarm seam; overlap the stitching at the underarm. (Fig. 221)

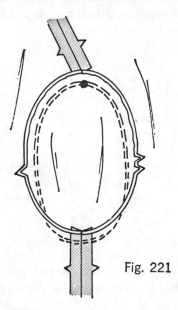

Fig. 221

Trim seam allowance to ⅜ inch (1 cm); finish seam.

Press the seam allowance toward the sleeve. Shrink out any fullness at the top of the sleeve. A tailor's ham or press mitt (which is held over the hand) is the most convenient base for pressing.

FINISHING THE SLEEVE

The sleeve finish varies with the fabric and style of the garment. The pattern guide sheet will include the necessary instructions. Some popular sleeve finishes are:

Plain Hem—Usually about 1 inch (2.5 cm) wide. It is used for short or long sleeves. The edge may be finished with seam binding, stitched and pinked, or the raw edge turned and stitched.

Turnback Cuff Cut with Sleeve—Made from a wide hem at least 4 to 6 inches (10 to 15 cm) deep. After the hem is finished, the double fold of fabric is turned back to the right side of the sleeve to form the cuff.

Turnback Cuff Cut Separately—This type of cuff can be stitched in place entirely by machine, or with a combination of machine stitching and hand hemming. With right sides together, stitch short ends of cuff, press seam open. Pin the right side of the cuff to the wrong side of the sleeve, matching notches and seams. Stitch. (Fig. 222)

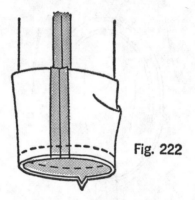

Fig. 222

Turn under the raw edge of the cuff and hem by hand or machine-stitch the edge to the seam line. Press. (Fig. 223)

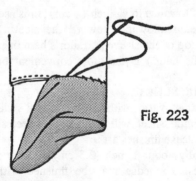

Fig. 223

Turn cuff and sleeve to right side; roll cuff up over sleeve—no stitching should show. Tack cuff at seam. (Fig. 224)

Cuff Applied with Bias Facing—Finish cuff and apply to right side of sleeve. Cut a strip of bias about 1¼ inches (3.2 cm) wide and

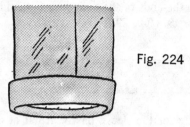

Fig. 224

long enough to fit over the cuff plus seam allowance. Join ends of bias in a plain seam. Pin and stitch bias strip to lower edge of sleeve, through all thicknesses. Turn under raw edge of bias and hem to inside of sleeve. (Fig. 225)

Roll cuff up over sleeve. (Fig. 226)

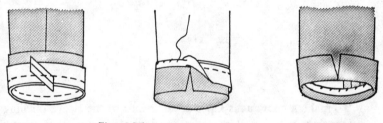

Fig. 225   Fig. 226

Tight Sleeve Opening Faced with Seam Binding—Stitch seam binding to raw edge of sleeve opening on the right side; miter binding at the corners, forming a neat triangle. Turn seam binding to wrong side of sleeve opening and hem. Sew on snaps to fasten opening. (Fig. 227)

Fig. 227

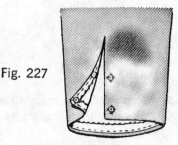

Band Cuff—Stitch the ends of the cuff, with right sides together. Turn to right side; press. (Fig. 228)

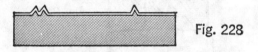

Fig. 228

If an opening for the sleeve has been left at the lower edge of the sleeve seam, make a narrow hem on each seam allowance. (Fig. 229)

Fig. 229

To make a continuous lap placket, reinforce the sleeve opening by machine-stitching along seam line indicated on pattern, taking one stitch across point of opening. Cut on slash line to point of stitching. (Fig. 230)

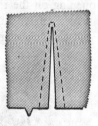

Fig. 230

Place right side of continuous lap to right side of sleeve opening and stitch along reinforcement line, taking up a ¼-inch (6 mm) seam on lap. (Fig. 231)

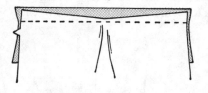

Fig. 231

Turn under ¼ inch (6 mm) on raw edge of lap and hem to seam on inside.

Turn front section of lap to inside, press, and baste in position at lower edge. Stitch diagonally across top of lap. (Fig. 232)

Fig. 232

Gather lower edge of sleeve with a double row of stitches. Pin the cuff to the right side of sleeve, distributing gathers evenly. Stitch. (Fig. 233)

Fig. 233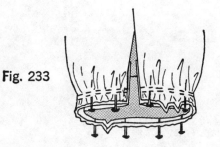

Turn under seam allowance on raw edge of cuff; hem by hand or edgestitch to seam line, enclosing the raw edges. (Fig. 234)

Fig. 234

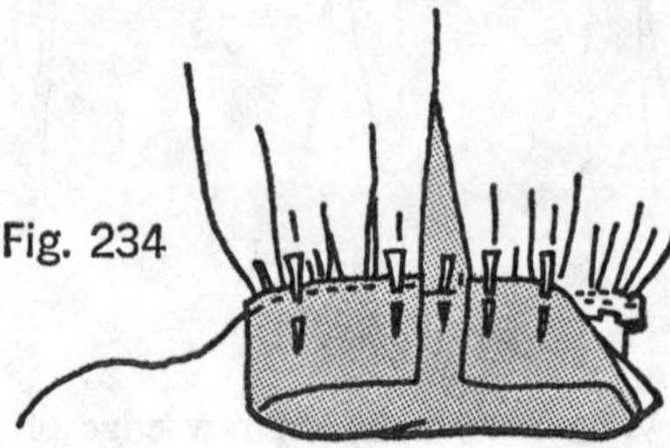

11 Facings and Hems

The difference between the homemade look and the professional appearance of the sewing you do often depends on such details as a facing, a row of scallops, or a hem. These are the finishing touches that not only add to the over-all appearance of your garment, but also reflect unmistakably the care and work that went into them.

TYPES OF FACINGS

A facing is a piece of material, matching or contrasting, that is used for finishing or decorating the edges. There are several types of facings:

Fitted Facing—A separate piece of fabric cut to the same shape and grain line as the garment. (Fig. 235)

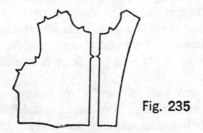

Fig. 235

Bias Facing—A bias strip of fabric applied to curved or shaped edges. (Fig. 236)

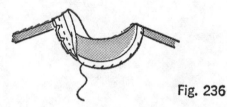

Fig. 236

Shaped Facing—Finished on the right side to add a decorative detail to the garment. (Fig. 237)

Fig. 237

Preparing the Facing

- Cut the facing pieces as indicated in the pattern; clip into the seam allowance at center front and center back neck edge for ease of matching.
- Cut the interfacing from the facing pattern, on the same grain as the facing, and clip center front and center back. (An interfacing is a piece of fabric used between the garment and the facing to give crispness or "body," to maintain permanent shaping, and to offset extra strain on the fabric in such places as under the buttons or buttonholes—see Chapter 5.) For the most professional shaped edge, consider the choice of an interfacing carefully, according to the design of the garment, the weight of the fabric, and the effect you wish to achieve (see chart in Chapter 5). Apply the interfacing to the wrong side of the garment.
- Join the pieces of the facing, if there is more than one; press seams open.
- Finish the outer edge of the facing, make a row of machine stitching ¼ inch (6 mm) from the edge, and finish the raw edge in one of the following methods, according to the weight of the fabric.
    - a. Clean-finish: fold on the stitching line and edgestitch. (Fig. 238)

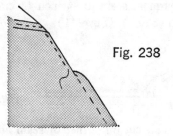

Fig. 238

b. Pink: pink edge beyond stitching line. (Fig. 239)

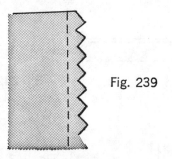

Fig. 239

c. Overcast: overcast raw edge by hand or machine. (Fig. 240)

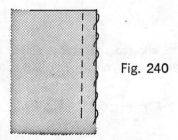

Fig. 240

Stitching the Facing
- Pin the right side of the facing to the right side of the garment and stitch.
- To reduce bulk, grade seam allowances (also called layering or staggering), to different widths; trim interfacing close to stitch-

ing, trim the garment seam to ⅜ inch (1 cm), trim the facing
seam to ¼ inch (6 mm). (Fig. 241)

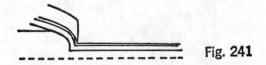

Fig. 241

- On outside corner, cut off corner of seam allowance almost to
  stitching line (Fig. 242); on inside corner, clip the seam allowance to the corner of the stitching to make the facing lie smooth
  (Fig. 243)

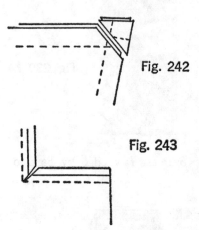

Fig. 242

Fig. 243

- For inside curve, clip seam allowance almost to stitching (Fig.
  244); for an outside curve, notch seam allowance. (Fig. 245)

Fig. 244

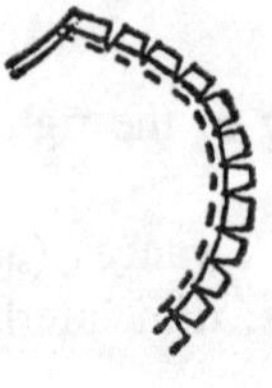

Fig. 245

Understitch the facing along the finished faced edge so that the edge will be sharp and firm and the facing will not roll to the outside of the garment. Place the garment at the machine right side up with the facing opened out. Turn seam allowances down toward facing and stitch along seam line, through all thicknesses of fabric. (Fig. 246)

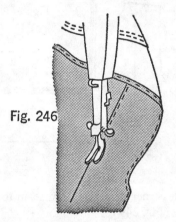

Fig. 246

Press the faced edge carefully. For top pressing, use a press cloth to avoid shine and ridges.

Anchor or Tack the free edge of the facing to the garment at seams and darts—use several catch-stitches. Do not fasten the facing by sewing it to the garment; sew only to the seam allowances.

Bias Facings—are used to finish necklines, sleeves, or hems on circular skirts. Cut the bias the desired width and length, plus seam allowances, and piece if necessary on the straight grain. Shape the bias pieces by "swirling" with a steam iron so that the outer edge will be wider than the inner edge. (Fig. 247)

Fig. 247

Make a line of stitching along outer edge ¼ inch (6 mm) from raw edge. Pin and stitch the bias facing in place. Turn under the outer edge on the stitching line and hem garment.

Facing for a Corner—Corners are usually faced or banded with two straight pieces of fabric that are mitered at the corner. This type of facing is often found on V and square necklines. Pin the facing to the garment, with right sides together, making a triangular fold with the facing at the corner. (Fig. 248)

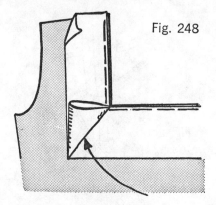

Fig. 248

Machine-stitch corner of facing; trim seam to ¼ inch (6 mm); press seam open. (Fig. 249)

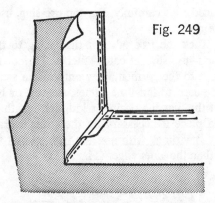

Fig. 249

Stitch the inner edge of the facing to the garment, and clip the seam allowance to the corner of the stitching. Grade seam allowances. Turn facing to inside; finish raw edges of facing; press and anchor to seams.

Facing for a Slashed Opening—Do not cut into fabric until stitching is completed. Mark position for slash on facing. Pin and baste facing to the garment with right sides together. Stitch a V, ¼ inch

(6 mm) from slash marking and taper stitching to a point; take one stitch across end at point of slash and continue stitching along other side of marking. (Fig. 250)

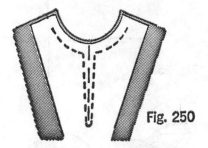

Fig. 250

Cut to point of slash; grade seam allowances; turn facing carefully to inside. Finish raw edge of facing and press. (Fig. 251)

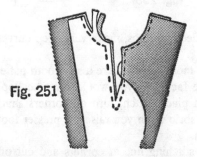

Fig. 251

Facing for a Scalloped Edge—This type of facing can be used on garments as well as household articles. If you have no pattern, make your own by cutting paper scallops in a set of three exactly alike. Cut a facing strip on the same grain as the edge to be faced. To mark the scallops, place the pattern on the facing and trace with pencil or chalk. Pin or baste the facing to the edge, with right sides together. (Fig. 252)

Stitch around curves; at corner of each scallop, leave the needle in the fabric, raise the presser foot, and pivot to the next scallop. Trim scallops to ¼ inch (6 mm). Clip into corners and notch curves so that the facing will lie flat and smooth when it is turned to the inside. Finish raw edge of facing; turn to wrong side and press. (Fig. 253)

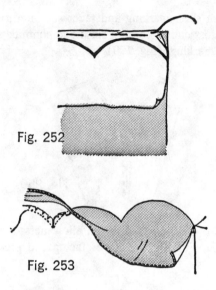

Fig. 252

Fig. 253

NOTE: For deep scallops, make very deep curves on your paper pattern.

Facing for a Saw-tooth Edge—Make a saw-tooth pattern of paper and mark it on the facing as you would for a scalloped edge. Pin or baste facing in place; stitch; turn all corners sharply, leaving the needle in the fabric when you raise the presser foot to pivot to the next saw tooth.

Clip to the stitching line at corners and cut off pointed tip of each tooth. (Fig. 254)

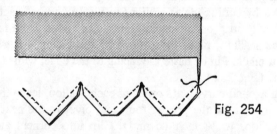

Fig. 254

Trim seams to ¼ inch (6 mm); finish raw edge of facing; turn to inside and press. (Fig. 255)

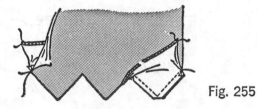

Fig. 255

BANDINGS

Bandings can serve the same purpose as facings, except that they are not always used at the edge of a piece of fabric. A banding may extend beyond the edge, or it may be used as a flat decoration.

Applied Band—Fold and press the seam allowance to the wrong side of the band. Pin the band in place and stitch along each edge by machine, or slip-stitch by hand. (Fig. 256)

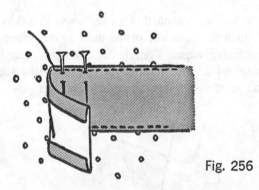

Fig. 256

If the banding is narrow or has a pointed or curved edge, it can be helpful to cut a pattern of cardboard and press the seam allowance over this for a sharp outline.

Extended Band

METHOD A: Fold the band in half, with wrong sides together. Pin the raw edges of the band to the raw edges of the fabric, with right sides together. Stitch ¼ inch (6 mm) from the edge. (Fig. 257)

Turn band up and press seam down. Edgestitch along seam line on the right side of the material for a neat finish. (Fig. 258)

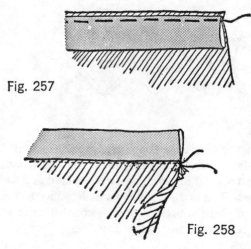

Fig. 257

Fig. 258

METHOD B: This is applied in the same way as a skirt waistband. Pin and stitch the right side of the band to the wrong side of the fabric, matching edges. Turn under the other edge and press. Pin this folded edge in position just covering the stitching line. The band must lie flat and smooth, without ripples. (Fig. 259)

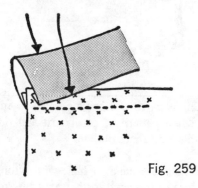

Fig. 259

Edgestitch band in place. (Fig. 260)

CASINGS

Casings can be referred to as "tunnels" to hold an elastic or drawstring.

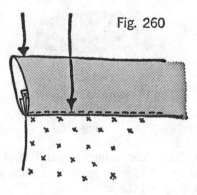

Fig. 260

Elastic Casing—Often used as a finish on a sleeve, neckline, or waistline of a skirt or pants. Narrow elastic ⅛ to ½ inch (3 mm to 1.3 cm) is used for sleeves, necklines, and children's clothes; ½ to 1 inch (1.3 to 2.5 cm) is recommended for waistline applications on skirts and pants. Cut the length of elastic the necessary measurement plus ½ inch (1.3 cm).

Turn in ¼ inch (6 mm) on edge of garment; press. The casing must be wide enough to accommodate the elastic easily; it should be at least ⅛ inch (3 mm) wider than the elastic you are using. Fold casing to inside of garment and stitch close to lower edge, leaving an opening at one seam to insert elastic. (Fig. 261) Use a

Fig. 261

bodkin or safety pin at end of elastic for ease of inserting it in casing. Lap ends of elastic ½ inch (1.3 cm) and sew securely. Stitch opening in casing, being careful not to stitch into elastic. (Fig. 262)

Fig. 262

To prevent elastic from rolling at waistline of skirts and pants, adjust fullness evenly between seams and stitch in crease of seam line through casing and elastic.

Applied Casing—For elastic or drawstring, normally used at the waistline of a garment. A strip of purchased bias binding or lightweight fabric wide enough to accommodate the elastic or drawstring, plus ½ inch (1.3 cm) for seams can be used. With fabric strip, turn under ¼ inch (6 mm) along both long edges; press. Pin casing in place on the inside of the garment and stitch along both edges of the strip. (Fig. 263)

Fig. 263

If the drawstring is to be tied on the outside of the garment, you will have to make two worked buttonholes or eyelets through a single thickness of the garment, positioning them 1 inch (2.5 cm) apart, within the width of the casing. The drawstring can then be inserted in the casing through the eyelets.

WAISTLINE FINISHES
The waistline of a skirt or pants must be finished with a waist-

band, fitted facing, or ribbon facing, to give a smooth, snug fit. Patterns will include a pattern piece for the waistband, front and back waistline facing pieces, or ribbon facing, according to the design.

Waistband—The finished edge of the waistband will be even with the zipper placket on one end and extend beyond the zipper on the other end to allow for a hook and eye closure. For a side or front closing, lap right over left; for a center back closing, lap left over right.

The waistband is interfaced for body and firmness; iron-on interfacings are excellent for this purpose. Cut interfacing to the fold line of the waistband pattern piece and baste or press to wrong side of waistband.

Turn under the seam allowance, ⅝ inch (1.5 cm), on long, unnotched edge of waistband; press. The waistline of the skirt or pants should be ½ to 1 inch (1.3 to 2.5 cm) more than the waist measurement and is eased to the waistband.

Pin waistband in place, matching notches and pattern markings; ease waistline to fit the waistband. Stitch, grade seam allowances, and press seam toward waistband.

Fold waistband right sides together along fold line; stitch short ends, trim seams. (Fig. 264) Turn waistband to right side and hem free edge to waistline seam. Press. Sew hook and eye to ends of waistband. (Fig. 265)

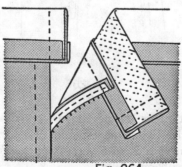

Fig. 264

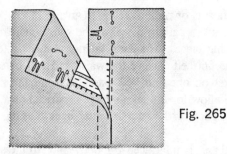

Fig. 265

Fitted Facing—The waistline facing is handled in the same manner as the neckline facing. The interfacing is applied to the wrong side of the skirt or pants section. The facing pieces are stitched, leaving one seam open for the zipper opening. Finish the outer edge of the facing according to the weight of the fabric.

Pin the right side of the facing to the right side of the waistline seam; stitch; grade seam allowances; understitch to keep facing from rolling out.

Turn facing to inside; press.

Turn under ends of facing and hem to zipper tape. Anchor or tack facing at side seams and darts. (Fig. 266) Sew hooks and eyes in place on waistband.

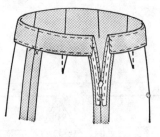

Fig. 266

Ribbon Facing—A ribbon facing eliminates additional bulk at the waistline and gives a smooth, snug fit. For a ribbon facing, use grosgrain ribbon ⅝ inch (1.5 cm) wide; transfer markings from pattern piece to ribbon.

Pin ribbon facing to right side of waistline, matching pattern markings. Facing should extend beyond the edges of the zipper opening.

Stitch close to the lower edge of ribbon; trim waistline seam allowance to ¼ inch (6 mm) from stitching. (Fig. 267)

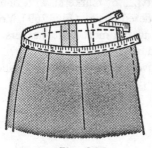

Fig. 267

Turn ribbon facing to inside; press. Hem edges of ribbon facing to zipper tape. Topstitch ⅛ inch (3 mm) from waistline through garment and ribbon. (Fig. 268) Sew a hook and eye above zipper.

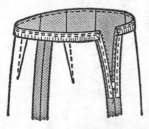

Fig. 268

HEMS

Each dress or skirt pattern includes a hem allowance about 2 to 3 inches (5 to 7.5 cm) deep, but you should try on the garment to mark a hemline that is becoming to you. Wear shoes with the heel height you expect to wear with the dress. If the dress requires a belt, wear one when the hemline is being marked.

Hemlines follow the dictates of fashion and may vary in length from season to season. There is no one "correct" length for a hemline. The right skirt length for you is the length that looks best on you and makes you feel comfortable. You may lengthen your skirts if hemlines are longer, you may shorten your skirts a little if hemlines go up, but always be guided by what is becoming to you rather than by what fashion "says."

Marking a Hem—The easiest way to mark a hem is with a skirt marker. It is an inexpensive sewing aid and a wise investment. There are several types of markers: with one type pins are used; with another, powdered chalk. (Fig. 269) You'll require the help of another person to use most skirt markers, although one chalk marker can be used by you alone.

If you do not have a skirt marker, a yardstick will do. Ask your

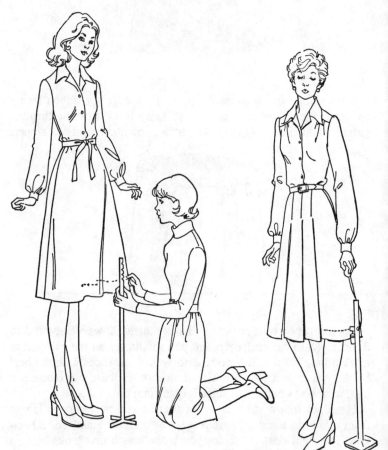

Fig. 269

helper to stand the yardstick upright on the floor against the garment and mark the hemline with pins placed parallel to the bottom of the skirt, about 3 inches (7.5 cm) apart. (Fig. 270)

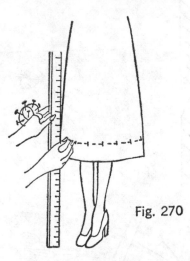

Fig. 270

Finishing a Hem—Most hems are from 2 to 3 inches (5 to 7.5 cm) deep. A very full skirt may have a narrower hem; a skirt for a growing girl may have a wider hem that can be let down.

• Turn up hem on marked hemline; pin and baste along fold line, straightening it if necessary to have an even line all around. (Fig. 271)

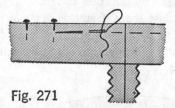

Fig. 271

• Decide the hem width you want and make yourself a hem gauge by notching a piece of cardboard to measure that width, or use an adjustable hem gauge. (Fig. 272)
• Measure from the fold the desired depth all around, mark with pins through one thickness of fabric only, or use tailor's chalk; trim the fabric along the marked line. (Fig. 273)

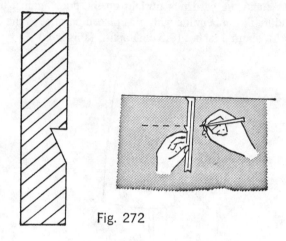

Fig. 272

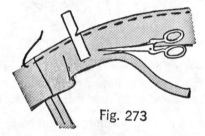

Fig. 273

- Reduce the excess fullness in the hem: make a line of machine stitching through one thickness of fabric only, ¼ inch (6 mm) below cut edge; use about 10 stitches to the inch (2.5 cm).
- Place garment on the ironing board, wrong side up; pull up bobbin thread gently with a pin, to adjust the fullness where necessary. (Fig. 274)

Fig. 274

- Press and finish hem; a piece of brown paper inserted between the garment and the hem will avoid ridge marks on the right side of the garment. (Fig. 275)

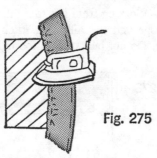

Fig. 275

Hem with Seam Binding—Stitch flat seam binding to right side of fabric, ¼ inch (6 mm) from cut edge; ease tape slightly. Pin or baste hem to garment. Finish hem by hand. (Fig. 276)

Fig. 276

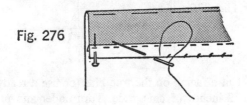

Bias seam binding is particularly good for circular skirts. It can be applied in the same manner as the flat seam binding, or as a facing.

Tailor's Hem—Make a line of stitching through one thickness of fabric ¼ inch (6 mm) from cut edge, and pink the edge. Pin or baste the hem to the garment, ¼ inch (6 mm) below the stitching line. Turn back the fabric and slip-stitch hem to garment. The catch-stitch may be used on knits or heavyweight fabrics. (Fig. 277)

Fig. 277

Catch-stitched Hem—Working from left to right, take a stitch in hem above the hem edge and the following stitch in the garment below the hem edge. Do not pull stitches too tight. (Fig. 278)

Fig. 278

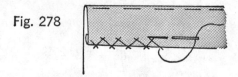

Turned and Stitched Hem—Make a line of machine stitching through one thickness of fabric about ¼ inch (6 mm) from edge. Fold on stitching line and edgestitch. Pin or baste hem in place and slip-stitch to garment. (Fig. 279)

Fig. 279

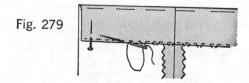

Faced Hem—Cut a facing on the true bias (or use a ready-made facing) about 2 inches (5 cm) wide. Turn under and press ¼ inch (6 mm) on one long edge of facing. Pin and stitch the other raw edge of the facing to the marked hemline with right sides together. Turn facing to inside, press along fold. Slip-stitch facing to garment. (Fig. 280)

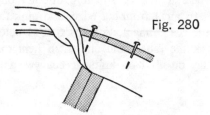

Fig. 280

For a shaped facing, cut the facing on the same grain as the pattern pieces and the exact shape of the edge of the garment; seam as necessary.

Rolled Hem—Machine-stitch along marked hemline. Trim fabric to ⅛ inch (3 mm) from stitching line. Roll the fabric between the thumb and finger of the left hand, take small slip stitches to hold roll in place. The tighter you roll, the narrower your hem will be. (Fig. 281)

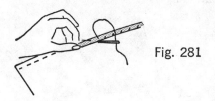

Fig. 281

Quick Rolled Hem—Trim fabric to ¼ inch (6 mm) from marked hemline. Fold raw edge under ⅛ inch (3 mm). Take a stitch in the fold, then catch a thread in fabric below raw edge, slip needle through fold again. Space stitches about ¼ inch (6 mm) apart, drawing thread up tightly to form a roll after every few stitches. (Fig. 282)

Fig. 282

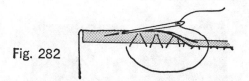

Whipped Hem—A narrow hem, somewhat like the rolled hem. The raw edge is not machine-stitched. The needle is inserted in one side of the material and brought out on the other side. Slanted thread is carried (whipped) over the rolled edge of the material. Stitches should be even and fairly tight. (Fig. 283)

Fig. 283

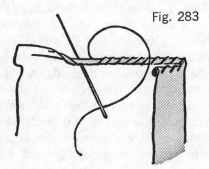

Edgestitched Hem—Fold fabric to wrong side on marked hemline. Stitch very close to the edge of the fold. Trim fabric close to stitching line. Turn stitched edge to wrong side, press, and edgestitch fold to garment. (Fig. 284)

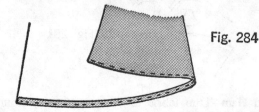

Fig. 284

Machine-stitched Hem—Fold fabric to one side on marked hemline, press, and edgestitch along fold line. Turn the skirt to the right side, make several rows of machine stitching evenly spaced, about ⅛ inch (3 mm) apart, around hemline; trim excess fabric close to last row of stitching. (Fig. 285)

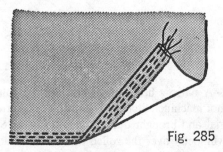

Fig. 285

Damask Hem—Used mostly for tablecloths and napkins. To be certain that the linen is cut on the straight grain of the cloth, pull a thread across the width of the material and cut on this line. Straighten fabric, if necessary (see Chapter 3). Make a ⅛-inch (3 mm) fold along the edge; make another fold ¼ inch (6 mm) wide. Crease the hem toward the right side exactly at the hemline. Point needle toward you as you hem; take a small straight stitch that catches both the hem and the folded material at the hemline. The stitches over the top of the folded ridge should be slanting and the thread drawn fairly tight. When the hem is pressed open, the stitches cannot be seen on the right side. (Fig. 286)

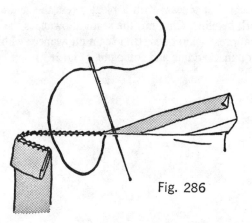

Fig. 286

Horsehair Braid—Mark hemline and trim fabric ¼ inch (6 mm) below marks. Stitch braid to the right side of the garment, with the edge of the braid on the marked hemline.

Narrow braid Fold braid to the inside of the garment and stitch around the edge through braid and garment. Catch loose edge of braid to seams only. (Fig. 287)

Fig. 287

Wide braid Fold braid to the inside of the garment, draw up top edge of braid to fit skirt, and hem in place. (Fig. 288)

Fig. 288

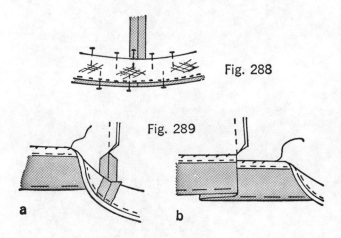

Fig. 289

a   b

Hem in Pleats—For a seam with a pleat, press the seam to one side, then mark hemline. Clip into the seam allowances the depth of the hem area; press seam open, trim seam allowances within hem; turn up hem on marked line and complete. (Fig. 289)

12   Buttons, Buttonholes, Zipper Applications, and Other Fastenings

———◆———

Among the tailoring details that will show off your work as a labor of love are buttonholes, buttons, and other fastenings. The time and effort spent in making these exactly right, instead of just about, will prove more than worthwhile to the finished appearance of any garment and the self-satisfaction you will realize.

BUTTONS

Buttons are used for decorative as well as utilitarian purposes, and you will find many types of buttons to choose from. The right selection for your particular garment depends not only upon the design of the pattern you have chosen, but upon such things as the texture and weight of the fabric, the color, and whether the garment will be dry-cleaned or laundered.

Buttons can be made of various materials such as wood, leather, bone, pearl, silver- or gold-colored metal, plastic, and rhinestone, and are found in many novelty shapes. Some are made with a shank, and others are made with holes. (Fig. 290)

Fabric Buttons—Can be covered with the garment fabric. Some types are easy to make at home, especially with one of the button-covering kits available at notion counters. Buttons can also be

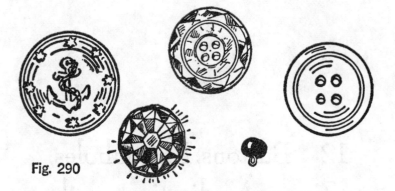

Fig. 290

made professionally at a minimal cost. If there is no button-making
store in your neighborhood, consult the fashion magazines or the
classified telephone directory for the addresses of firms that cover
buttons. Mail them the fabric, details of button size and style, and
money. The material required will, of course, vary with the size
and number of buttons needed. It is also a good idea to order several extra buttons to replace any you may lose.

Making Covered Buttons—Buy wooden molds in the size needed and
use a soft, firm material, such as outing flannel, to pad the buttons.
Cut the fabric covering for the button larger than the mold and run
a gathering thread around the edge. (Fig. 291a)

Cut each pad slightly smaller than the fabric covering. Place the
pad over the mold and hold it in place with stitches taken across
the back of the mold. Then cover with the circle of fabric, drawing
the gathering thread tight, so that the surface of the button will be
smooth. (Fig. 291b)

Fig. 291

Fasten the thread on the underside of the button; cover the raw edges with a circle of fabric. For additional interest, the fabric could be embroidered before covering the mold. (Fig. 292)

Fig. 292

A variety of interesting buttons can be made with bone rings covered in the same manner as the wooden mold and trimmed with embroidery thread. (Fig. 293a–e)

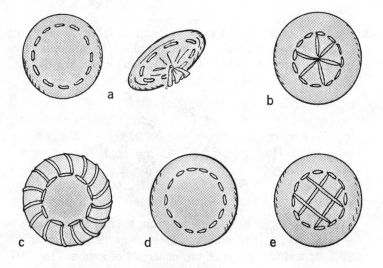

Fig. 293

Fabric-covered Ball Buttons—Can be made by covering old-fashioned shoe buttons with a circle of fabric, gathered and fastened to the shank of the button. (Fig. 294) Rows of these are very decora-

Fig. 294

tive on a dress, or used at sleeve openings. Fabric loops, instead of
buttonholes, are generally used with ball buttons.

Crocheted Buttons—Can be made easily by crocheting over a button
mold. (Fig. 295a–c)

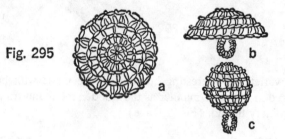

Fig. 295

Chinese Ball Buttons—Use a soutache braid or fabric-covered cord.
The size of the button will be determined by the thickness of the
cord. Cut a piece of cord 10 inches (25.5 cm) long and make loops
following the diagrams carefully. (Fig. 296a–c)

Fig. 296

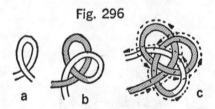

Keep loops open while working; then, holding the two ends of
the cord together, ease the loops together in the shape of a ball.
Clip ends and fasten securely to underside of button. (Fig. 297)

Fig. 297

Making Frogs—Frogs can be made of braid or fabric-covered cord to use with Chinese ball buttons. Draw the outline for the frog design on a piece of firm paper; the size of the loops can vary with the design. Extend the loop on one end of the frog to fit over the button.

Baste the cord to the paper, following the outline. Sew securely at crossings and tack ends of cord in place. Remove frog from paper carefully—a few extra stitches may be necessary at the cross points. Slip-stitch in place on the garment with button loop extending beyond edge on right side. (Fig. 298)

Fig. 298

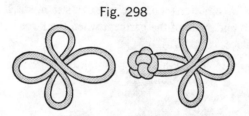

Sewing on Buttons—A shank is a necessity when you are sewing a button on. The extra space allowed by a shank is needed for the overlapping of the material between button and garment.

Some buttons are made with shanks of metal or plastic. Sew the button on with small stitches through the eye of the shank. (Fig. 299)

Fig. 299

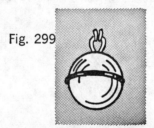

For buttons with holes, make a thread shank by sewing the button over a pin. Use single thread, with the knot on the underside of the button. Take at least six or eight stitches through the holes in the button; remove the pin; wind the thread around the stem of thread beneath the button. Fasten the thread on the underside of

the garment and cut the thread end—do not pull and break off.
(Fig. 300)

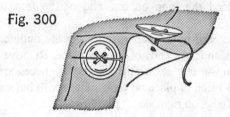

Fig. 300

To reinforce buttons that receive extra strain, stitch a small button on the underside of the garment when the large button is being
sewn in place. (Fig. 301)

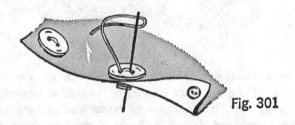

Fig. 301

You can link two buttons together to use as cuff links, or to join
a neck opening, by covering the threads that join the buttons together with a blanket stitch (see Chapter 17). (Fig. 302a, b)

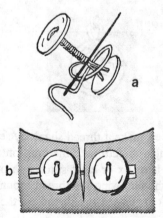

Fig. 302

BUTTONHOLES

There are two types of buttonhole, the bound buttonhole and the worked buttonhole, which can be made by hand or machine. The type you use on your garment will depend upon its style and the fabric. In most cases you will be guided by the instructions in your pattern.

Measuring for Buttonholes—To determine the correct size for a buttonhole, measure the diameter of the button, plus ⅛ inch (3 mm) or the thickness of the button. Make a slit this length in a scrap of the material to try the button; it should slide in easily. The length of the slit will be the length of the buttonhole. Always make one or two test buttonholes in scrap fabric before you begin to make them in the garment itself. A word of caution: when making buttonholes, be careful not to pull or tug the material so that the buttonhole will be stretched out of shape and spoil the appearance of your garment. (Fig. 303)

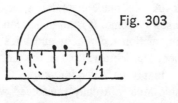

Fig. 303

Spacing Buttonholes—Your pattern will have markings for the position of the buttonholes, but a pattern alteration may have thrown the original spacing out of line, so it is wise to re-mark them, making sure that the spaces between are even.

Mark the position of the buttonholes accurately on the wrong side of the garment. With horizontal buttonholes, make two vertical lines the width of the buttonhole; the end line should extend ⅛ inch (3 mm) beyond the center front line. Make horizontal lines to indicate the placement of the buttonholes. (Fig. 304)

With vertical buttonholes, the size of the buttonhole should be indicated directly on the center front line.

Machine-baste (hand-baste fabrics that mark easily) through these markings so they are visible on the right side. If an interfacing is used, make the markings on the interfacing, then pin the in-

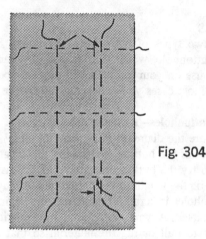

Fig. 304

terfacing to the wrong side of the garment and machine-baste through the markings.

Bound Buttonhole—A well-made bound buttonhole adds quality to the clothes you sew at home. It is an indication that care was given to the finer construction techniques and adds that difference between the garment that is turned out in the "mass-production" factory, and the one that is made just for you.

The buttonhole area is usually reinforced with interfacing and is made in the garment before the facing is applied; use a small machine stitch, eighteen to twenty per inch (2.5 cm).

Patch Method I

a. Cut a patch of fabric, on either the straight grain or the true bias, 2 inches (5 cm) wide and 1 inch (2.5 cm) longer than the length of the buttonhole. Crease through center of patch.

b. Place the right side of the patch to the right side of the garment, match crease of patch to buttonhole marking, and baste patch in place. (Fig. 305)

c. Machine-stitch ⅛ inch (3 mm) on each side of basting and across ends; start and end stitching at center of buttonhole. (Fig. 306)

d. Cut in the center of the two rows of stitching, cutting to ¼ inch (6 mm) from the end lines; clip diagonally into each corner. Cut through patch and garment. (Fig. 307)

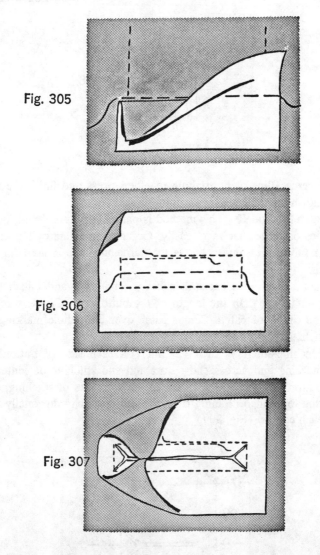

Fig. 305

Fig. 306

Fig. 307

e. Turn the patch to the wrong side of the garment carefully, through slit, and pull into shape.

f. With right side of the garment up, fold garment over buttonhole and stitch triangular ends of patch, by hand or machine. (Fig. 308)

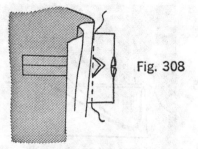

Fig. 308

g. Overcast lips of buttonhole together; press and finish the facing on the underside of the buttonhole.

Patch Method II This method is particularly useful with bulky fabrics or those that ravel easily. Organza or a lightweight crisp, sheer fabric the same color as the garment fabric is used for the patch.

a. Cut a patch of organza 2 inches (5 cm) wide and 1 inch (2.5 cm) longer than the length of the buttonhole. Crease through the center of patch. Center patch over buttonhole marking on right side of the garment; pin in place.

b. Machine-stitch ⅛ inch (3 mm) on each side of buttonhole marking and across ends; start and end stitching at center of buttonhole. Cut in the center of the two rows of stitching, cutting to ¼ inch (6 mm) from the end lines; clip diagonally into each corner. (Fig. 309)

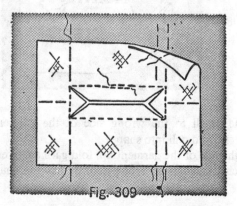

Fig. 309

c. Turn the patch to wrong side of garment through slit; press seam allowances, forming an opening the size of the finished buttonhole. (Fig. 310)

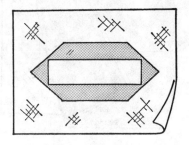

Fig. 310

d. Cut two pieces of garment fabric the same size as the patch. Place pieces with right sides together and baste on lengthwise center. Press seam open. (Fig. 311)

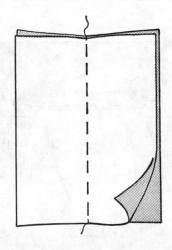

Fig. 311

e. Place the basted pieces over the opening; be sure the seam is in the center of the opening, since this will form the lips of the buttonhole. (Fig. 312) Pin close to each end.

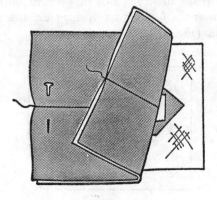

Fig. 312

f. Turn garment back over buttonhole. Pin at center of long edge to hold lip in place. Pin and stitch over previous stitching, extending the stitching lines on each end. Repeat for other lip. (Fig. 313)

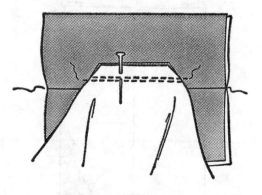

Fig. 313

g. Stitch across triangular ends as shown in Fig. 308. Press and finish the facing on the underside of the buttonhole. Remove basting from lips.

Two-piece Bound Buttonhole or Piped Buttonhole

a. Cut a strip of fabric 1 inch (2.5 cm) wide and twice the total

length of all buttonholes plus 2 inches (5 cm) for each buttonhole, on the straight grain or true bias. Fold the strip in half
lengthwise, with wrong sides together, and stitch ⅛ inch (3
mm) from folded edge. Trim raw edge ⅛ inch (3 mm) from
stitching line. (Fig. 314)

Fig. 314

b. For each buttonhole, cut two strips 1 inch (2.5 cm) longer than
buttonhole length. Pin strips in place on right side of garment,
with raw edges of strip on the marked buttonhole line. Stitch
the exact length of the buttonhole, using the stitched line on
the strip as a guideline—do not stitch across ends. Reinforce
stitching at ends or fasten threads on wrong side. (Fig. 315)

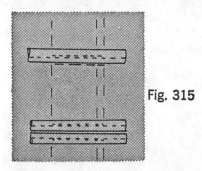

Fig. 315

c. Lift the strips and, starting at the center, cut the garment between the stitched lines to ¼ inch (6 mm) from the ends; clip
diagonally to each end. (Fig. 316)

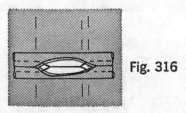

Fig. 316

d. Turn the stitched pieces through the opening to the wrong side
of the buttonhole. Stitch across triangular ends as shown in Fig.

308. Overcast lips of buttonhole together and press. Finish the facing on the underside.

Corded Bound Buttonhole is made the same way as the two-piece buttonhole. A soft cotton cord or yarn is inserted in each folded strip before it is stitched in place. (Fig. 317)

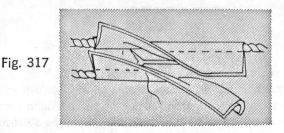

Fig. 317

Facing the Bound Buttonhole

METHOD A: From the outside of the garment, stick a pin through each end of the buttonhole. Turn garment over; slash the facing under the buttonhole from pin to pin. Turn under raw edges and hem to buttonhole. (Fig. 318)

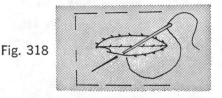

Fig. 318

METHOD B: From the outside of the garment, stick a pin through each corner of the buttonhole. Turn garment over; slash the facing under the buttonhole through the center and clip into pins at corners. Turn under raw edges and hem to buttonhole. (Fig. 319)

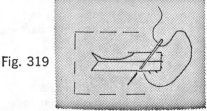

Fig. 319

Worked Buttonhole—Worked buttonholes are made after the garment is completed with facings. The horizontal buttonhole has a bar at one end and a fan at the end near the garment edge; a vertical buttonhole has a bar at each end.

a. Mark each buttonhole position; make a row of machine stitching, eighteen to twenty stitches per inch (2.5 cm), ⅛ inch (3 mm) either side of the buttonhole line. (Fig. 320)

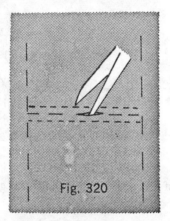

Fig. 320

The depth, or height of the stitches, is determined by the size of the buttonhole and the type of fabric used. A large buttonhole on a heavy fabric will have stitches that go deeper into the material than those in a small buttonhole on a lightweight fabric.

b. Cut the buttonhole from the center to each end and overcast the raw edges to prevent raveling. (Fig. 321)

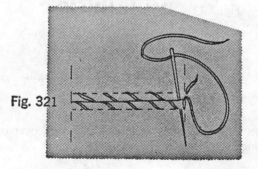

Fig. 321

c. Work the buttonhole stitch over the edges from right to left. The buttonhole stitch resembles the blanket stitch, but differs in that it has an extra ridge of thread called a purl. Make the stitches close together so that you cannot see the fabric between the stitches and use the stitched line as a guide for the depth of the buttonhole stitch. (Fig. 322)

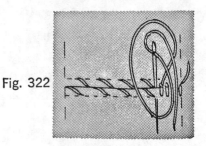

Fig. 322

d. Fan stitches of a horizontal buttonhole near garment edge. (Fig. 323)

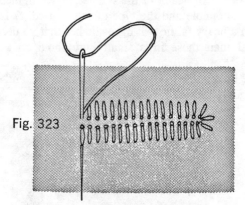

Fig. 323

e. Make a bar tack at opposite end and work over the threads, catching thread and garment cloth. (Fig. 324)

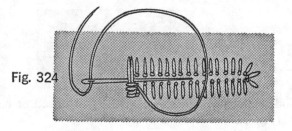

Fig. 324

On vertical buttonholes, make a bar at each end. (Fig. 325)

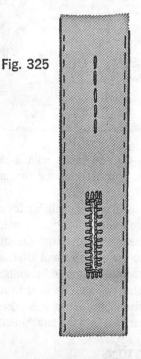

Fig. 325

Tailored Buttonhole—A tailored buttonhole is used on men's suits and on coats of heavy material. It differs from the ordinary worked buttonhole in one way. Before the tailored buttonhole is cut, a hole is punched at the end that will get the greater strain of the button, near the garment edge. The hole can be punched with a stiletto, an awl, a crochet hook, or a knitting needle. (Fig. 326)

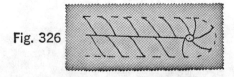

Fig. 326

Work buttonhole stitch over a strand of thread or buttonhole twist. (Fig. 327)

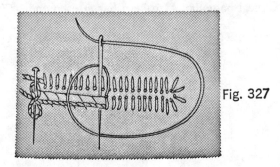

Fig. 327

Machine Buttonhole—Can be made with a zigzag machine. Follow the instructions in your manual for the proper adjustments and stitch settings.

A buttonhole attachment is available for most straight-stitch machines. Various size buttonholes can be made by inserting a different cam. Follow the instructions with the attachment for the necessary adjustments to the machine and attachment. We have found it useful to make a sample swatch of buttonholes with each size indicated on the sample. This can be used to test the button to determine the correct size of the buttonhole; then all you need do is to insert that particular cam into the attachment.

ZIPPER APPLICATIONS

When buying a zipper, look for the length specified in the pattern, a color to match the fabric, and a good metal chain or polyester coil. There are special zippers for special jobs, such as a separating jacket zipper for light- or heavyweight jackets, trouser zippers, blue jean zippers, and slipcover zippers with extra-heavy chain and wider tapes.

If you decide to use a length different from that suggested in the pattern, change the placket opening accordingly.

Lapped Application—This technique is used at the side seam of a skirt or pants or at the center back of a garment. If the seam allowance is less than ⅝ inch (1.5 cm), or if the fabric ravels easily, widen the front seam allowance by stitching a piece of seam tape to it. (Fig. 328)

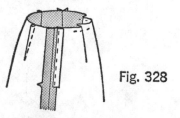

Fig. 328

The Length of the Opening for a skirt or pants should be the length of the closed zipper from the lower edge of bottom stop to top of the slider plus ⅜ inch (1 cm) and waist seam allowance; for a dress side opening add ⅜ inch (1 cm); for a neckline opening add ½ inch (1.3 cm) plus seam allowance if neck edge is unfinished.

Preparing the Placket   Machine-baste opening along seam line. (Fig. 329) All stitching is done on the inside of the garment; stitch

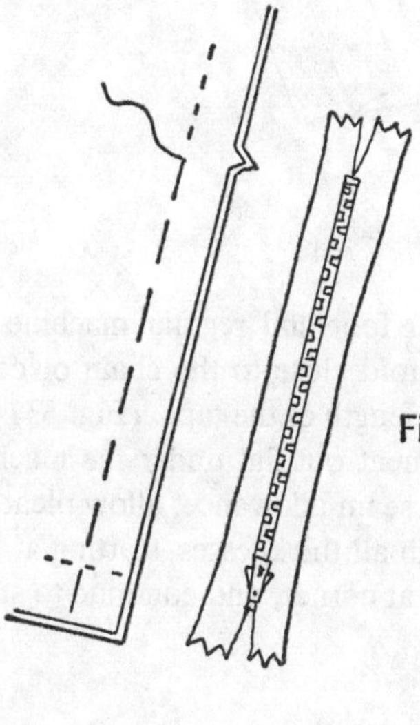

Fig. 329

from the bottom to the top of the placket. Use a zipper foot where indicated so that you can stitch close to the zipper.

STEP 1. Use regular presser foot and long machine stitch. Place closed zipper face down on the single seam allowance; bottom-stop at end of placket with the full width of the zipper chain or coil on the extended seam allowance and its edge against seam line. Stitch along tape, checking position of zipper every inch (2.5 cm) or so. (Fig. 330)

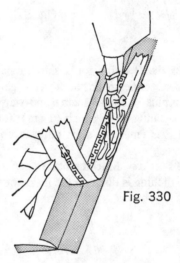

Fig. 330

STEP 2. Use zipper foot and regular machine stitch. Turn zipper face up; make a fold close to the chain or coil and stitch fold to zipper tape the full length of the tape. (Fig. 331)

STEP 3. Open garment out flat under the machine, place zipper face down over other seam allowance, allow pleat to form at end of placket. Stitch through all thicknesses, starting at the bottom across tape, pivot on needle at corner, and continue to stitch along zipper. (Fig. 332)

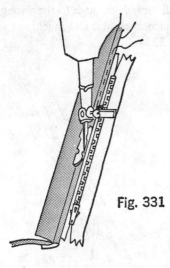

Fig. 331

Fig. 332

To Finish Pull threads through to the wrong side and tie. Turn back seam allowance over, and clip machine basting; remove basting threads. (Fig. 333)

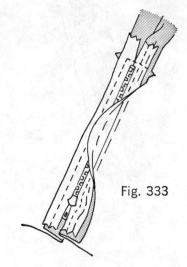

Fig. 333

Press placket on right side, over a tailor's ham. (Fig. 334)

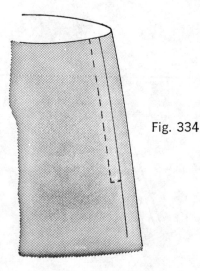

Fig. 334

Center Seam Application—This technique is appropriate for all placket openings, particularly in a neck placket. Check the length of the opening and prepare the seam as in the lapped application. Machine-baste the seam; clip basting every 2 inches (5 cm); press seam open.

STEP 1. Use the regular presser foot and long machine stitch. Work on the inside of the garment with the zipper open. Starting at bottom of placket, place open zipper face down on a single seam allowance—have teeth or coil of zipper against seam line. Machine-baste along tape. (Fig. 335a)

NOTE: The tape may be trimmed at the neckline seam to eliminate bulk with the facing. (Fig. 335b)

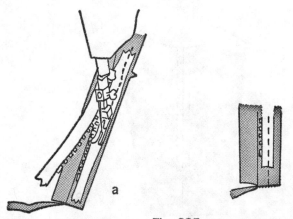

Fig. 335

STEP 2. Close zipper. Extend other seam allowance and baste zipper tape in place, stitching from the top down. (Fig. 336)

STEP 3. Work on outside of garment. Mark bottom of zipper tape with a pin. Spread garment flat and stitch evenly on either side of seam line. (Fig. 337) To mark the final stitching, you may find it necessary to use a line of basting or a special tape designed as a guide for topstitching.

To Finish Bring thread ends to wrong side; tie. Remove machine basting; press placket.

Zipper in a Slashed Placket—Finish neckline slash and slip-baste placket opening. Open zipper and hand-baste one tape to garment, using seam line as a guide; fold end of tape under at neckline, close

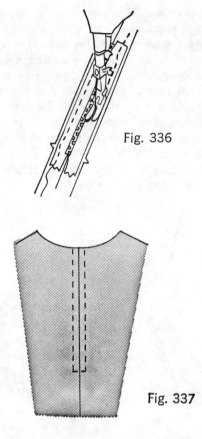

Fig. 336

Fig. 337

zipper, and baste other tape in place. (Fig. 338) Turn garment to right side and machine-stitch evenly on either side of the seam line.

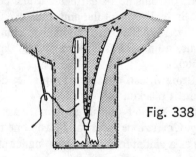

Fig. 338

Hand Application—For a custom look or with delicate fabrics that can mar easily, such as chiffon, velvet, lace, it is preferable to do the last stitching by hand on the right side of the garment. Use a half backstitch or pick stitch, spaced about ¼ inch (6 mm) apart. (Fig. 339)

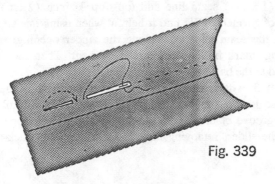

Fig. 339

Invisible Zipper Application—This technique is called "invisible" because the zipper is hidden in the seam, with no visible stitching lines appearing on the right side of the garment. (Fig. 340) The

Fig. 340

zipper is applied before the seam is stitched. A special zipper foot is required to fit the zipper brand. You can purchase one of these when you purchase the zipper, and then keep it with your other attachments for future use.

STEP 1. Open zipper; from the wrong side, press coils flat, using a synthetic setting on the iron.

STEP 2. Remember, the seam is not stitched for this application, therefore you will be working with two pieces of the garment. Pin open zipper face down on right side of fabric. Place coil on ⅝-inch (1.5 cm) seam line and top-stop ¾ inch (2 cm) from raw edge of garment. (We find it helpful when using this application to mark the seam allowance along the zipper opening with a hand basting; mark both pieces of the garment. Then the coil can be placed at the basted line.)

STEP 3. Attach invisible zipper foot to the machine, adjusting the foot so that the machine needle is centered in the hole. Position right groove of foot over coil; stitch from top of zipper until foot hits the slider, removing the pins as you stitch. Back-tack. (Fig. 341)

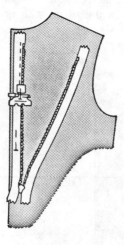

Fig. 341

STEP 4. Pin other side of zipper, face down, to right side of other garment section. Place coil on ⅝-inch (1.5 cm) seam line and top-stop ¾ inch (2 cm) below raw edge; check to be sure zipper is not twisted at bottom.

STEP 5. Position left groove of foot over coil, and stitch zipper until the foot hits slider. Back-tack. (Fig. 342)

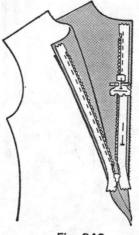

Fig. 342

STEP 6. Close the zipper. Pin garment sections right sides together along seam line below zipper, pull end of zipper out of the way. Adjust zipper foot to the left so that the needle is in line with the edge of the foot. Insert needle slightly above and to the left of previous stitching; stitch seam. Pull thread ends to one side and tie. You may find it easier to stitch this seam for about 2 inches (5 cm) with the zipper foot, then change to the regular presser foot to complete the seam. (Fig. 343)

To Finish Stitch ends of zipper tape to each seam allowance only. (Fig. 344)

Replacing a Zipper—Always measure the length of the old zipper; buy a new zipper the same length or slightly shorter. Remove the old zipper carefully, examine the garment to see how the zipper was put in. Try to utilize the fold lines and previous stitching lines.

Care of Zippers—Careful consideration for your zippers will mean longer life and fewer replacements.

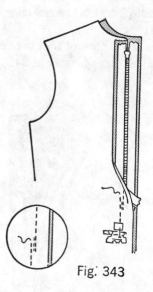

Fig. 343

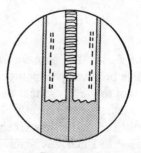

Fig. 344

- Close zipper before washing or dry-cleaning a garment.
- Open zipper all the way when putting on or removing the garment.
- Keep zipper closed in garments not in use to help retain the shape of the garment.
- Use beeswax or a lubricant if zipper has become stiff.
- Set iron at synthetic setting when using coil zipper.

OTHER FASTENINGS

Snaps and hooks and eyes are used to put the finishing touches to your garment. They are one of the small details that should not be neglected if you are working toward perfection.

Snaps—Sew-on snaps can be used as a fastening where there is little strain. They are available on cards, in sizes varying from 4/0 (smallest) to 1 (large); black or nickel.

The section with the socket corresponds to a button as to position. It is usually sewn on the left side of the garment. The section with the ball corresponds to the buttonhole and is placed on the right side. Position the ball section of the snap and sew it in place. (Fig. 345) You can place the socket accurately by marking the

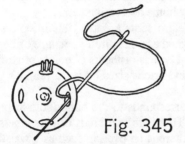

Fig. 345

ball section with tailor's chalk and pressing it to the facing piece of material. The chalk will mark the correct position for the socket portion of the snap. (Fig. 346) Make several stitches in each hole of the snap, and carry the thread under the snap to the next hole.

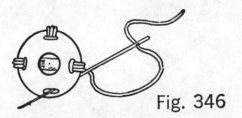

Fig. 346

Hammer-on Snaps—For children's clothes, sportswear, shirts, pajamas, and home furnishings, there are snaps that are attached with a few quick strokes of a hammer. These are available in kits containing snaps, a metal bracket, socket, and stud tools. Directions in the kit will tell you how to attach snaps.

Nylon Tape Closure—This looks like two pieces of velvet ribbon with the nap sides laid face to face. However, the nap is different on each tape; one is rather flat and the other is fuzzy with little burrs on it. Their threads interlock when they are pressed together, to form a fastening, and all you need do to open it, is to pull the two tapes apart, with the same motion as that of peeling a banana. Velcro (a trade name) is made of nylon and can be purchased in a package or by the yard in 1-inch (2.5 cm) widths. It is sewn flat to the garment by hand or machine; check the directions on the package. This tape should not be used on sheer or very light-weight fabrics. It has a useful place on sports jackets, on the belt lines of wrap-around skirts, on maternity clothes where it allows for easy waistline adjustments, and on children's clothes. It is also an aid for many home decorating items.

Packaged Velcro spots are available in colors and several sizes. These are designed as a substitute for snaps or buttons.

Hooks and Eyes—Used as fasteners at points of strain. They are available on cards in various sizes from 00 (small) to 4 (large); black or nickel.

The hook corresponds to the buttonhole in position and the eye to the button. There are two kinds of eyes—the straight eye, which is used where there is an overlap such as a waistband (Fig. 347a); and the round eye, which is used when two edges meet, such as at a neckline. (Fig. 347b)

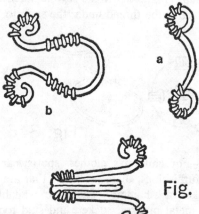

Fig. 347

Sew them as shown. It is important to fasten the hook (Fig. 347c) under the curved section, to hold it firmly in place. Use single thread and start on the wrong side of the fabric. Fasten the thread with several small stitches.

A thread loop can be used in place of the metal eye, as a custom finish; see Chapter 14 on how to make this kind of loop.

There are special heavy-duty, flat hooks and eyes used on the waistbands of pants and skirts. Position them as you would the regular hook and eye, and sew in place through holes.

13 Pockets

Pockets can be both useful and ornamental. Here are several types of pockets, which begin with a simple-to-make one and become progressively more difficult. These pockets could be used to change the appearance of the original pattern style. The cut and sew guide sheet in your pattern will describe a pocket designed for the garment, and you should follow the instructions for making it.

Patch Pocket—This is the easiest pocket of all to make, yet it is adaptable to almost every type of garment. Its purpose may be entirely utilitarian but it is more often used for decoration. Patch pockets are made in every conceivable shape from the simple square outline to the more intricate detail of a petal design. Be sure to mark the position of the pocket carefully on the outside of the garment (see Chapter 3).

TO MAKE:

a. Turn under the top edge of the pocket ¼ inch (6 mm) and stitch. (Fig. 348)

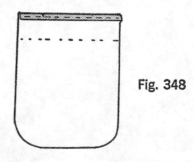

Fig. 348

b. Turn top edge to right side along fold line to make facing. Stitch around pocket on seam line. (Fig. 349)

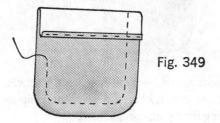

Fig. 349

c. Cut off top corners and trim seam allowance to about ⅜ inch (1 cm). Notch curves as shown. (Fig. 350)

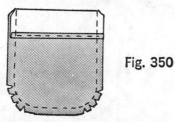

Fig. 350

d. Turn facing to wrong side and press. Turn and press seam allowance to wrong side, rolling stitching line slightly to inside. (Fig. 351)

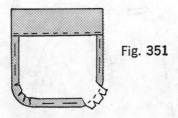

Fig. 351

e. Pin and baste pocket in place on garment and edgestitch, reinforcing top corners as shown. (Fig. 352)

Fig. 352

A patch pocket can be hand-sewn to a garment. Complete the pocket as above, pin and baste in place, and slip-stitch around the edges, catching both garment and pocket.

Side Seam Pocket—Stitch side seam to pocket marking.

    a. Pin one pocket section to the skirt back and the other to the skirt front. Stitch from side seam to waistline edges. (Fig. 353)

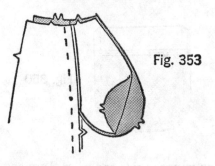

Fig. 353

    b. With right sides together, stitch around pocket from side seam opening to waistline edge. (Fig. 354)

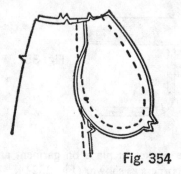

Fig. 354

c. Press pocket toward front; baste pocket opening along seam line on skirt front and press.

Slot Pocket—Made exactly like a bound buttonhole.

TO MAKE: Mark the position of the pocket and the length of the opening on the garment. (Fig. 355)

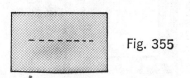

Fig. 355

a. Cut a piece of fabric for the pocket 1 inch (2.5 cm) wider than the opening and twice the desired depth of the pocket plus 1 inch (2.5 cm) for seam allowance. Mark the pocket line on the pocket piece about 1 inch (2.5 cm) below center. (Fig. 356)

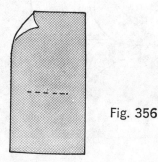

Fig. 356

b. With right sides together, place pocket piece over garment, matching marked line on pocket piece to marked line on garment, and baste through marking. Stitch ¼ inch (6 mm) either side of the line and across the ends; slash on line to within ½ inch (1.3 cm) of the ends and clip diagonally into corners. (Fig. 357)

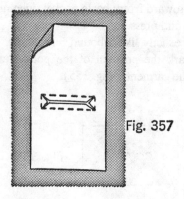

Fig. 357

c. Turn the pocket through the slit to the wrong side. (Fig. 358)

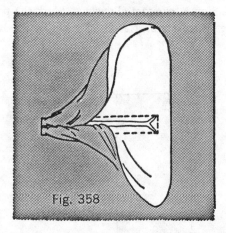

Fig. 358

d. Adjust lips of pocket evenly and stitch around the finished pocket on the right side; press. (Fig. 359)

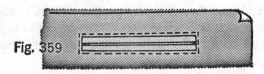

Fig. 359

e. On the inside of the garment, stitch the side seams and bottom of the pocket strip together as shown. Do not stitch pocket section to garment. (Fig. 360)

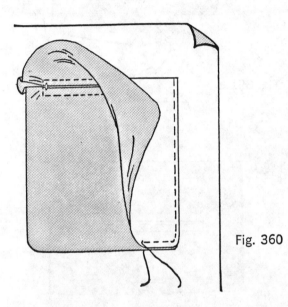

Fig. 360

Slot Pocket for Tailored Garments Pockets in bulky fabrics, such as heavy woolens or corduroy, do not make up smoothly when a self-fabric pocket lining is used. It is better to use a lighter-weight lining material with these types of fabrics.

The pocket is made as described above, using self fabric for the binding, up to the point where the bound buttonhole opening is completed. Then a separate pocket of lining material is made, on the inside of the garment. Use two pieces of lining fabric for the pocket sections and stitch to the opening as illustrated. (Figs. 361a, b)

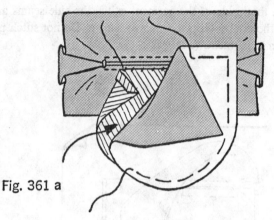

Fig. 361 a

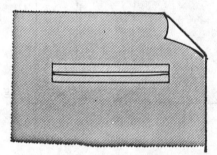

Fig. 361 b

Welt Pocket—The welt pocket is used on tailored garments, particularly jackets.

TO MAKE:

a. Mark the pocket opening on the garment with a basting. Cut a pocket piece 1 inch (2.5 cm) wider than the pocket opening, and twice the depth of the pocket plus 1 inch (2.5 cm) for seam allowance. Mark the pocket line on the pocket piece about 1 inch (2.5 cm) below the center.

b. Place the piece right side down on the right side of the garment; match marked lines carefully. Baste through markings; stitch ¼ inch (6 mm) on each side of line and across ends. Slash to within ¼ inch (6 mm) of the end, then clip diagonally into corners. (Fig. 362)

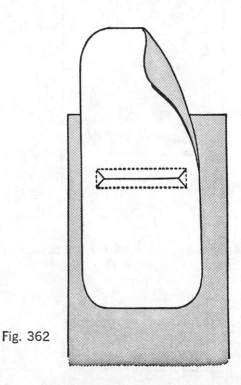

Fig. 362

c. Turn the pocket through to the wrong side and make the welt by folding the lower section of the pocket so that it meets the pocket opening exactly. (Fig. 363)

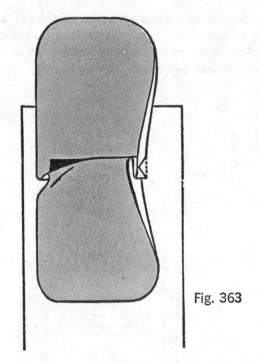

Fig. 363

d. On outside of garment, stitch the welt in place, stitching across each end for added strength. (Fig. 364)

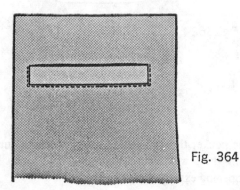

Fig. 364

e. On the inside, sew pocket sections together around sides; overcast raw edges together. Turn down seam allowances on upper part of pocket and sew to pocket. (Fig. 365)

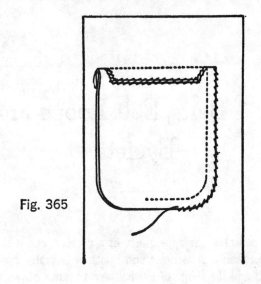

Fig. 365

14   Belts, Belt Loops, and Eyelets

BELTS

A belt can alter the appearance of a dress; it can make the difference between a soso dress and one that is really eye-catching. The width and the shape of the belt are a matter of personal taste and should be guided by your size and figure. Wide belts and shaped belts attract attention to the waistline; they are good for the long-waisted, slender figure. As a rule, the larger waist looks better with a narrower belt. A matching belt made of the same material as the dress is becoming for most figures.

You can have a fabric belt and covered buckle made by a commercial concern, or you can make your own. There are kits available that include the buckle and necessary belting in widths from ¾ inch (2 cm) to 2 inches (5 cm), for a straight or contour (shaped) belt. A note of caution: be sure that the belting you use can be laundered, for washable fabrics, or dry-cleaned. Check the buckle frame to be sure it is rustproof.

Belt Without Stiffening—Material for the belt should be cut on the lengthwise grain. It should be twice as wide as the finished belt plus ½ inch (1.3 cm) for seams, and have sufficient length for lap-over. Shape one end to make a point. With right sides together, fold the belt in half lengthwise and stitch ¼ inch (6 mm) from edge along edges, leaving an opening for turning. (Fig. 366)

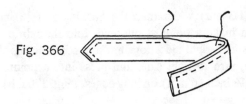

Fig. 366

Turn to right side, slip-stitch opening, and press. Attach the buckle to the belt at one end and sew in place. (Fig. 367)

Fig. 367

If the buckle is a prong type you will have to make a cut in the belt to fit the prong and make eyelets in the other end of the belt. (Fig. 368)

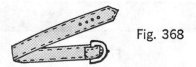

Fig. 368

Tie Belt—A tie belt is constructed in the same way; you must have sufficient length to go around your waistline plus enough fabric for ties. If you lack the necessary length of material, piece the belt at the center back. Stitch diagonally across each end of belt. Top-stitch the edges for added interest.

Belt with Interfacing—If the belt needs stiffening, cut a strip of interfacing the width of the finished belt. Pin and stitch to wrong side of belt and complete the belt as directed above. Iron-on interfacing is a quick and easy technique for stiffening the belt. (Fig. 369)

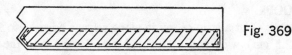

Fig. 369

Belt with Backing—Cut a piece of backing to your waist measurement plus 5 inches (12.5 cm). Cut the fabric strip on the straight grain,

½ inch (1.3 cm) wider than the backing and ¼ inch (6 mm) longer. To make a point at one end, fold the fabric strip in half lengthwise with right sides together and stitch across the end. Cut off corner, turn to right side, and press into a point. Turn under and press ¼ inch (6 mm) on long edges. (Fig. 370a, b)

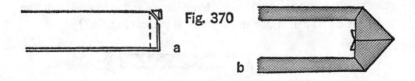

Fig. 370

Cut a point at one end of backing. Pin and baste backing to wrong side of fabric strip. Edgestitch belt from the fabric side. (Fig. 371)

Fig. 371

Cover the buckle according to the instructions in the kit, or have one covered. Sew buckle to straight end of belt. (Fig. 372)

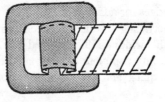

Fig. 372

BELT LOOPS

Fabric Carrier—Cut a strip of fabric along selvage edge ¾ to 1 inch (2 to 2.5 cm) wide and ¾ inch (2 cm) longer than the width of the belt. Fold piece in thirds, as shown, with selvage edge on top. Stitch along both edges and stitch in place on garment. (Fig. 373a, b)

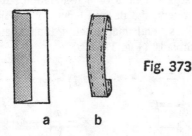

Fig. 373

a   b

Fabric Loops—Can be made of bias tubing as described in Chapter 16. Cut into pieces the necessary length and sew in place at waistline seams.

Chain Loop—Secure thread in side seam with several small stitches. Take another stitch, leaving a loop of thread. Using fingers, pull thread through loops to form a chain. (Fig. 374)

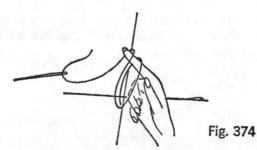

Fig. 374

Bring needle through last loop, pull thread tight. Take several small stitches to fasten thread at opposite end. (Fig. 375)

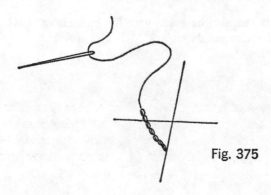

Fig. 375

Thread Loop—Make a bar of 3 or 4 foundation stitches in the side seams of the garment, the desired length of the finished loop; secure the ends with several small stitches. Blanket-stitch closely over the foundation threads. (Fig. 376a, b)

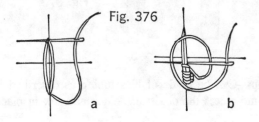

Fig. 376

a   b

Thread loops can be made at the edge of a garment to be used as loops for ball buttons.

EYELETS

Outline a circle on the fabric with small running stitches. Make hole in the fabric with a stiletto. Work over raw edges of hole with close blanket stitch. (Fig. 377)

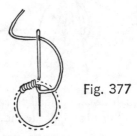

Fig. 377

Eyelets can also be made with the buttonhole attachment and a special eyelet template.

15   Gathering, Shirring, and Ruffles

GATHERS

Gathers can be used to add fullness or to control fullness. They can be functional or they can be decorative. Functional gathers are those that ease in fullness. Gathers used for decorative purposes include shirrings, ruffles, and headings.

Gathering by Hand—Use a thin needle and a fine, strong thread that will not break when the gathers are pulled into place. Always knot the thread. Take small running stitches across the material to be gathered and pull thread up gently until the gathering measures the desired length. (Fig. 378)

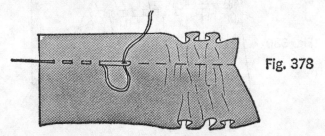

Fig. 378

Gathering by Machine—Gathers on the machine are made by loosening the top tension slightly and using a longer stitch. Stitch on the right side of the garment, leave the thread ends long enough to work with. Pull the bobbin thread carefully, pushing the material along this thread until you have the desired fullness. If you want a double or triple row of stitches, space the machine stitching about ¼ inch (6 mm) apart—the width of the presser foot makes a good guide; pull all the bobbin threads evenly to form the gathers. Pull thread ends through to the wrong side and tie each row separately.

The gathering foot can also be used on the machine—the amount of fullness is determined by the stitch length. Test a piece of fabric until you obtain the desired amount of fullness. (Fig. 379)

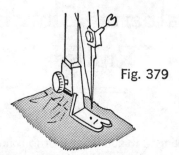

Fig. 379

Gathers to Hold Fullness—When gathers are used to adjust fullness, make two rows of gathers ⅛ inch (3 mm) apart and pull the gathered edge until it measures the same as the straight edge. Pull threads through to the wrong side and tie each row separately. (Fig. 380)

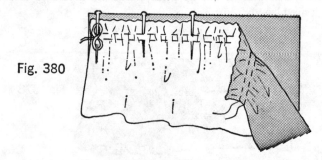

Fig. 380

SHIRRING

Shirring is made up of rows and rows of gathers, usually about ⅛ inch (3 mm) apart. It may be used in narrow or wide bands as trimming, or shaped for a particular area such as a yoke of a blouse or skirt. It is best suited to sheer or lightweight fabrics. (Fig. 381)

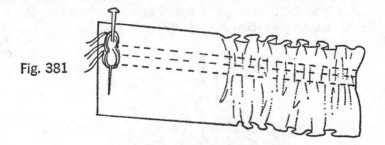

Fig. 381

Using a Stay Under Shirring—Cut a strip of material the width of the shirring, allowing at least 1 inch (2.5 cm) for seam allowances. Turn under the seam allowances on the long edges of the strip and baste it over the shirring on the wrong side. Stitch invisibly to the first and last rows of gathers. (Fig. 382)

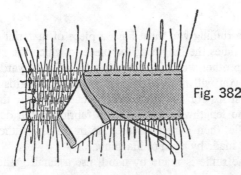

Fig. 382

Shirring by Machine—This is done the same way as gathering by machine. Space the rows of stitching evenly, from ⅛ to ¼ inch (3 to 6 mm) apart. When all the rows have been stitched, pull each bobbin thread separately to form the shirring. Pull thread ends to wrong side and tie each row separately. The gathering foot may also be used.

Using Elastic Thread—Wind the elastic thread by hand, stretching it slightly, until the bobbin is almost full. The tension of the bobbin case should be tight so that the elastic thread pulls out with considerable stretch. Use regular sewing thread on top; set the machine for a long stitch. Test stitching on a scrap of the material to be used. When making more than one row of gathers, continue to stretch the fabric as you stitch each row. Fasten the thread ends securely at the beginning and end of each row—from four to six rows makes a good shirring. (Fig. 383)

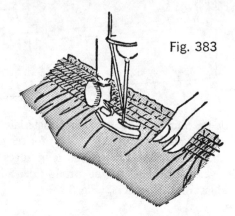

Fig. 383

RUFFLING

To make ruffling you must have a piece of material at least one and a half times the length of the piece to which the ruffle will be attached. In other words, if you want to make 10 yards (9.15 m) of ruffling you will need a strip of material 15 yards (13.75 m) long. The strips for the ruffle can be cut on either the crosswise grain or the lengthwise grain of the fabric, in the desired width for the ruffle, then joined for use. As in making gathers, the ruffling can be made by hand or machine.

When the ruffle is made by hand, use a small gathering stitch. (Fig. 384)

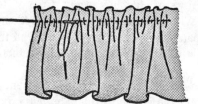

Fig. 384

When the ruffle is made by machine, the ruffler attachment can be used. The amount of fullness is controlled by the stitch length and an adjusting screw. Test for correct fullness and adjustments, using a strip of the same fabric; follow the instructions in the machine manual. This attachment can also be adjusted to do even pleating or groups of spaced pleats. (Fig. 385)

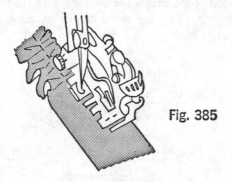

Fig. 385

When making yards and yards of ruffling, use the narrow hemmer on the machine for those small hems on the long edges. (Fig. 386)

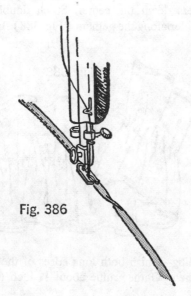

Fig. 386

Circular Ruffle—You may sometimes want to make a ruffle without the extra fullness at the top, so you would use a circular ruffle. This type is often recommended for use on stiff fabrics. Experiment with the circular shape by cutting it in paper first. When you have worked out the shape and length of ruffle you need, cut the fabric. Finish one long edge with a narrow hem; snip the top edge of the ruffle every inch (2.5 cm) or so before attaching it, to prevent pulling. (Fig. 387a, b)

Fig. 387

Double Ruffle—Make a continuous strip of material as you would for a single ruffle; hem both long edges of the strip. Make two or three rows of gathers down the center. Stitch double ruffle in place through the center along the gathers. (Fig. 388)

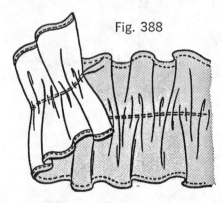

Fig. 388

Ruffle with Heading—Finish both long edges of the strip with a narrow machine hem. Gather ruffle about ¼ inch (6 mm) from top edge to desired fullness. Pin wrong side of ruffle to the right side of hemmed fabric and stitch on gathering line of ruffle. (Fig. 389)

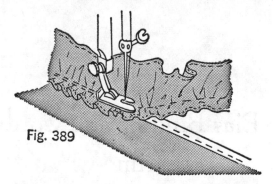

Fig. 389

16 Bias Binding and Cording Trim

BIAS BINDING

Binding is a narrow strip of matching or contrasting fabric used to finish the raw edges of a garment or a household article. Binding or cording is also used as a decorative trim. Most bindings are bias in order to fit smoothly and to turn around corners and curves easily. Bias binding, often called bias tape or bias fold, comes in cotton and rayon; it can be purchased by the package in many colors.

Trimming a garment with binding of self fabric gives an attractive, custom look, especially when the fabric is striped since the bias trimming will show the stripe at a slant.

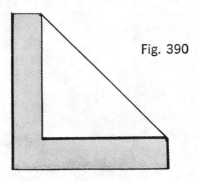

Fig. 390

The word "bias" indicates the way in which the piece of fabric is cut to make the strips for the binding. To find this bias grain of cloth, fold the selvage edge of the fabric at right angles to a straight crosswise thread of the fabric. The folded edge of the triangle formed is the bias grain of the fabric. (Fig. 390)

If you will take this folded edge between your two hands and pull gently, you will see that the bias grain stretches very easily. This stretch or give makes the fabric pliable in places where a straight piece of fabric could not be handled as readily.

Cutting a Bias Strip—Measure and mark from the fold the width of the strip you need. Cut along marked lines. (Fig. 391)

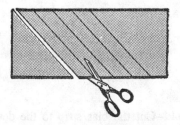

Fig. 391

Joining Two Bias Strips—Place the right side of the bias strips together on the straight grain of the fabric so that the edges of the finished strip will be in a straight line, and stitch across the short ends. Trim off slanting ends of fabric. (Fig. 392)

Fig. 392

Making a Continuous Bias Strip—Use a rectangular piece of material. Fold opposite ends of the material on a true bias. (Fig. 390) Cut along each diagonal fold line. Mark the wrong side of the material the desired width of the strip, using tailor's chalk.

With right sides together, join the ends of the rectangle, forming a tube; one strip width should extend beyond the edge at each end. Cut along last marking and continue cutting in a circular fashion. (Fig. 393)

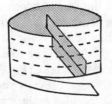

Fig. 393

How to Stretch Bias—Before applying the bias, stretch the strip at the ironing board, using a steam iron and even pressure. When the bias is to be applied to a curve, shape the strip in a "swirling" technique as you press. (Fig. 394)

Fig. 394

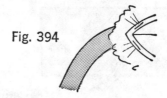

Making a Single Bias Fold—Cut the bias strip to the desired width, usually twice the finished width you want plus ½ inch (1.3 cm) for two seam allowances. Turn under ¼ inch (6 mm) on each raw edge of the strip to the wrong side; press. (Fig. 395) This bias binding is now ready to be used for binding seams or edges.

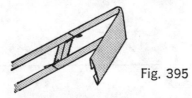

Fig. 395

Topstitching Bias Binding—If bias binding must be joined (as when binding an armhole or pillow), estimate the amount of binding needed by easing it slightly around the outer edge of the piece to be bound. Allow ½ inch (1.3 cm) for seams. Cut the binding on the straight grain and stitch the ends as you did when joining the bias strip. Fold the binding slightly off center, making the underside of the binding ⅛ inch (3 mm) wider than the top. This is to make sure that both sides of the binding will be caught in a single stitching. Stitch along the edge of the binding, on the right side of the garment. (Fig. 396)

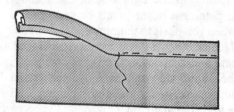

Fig. 396

Hand-hemming Bias Binding—If bias binding is to be finished by hand, it is opened flat and placed on the material with right sides together. Machine-stitch about ¼ inch (6 mm) from the edge. Turn the bias binding over the raw edge of the material and sew it in place, using a slip stitch or hemming stitch. The hand stitching should cover the machine stitching on the underside. (Fig. 397)

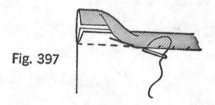

Fig. 397

Double Bias Binding or French Binding—For this type of binding, cut the strips six times the width of the finished binding. Fold strip in half lengthwise with wrong sides together and press. Pin and stitch bias to right side of garment, matching raw edges. Turn bias over raw edges and sew along stitching line. (Fig. 398) This technique is preferred as a finish for sheer fabrics.

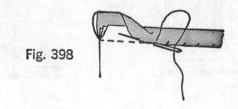

Fig. 398

To Bind Scallops—You can use ready-made binding or cut strips not more than 1 inch (2.5 cm) wide. Pin and baste the right side of the binding to the right side of the scallops. Stretch the binding when pinning it in the points between each scallop; ease the binding when you pin it to the curves. (Fig. 399a)

Machine-stitch as you would a scalloped facing. Clip into the corners and trim seams. Fold the bias binding over the raw edges to the wrong side and hem. At each point between the curved scallops, make a crease in the binding and take an extra stitch there to hold that crease. (Fig. 399b) Press carefully.

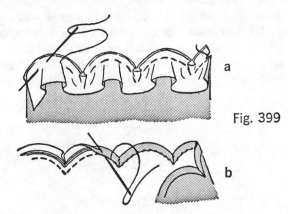

Fig. 399

To Bind an Outside Corner—Place right side of binding to right side of fabric, and stitch the binding to fit the corner, making a fold at the corner. Turn binding to wrong side, over raw edge; miter corner and sew to stitching line. (Fig. 400a, b)

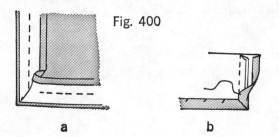

Fig. 400

a   b

To Bind an Inside Corner—Place right side of binding to right side
of fabric; leave needle down in fabric at corner, pivot on needle
to turn corner. Turn binding to wrong side and sew to stitching
line; miter corner. (Fig. 401a, b)

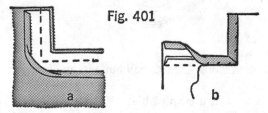

Fig. 401

CORDED PIPING

A corded piping is a "plus" detail at neckline, collar, cuffs, armholes, or the waistline of a beltless dress. It can be of the same
material or a contrasting fabric.

To Cover the Cord—Cut bias strips to the desired width and stretch
the strip. Fold strip in half lengthwise, wrong sides together; en-
close the cord in fold of bias and stitch close to the cord, using
the zipper-cording foot. (Fig. 402) Place cording to garment edge

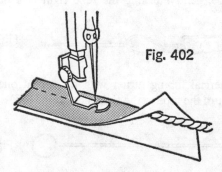

Fig. 402

to be trimmed, with raw edges together. (Fig. 403) Face garment
section following directions for stitching a corded seam in Chapter 7.

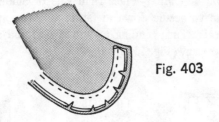

Fig. 403

TUBING

For button loops, Chinese ball buttons, and frogs, prepare fabric loops.

TO MAKE: Cut a strip of bias 1½ inches (3.8 cm) wide. Fold strip in half lengthwise, with right sides together. Machine-stitch ⅛ to ¼ inch (3 to 6 mm) from fold (depending on weight of fabric); stretch bias strip as you stitch and stitch out at each end as shown. (Fig. 404) Trim seam. Fasten a strong thread at one

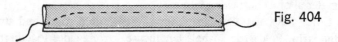

Fig. 404

end and attach thread to a bodkin (a blunt needle used to thread tape or ribbon through a casing), and work bodkin and thread through tube, gently turning the tube right side out. (Fig. 405)

Fig. 405

A commercial tubing turner with a hook at one end can also be used to turn the tube to the right side. (Fig. 406)

Fig. 406

To Make a Corded Tubing—Determine the size of the cord to be covered and secure a smaller cord to it. Cut a bias strip to fit over cord; attach one end of strip to the end of the small cord where it is fastened to the larger cord. (Fig. 407)

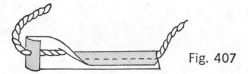

Fig. 407

Fold right sides of bias strip over small cord and stitch, using a zipper-cording foot—do not catch cord in stitching. Trim seam. Pull smaller cord through the tubing, turning the tubing to the right side and enclosing the larger cord in it. (Fig. 408)

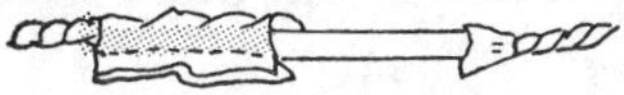

Fig. 408

Bias Cord Loops—Corded tubing can be made into a single loop or a series of loops to be used as a decorative closing with ball buttons. Loops can also be arranged in an interesting design to be used as a trimming on a neckline or sleeve.

Plan the placement and design for the loops on a piece of firm paper, about 2 inches (5 cm) wide, in the length you will need.

Mark ⅝-inch (1.5 cm) seam allowance on one long edge of the paper. Form the loops with the seam of corded tubing uppermost. Tape the loops in place; stitch them to the paper on the seam line.

Pin the paper with the loops to the right side of the garment, matching seam lines; stitch through paper and loops over previous stitching. Tear paper away carefully. Finish the garment edge with a facing. (Fig. 409)

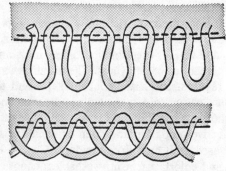

Fig. 409

17 Decorative Stitches and Techniques

———◆———

A touch of embroidery or decorative stitching is enough to transform a simple garment into something very special. Embroidery can be a challenge to your imagination and makes it possible for you to express ideas with a needle. It is a fascinating experience to take odds and ends of thread and a piece of cloth and translate them into designs using combinations of the elementary stitches shown in this chapter. Try a few on some scraps of material. Then, when your needle knows its way around, put it to work to add touches of beauty to blue jeans, shirts, jackets, blouses, and smocks, as well as many household articles.

Modern machinery and chemicals have given us a new world of threads, from the most delicate to heavy—soft yarns, textured yarns, metallic yarns, and fabrics woven with threads of new fibers. The yarns and threads used for embroidery may range from a spool of sewing thread to woolen yarns. The usual six-strand embroidery floss and rayon strand sheen sold in skeins and the single-strand heavier pearl cotton sold by the ball can be used on most materials. Woolen yarn is generally used for decorating woolen materials and is very effective on burlap and linen or linen-like fabrics; it is traditionally used with crewel embroidery. Choose threads that are washable and colorfast to trim washables; choose a needle to accommodate the thread you are using. Embroidery needles have extra-long eyes for easier threading.

Plan the color combinations for your fancy stitches carefully, harmonizing or contrasting the colors with your materials. Design inspiration is abundant—motifs and repeat patterns can be adapted from a drapery fabric, wallpaper repeat, or museum textile. If you use a transfer, you will find the design printed in color on the pattern envelope along with a suggested color guide. The areas of color as well as the colors themselves will determine the attractiveness of your finished work.

The fabric must be held taut in an embroidery hoop; hoops come in various sizes and are made of metal or wood, with an adjustable screw for securing the fabric. Work out your ideas on a sample swatch before applying them to the finished piece.

Press the finished embroidery right side down on a padding of turkish towel to prevent flattening of the stitches and thread.

EMBROIDERY STITCHES
Satin Stitches (Fig. 410)—are even, flat, smooth stitches placed

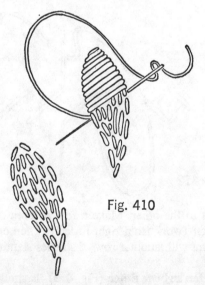

Fig. 410

closely side by side. This decorative touch is used for solid work such as leaves and flowers. First, pad the area with small, even running stitches. This "raises" the finished design. The padding stitches are covered with close, even, overcast stitches that follow the outline of the design.

Outline Stitch (Fig. 411)—is a solid row of stitching made by taking

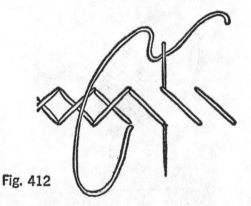

Fig. 411

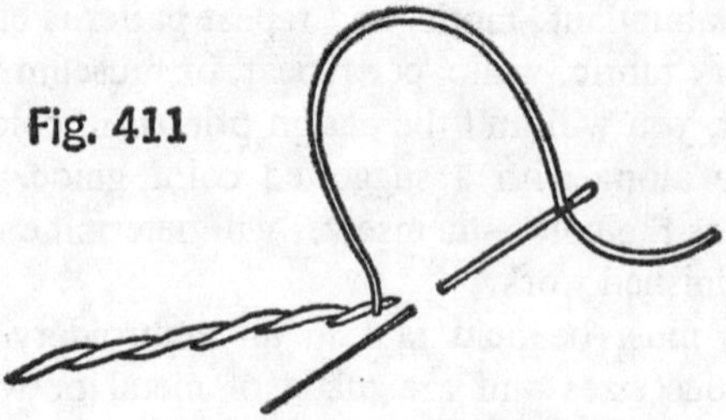

a stitch about ¼ inch (6 mm) long on the right side of the material, then a short backstitch that comes up very close to the first stitch. The outline stitch gives the appearance of one continuous line; it is used for a border, and for leaves and stems in a flower design.

Cross-Stitch (Fig. 412)—is actually two stitches taken one across and

Fig. 412

at right angles to the other. Make a row of even stitches slanting in one direction (work from right to left). Then cross each stitch at the mid-point with another row of stitches slanting in the opposite direction.

Catch Stitch or Herringbone Stitch (Fig. 413)—is similar to the cross-stitch and can be used for many of the same purposes. Work from left to right. Bring the needle up from the lower line, carry the thread diagonally to the upper line and take a small backstitch. Carry the thread down and take another small backstitch. The stitches can be made as long or as close together as you desire.

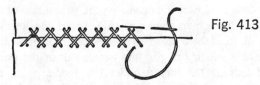

Fig. 413

Chain Stitch (Fig. 414)—is another outline stitch. Insert the needle

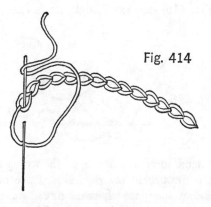

Fig. 414

on the wrong side of the fabric and bring it through to the right side. Hold the thread with the thumb of one hand and insert the needle very close to the place where the thread came up.

Take a short stitch through the material, keeping the thread under the needle so that it forms a loop. Do not pull the thread too tight. Take each successive stitch inserting the needle inside the loop and bringing it into position for the next loop, as shown in the illustration.

Lazy Daisy Stitch (Fig. 415)—is a loop stitch used chiefly in work-

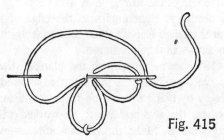

Fig. 415

ing flower designs. Insert the needle on the wrong side of the fabric and bring it through to the right side. Insert the needle on the right side of the fabric close to the place through which it was drawn. Take a stitch, bringing the needle out at the point of the petal, and looping the thread under the needle point, as shown in the illustration. Pull the needle through and catch the petal loop with a tiny stitch, bringing the needle into the position for the next stitch.

French Knots (Fig. 416)—are small, tight knots that can be worked

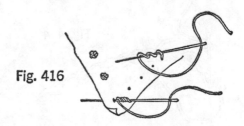

Fig. 416

in intricate designs. Insert the needle on the wrong side of the fabric and bring it through to the right side. Place the point of the needle very close to the place where the thread was pushed through the fabric, but do not insert it into the fabric. With the thread held taut in the other hand, wind it one or two times around the point of the needle. Continue to hold the thread tight while you push the needle through carefully, pulling the thread through the loop until it is knotted. Repeat the process, as close to or as far apart from the first French knot as the design indicates. The heavier the thread, the larger the knot will be.

Blanket Stitch (Fig. 417a–c)—may be evenly spaced with one stitch exactly like the stitch next to it, or spaced irregularly, with three stitches together, then a space, then three more stitches grouped together. The length of the stitches may also vary.

Insert the needle at right angles to the edge of the piece and bring it out at the edge. Repeat, each time passing the needle over the thread, as shown in the illustration.

Scallops (Fig. 418)—can be made with the blanket stitch. The exact space for the scallops should be marked along the edge of the material, preferably by being pressed on from a transfer pattern. Pad the section where the scallops are to be worked with a series of small running stitches. Make the blanket stitches even and close

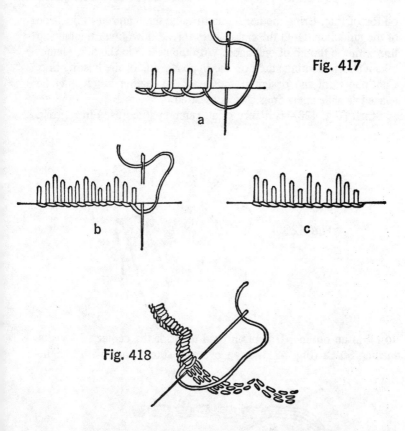

Fig. 417

a

b   c

Fig. 418

together. Do not cut the edge of the material along the curved
outer edge until the scallops are completely finished.

Feather Stitch (Fig. 419)—is a variety of the outline stitch. First run
a basting line as a guide for your design, and do the feather stitch

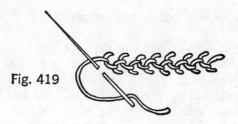

Fig. 419

on top of that. Bring the needle up through the material to one side
of the guideline. Hold the embroidery thread down over the basting
line with the thumb of one hand. With the needle in the other hand,
take a short, slanting stitch on the opposite side of the basting line.
Continue until the design is finished. The feather stitch may be
spaced as wide apart or as close as desired.

Seed Stitch (Fig. 420)—is a very small running stitch used in a group

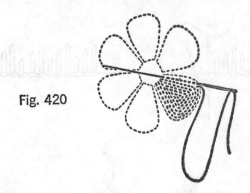

Fig. 420

to fill in an outline. It is often used to work the center of flowers.

Couching Stitch (Fig. 421)—is an overcast stitch made with a light-

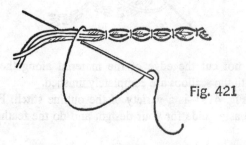

Fig. 421

weight thread, to hold one or two strands of heavier thread in
place.

Bullion Stitch (Fig. 422)—is made in the same way as the French
knot, but the threads are not wound so tightly and the needle is
pushed down through the material somewhat farther from the point
at which it was picked up. The twisted threads will then lie flat, as
shown in the illustration.

Fig. 422

Saddle Stitch or Cable Stitch (Fig. 423)—is a row of straight stitch-

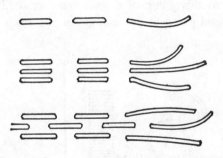

Fig. 423

ing taken by hand, with the upper stitch slightly longer than the one on the underside of the material. Saddle stitching is almost like uneven basting. The size of the stitch is determined by the size of the thread and the space to be stitched.

Hemstitching or Drawn Work—must be done on the straight grain of the fabric. It makes a fine finish just above a hem. Turn up the hem to the right side and crease it, so you know just where the top of the hem will be. Starting at the top of the hem, pull crosswise threads until you have the width you desire to hemstitch. Then baste the hem in place. To do the hemstitching, secure thread in hem on wrong side, pick up three or more threads with your needle and then draw the thread through. (Fig. 424) Bring the needle around over the small group of cross threads and pick up a small stitch of the hem from the back at the point where the needle was first

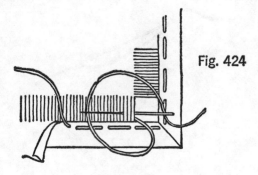

Fig. 424

inserted. Draw this group of threads together. Pull your sewing thread tight and go on to the next group of threads. (Fig. 425)

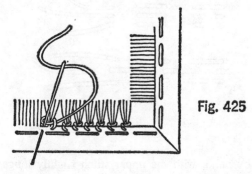

Fig. 425

Continue until the row of hemstitching is completed, making each group of threads uniform. This is known as single hemstitching.

For **Double Hemstitching** the threads are caught down and fastened on each side of the pulled cross threads. These groups of thread resemble spokes. (Fig. 426)

Diagonal Hemstitching is done in the same way as single and double hemstitching except that the threads are separated as they are caught down and fastened. One half of a group joins half of the next group of threads, to form a diagonal line rather than a straight spoke. (Fig. 427)

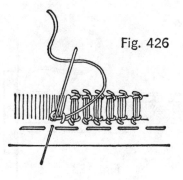

Fig. 426

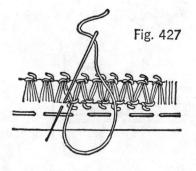

Fig. 427

Fagoting—is a decorative method of joining seams. There are two methods of fagoting, the crisscross and the bar or spoke. The material is prepared the same way for each method. The two edges of the fabric are turned under ¼ inch (6 mm) to the wrong side; press. Baste the folded edges to a piece of paper, leaving a space between the two edges. Usually a ¼ inch (6 mm) space is left. Pearl cotton or buttonhole twist is a good thread to use for fagoting.

Crisscross Fagoting (Fig. 428) Start on the wrong side and bring thread through close to one edge. Start the needle downward and take a stitch about ¼ inch (6 mm) away on the opposite edge of the fabric. Pass the needle over the thread, as shown, and pull the thread through. Take the next stitch on the opposite side, continuing to alternate the stitches for the length of the space.

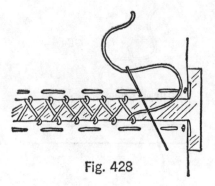

Fig. 428

Bar or Spoke Fagoting (Fig. 429) is made by bringing the nee-

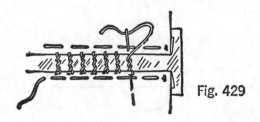

Fig. 429

dle through from the wrong side, close to the edge, and tacking the
thread by going through once more. Directly opposite, on the other
edge, take a small stitch and again fasten it by tacking. Bring the
needle over and over this "foundation bar," winding the thread
around it until the other edge is reached. Fasten by tacking. Repeat, making the bars ⅛ inch (3 mm) apart.

Smocking—is a decorative technique for gathering widths of material
into regular folds to control fullness. Silk, cotton, blends, and lightweight wool fabrics can be used. Six-strand embroidery floss or silk
thread is used for the embroidery. All smocking should be worked
before the garment or article is made up. The width of material
required for smocking is approximately three times the width of the
finished piece of work. Mark out the position for the gathering
stitches on the material; this can be done with a ruler and sharp
dressmaker's pencil or a printed transfer pattern. The spacing of

the dots can vary from ½ inch (1.3 cm) on thick materials to ⅜ inch (1 cm) or ¼ inch (6 mm) on finer fabrics; however, the space between the horizontal and vertical rows of dots must be equal.

A fabric with an evenly spaced pattern, such as gingham, affords a mechanical guide for the stitches. Smocking worked on gingham gives a special look.

Most smocking patterns are worked from left to right on the right side of the material. Once the basic stitches are learned, there is no end to the decorative borders you can design by grouping these stitches in various ways.

Outline Stitch (Fig. 430)   Knot thread and bring needle up

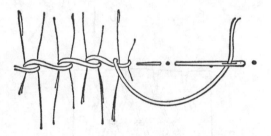

Fig. 430

through fabric at first dot. With thread below the needle, insert in fabric at second dot. Pull thread taut to form a fold in fabric. Continue across row in this manner making one stitch at each dot; always keep thread below needle.

Cable Stitch (Fig. 431a, b)   Knot thread and bring needle to right side at dot 1. With the thread *above* needle, insert in fabric under dot 2. Bring needle out and draw up thread. With thread *below* needle, make a stitch at dot 3. Complete the row, alternating the thread above and below the needle.

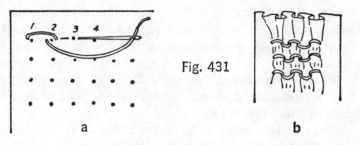

Fig. 431

a   b

Honeycomb Stitch (Fig. 432a–c) This pattern gives greater

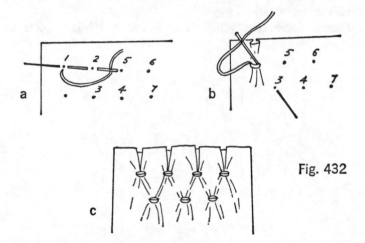

Fig. 432

elasticity to the smocking and completes two rows of stitching in one operation. Bring the needle through to the right side at dot 1. Make a small stitch at dot 2, another at dot 1. Draw thread up tightly. Insert needle at dot 2, slip down on the wrong side of fabric, and bring needle up at dot 3. Take a small stitch at dot 3 and dot 4; proceed to dots 5 and 6. Continue to work in this manner.

A variation of the honeycomb stitch is produced by having the thread pass from stitch to stitch on the surface of the fabric. (Fig. 433)

Smocking should be steam-pressed. Use a steam iron, holding it above the work and allowing the steam to penetrate, or use a damp cloth over a hot iron to make the steam. Do not press the work flat.

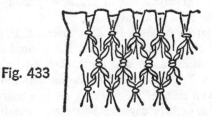

Fig. 433

Quilting—is the old art of stitching several layers of fabric held together to form decoration. Many years ago, quilted garments were worn by the Chinese; quilted mattresses and bedclothes were used by Europeans for warmth; a quilted shirt was worn under a knight's armor; gowns were quilted for royalty to support the weight of their jewels. Fabrics used for quilting should be firmly woven, soft in texture, and smooth; for the padding, use cotton or polyester batting, flannel, or lightweight wool. The lining fabric should be of the same quality and laundering characteristics as the upper fabric—a good muslin, percale, or broadcloth is usually sufficient.

To prepare the fabric for quilting, arrange the material in layers, one above the other—the lining fabric, the padding, and the upper fabric—and baste all three together. (Fig. 434) Baste from the cen-

Fig. 434

ter to the side, keeping the fabric smooth. Tack the entire surface to prevent layers of fabric from shifting. If a design motif is used, it should be transferred to the back of the lining fabric before the layers are basted together.

Choose a quilting thread to correspond with the material used:

mercerized cotton thread, silk thread, or a specially prepared quilting thread that has a resin finish.

Quilting can be done by hand or machine. For hand quilting, use a backstitch or a running stitch. Each stitch should be made in two movements, down and up through all layers of material. This technique keeps the materials in position and produces even stitches on both sides of the work. A quilting frame must be used for a large size quilt or coverlet. Small items can be worked in an embroidery hoop.

For machine quilting, replace the presser foot with the quilting attachment, which is designed with a short open foot and an adjustable as well as removable space guide. Quilting can be done in square or diamond patterns; use a medium-length stitch, increase the pressure on the presser foot, and adjust the space guide on the attachment to the desired width of the block pattern. (Fig. 435)

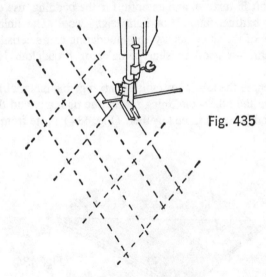

Fig. 435

A touch of quilting—a yoke, collar, cuffs, pocket—added to a garment can give it an elegant and unusual look. If the quilting is to fit a shaped area, prepare and quilt the fabric in sections, then cut the pattern piece from the quilted fabric section.

Trapunto or Italian Quilting (Fig. 436) With this quilting technique the design is outlined in a double row of stitching through two layers of fabric, the outer fabric and the lining, form-

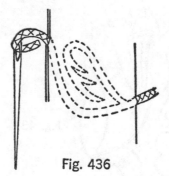

Fig. 436

ing a narrow channel through which a cord or thick yarn is threaded through from the wrong side, to produce a pattern in relief on the right side. The inside areas of the design may be padded for depth and dimension. To pad an area of the design, slash the motif on the back through the lining only, and stuff evenly with cotton or polyester stuffing. Close slash in lining with an overcast stitch. Pad each motif separately; avoid using large shapes since they are difficult to pad evenly.

If the design is planned for a section of a garment, such as a blouse front, do all the quilting in the desired area before the garment is stitched together.

Appliqué—is the technique of applying a piece of material in the shape of a design to a contrasting fabric with decorative stitching. You can use design motifs cut from patterned materials or designs traced or transferred to the fabric. It may be done by hand or machine.

For Hand Appliqué, cut out the design, allowing ¼ inch (6 mm) on all edges. Machine-stitch around seam line. Fold under seam allowance on design motif and pin in place. Sew around edges with one of the decorative embroidery stitches described, or use a slip stitch. (Fig. 437)

Use fine thread the color of the appliqué if you want the stitching to be inconspicuous, heavier thread in a contrasting color if you want the stitches to stand out in relief against the background.

For Machine Appliqué there are two techniques you can use.

METHOD A: The design is transferred to the appliqué fabric, allowing ½ inch (1.3 cm) all around the design. Pin or baste the

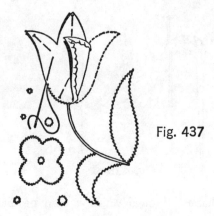

Fig. 437

appliqué in place. Set the machine for a close satin stitch and stitch around the seam line. Trim extra fabric close to stitching line. (Fig. 438)

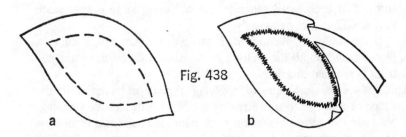

Fig. 438

a

b

METHOD B: Allow ¼ inch (6 mm) all around the design. Pin or baste the appliqué in place. Stitch around seam line, using a regular machine stitch. Trim extra fabric close to stitching line. Stitch over raw edges of fabric and line of regular stitching, using a close satin stitch. (Fig. 439)

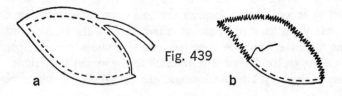

Fig. 439

a

b

MACHINE EMBROIDERY

The sewing machine of today can do more than sew a straight seam. With slight adjustments, the machine can vary from straight sewing to a zigzag stitch—in this action, the needle moves from right to left of center in a zigzag pattern as the fabric is guided under the presser foot. (Fig. 440) This zigzag stitch can be adjusted for width (Fig. 441) and for closeness of stitch. (Fig. 442)

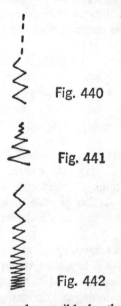

Fig. 440

Fig. 441

Fig. 442

These changes are made possible by the lever controls on the zigzag machine. The stitch length lever controls the number of stitches per inch for straight sewing and also controls the closeness or bight of the zigzag stitch. An additional lever, usually located in the center of the arm section of the machine, controls the width of the zigzag stitch. The needle can be positioned to stitch in the center, to the right of center, or to the left of center. The controls and capabilities will vary with the model and make of the machine, so make it a habit to study your machine manual carefully for the proper settings.

With the automatic zigzag machines, a variety of decorative stitches can be accomplished with the simple insertion of a disk or cam in the head of the machine. There are so many unusual stitch patterns, some designed especially to look like delicate hand embroidery. Combinations of these stitches make interesting border designs.

A double needle can replace the single needle to give you a double row of stitching, evenly spaced, similar to fine tucking.

Block or script monograms can be done on sheer or coarse fabrics, using a close satin stitch. The script monogram requires practice and skill, since the presser foot is removed, the feed is dropped, and the fabric held taut in an embroidery hoop while the operator guides the hoop in the machine with the needle as the writing instrument.

A special attachment is available for use on the straight-stitch machine that also produces some varied zigzag stitch patterns. With the attachment, the fabric is moved from side to side to create decorative stitches.

PATCHWORK

Patchwork is the art of joining small pieces of material in patterns using diamonds, triangles, squares, and similar geometric shapes. We tend to think of patchwork as using bits and pieces of soft-textured cloth—calico, percale, muslin—but some very elegant patchwork designs can be developed using silk or textured fabrics.

One need not make something as large as a quilt to learn to appreciate this art form—a pillow, skirt, or vest could whet your appetite. Then, once you have learned what a pleasant hobby this can be, you can go on to planning and designing your "heirloom piece," a patchwork quilt or bedspread.

Choose or design the pattern you want to use; you can buy patchwork designs that give you full directions, or you can make your own patterns. Old patchwork designs have names and stories attached to them; it is fun to read the history of these designs and learn a little about how they came to be. Sort out the fabric; use the same weight, such as all gingham or percale, or all silk or satin. Leftover scraps of material from sewing projects, discarded ties from the wardrobe of the man in your family, may find a new life in patchwork.

All pieces must be cut accurately, preferably from a cardboard pattern piece; allow ¼ inch (6 mm) for seams on all edges. The patchwork pattern is made by pinning and stitching the patches together in small groups to form the design. Because of the odd-shaped pieces, you will find it easier to get into the points and corners by using small, even, hand running stitches rather than the machine. The seams are pressed to one side. Interesting effects can be achieved by outlining the seams of the patchwork pattern with some of the decorative stitches described previously; use pearl cotton, embroidery floss, or buttonhole twist.

If you are planning to make a shirt or vest in patchwork, prepare the patchwork according to the shape of the pattern pieces to be used.

To make a quilt, join the small groups of your patchwork design. Cut a piece of lining material for the underside to the desired size—you can use figured material, unbleached muslin, percale, or cotton broadcloth. Place an interlining or padding (polyester batting is best for quilts) on top of this; cut the interlining 1 inch (2.5 cm) shorter on all sides. Now place the finished patchwork over the lining and interlining and tack or quilt through all layers,

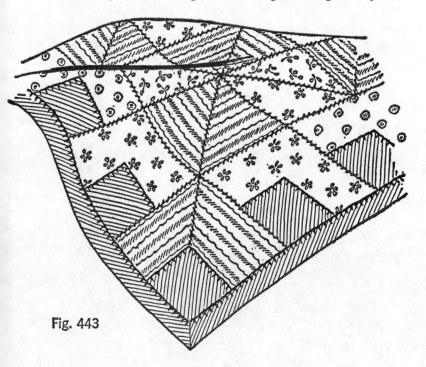

Fig. 443

at evenly spaced intervals. A large quilt should be placed on a quilting frame so that all layers of fabric are held in place for the tacking or quilting.

Finish the raw edges with a binding applied with a decorative stitch. (Fig. 443)

18 Decorative Trimming Tricks

———◆———

Trimmings are a means of adding color, texture, and interest to clothes; decide where, when, and how much trimming you will use according to the design of the garment. The simple garment with few construction details offers the best background for decoration.

Lace Edging—Lace adds a touch of elegance to any garment. Lace edging is available in many widths; it is applied to the edge of the fabric and can be sewn on by hand or machine. Before applying lace edging you must decide whether you want it to be straight or gathered. If you put lace edging on a shaped or curved area it is best to gather the lace slightly, because a straight edge cannot be applied neatly to a curved edge.

To gather lace edging, look for the heavy thread that is woven close to the straight edge or selvage. Take hold of the thread with one hand and with the other hand push the lace gently along this thread; you will find the lace gathers quite easily in this way.

Applying Lace to a Raw Edge Baste the lace about ½ inch (1.3 cm) from the edge on the right side of the fabric. On the wrong side, roll the edge of the fabric and catch the lace with each stitch you take in the hem. (Fig. 444) It takes a little skill to become adept with this technique.

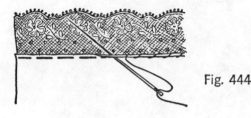

Fig. 444

Applying Lace to a Hemmed Edge   Place the lace to the fabric with wrong sides together. Hold the fabric with the lace toward you; use small, loose overcast stitches to whip the lace to the edge. After stitching, spread the lace out flat. (Fig. 445)

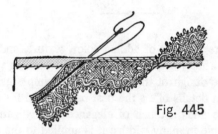

Fig. 445

To apply lace edging by machine, place edge of lace slightly over the edge of the fabric, with right sides up, and use a narrow, open zigzag stitch or a straight stitch.

Lace Inserts or Bands—Baste the lace insert or flat lace band to the right side of the material. Use small running stitches around the edges of the lace, or stitch around the edges by machine. If the material is to remain under the lace, no other sewing is necessary.

For a cut-out lace insertion or laceband, trim away the material under the lace very carefully with small embroidery scissors; leave only enough fabric, about ½ inch (1.3 cm), to be able to roll and whip the edges. (Fig. 446)

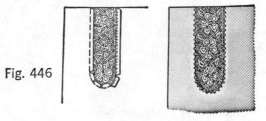

Fig. 446

Braid (Passementeries)

Novelty braid is available in a variety of types, widths, colors, and materials; it may be applied either by hand or by machine. You may find it easier to manipulate intricate curves when applying the braid by hand; but if extra firmness is required, machine stitching will be more secure.

With soutache or narrow braid, trace the design on the right side of the fabric; the stitching is done through the center of the braid. Stitch along the outer edges of wider braids. (Fig. 447)

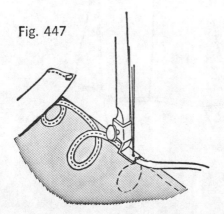

Fig. 447

Used with taste and discrimination, braid will add smartness to an otherwise plain outfit. (Fig. 448)

Fig. 448

Arrowhead

It can be used on the corners of tailored pockets, at the top of a pleat, or at the end of a row of saddle stitching. To make it, use buttonhole twist or embroidery thread, and mark a triangle on the fabric, ⅜ inch (1 cm) to ½ inch (1.3 cm) wide at the base. Take three or four small stitches within the triangle, bringing the thread out at the corner. Take a small horizontal stitch at the point of the triangle. (Fig. 449)

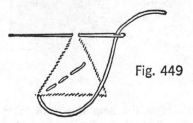

Fig. 449

Then take a horizontal stitch across the base of the triangle, forming a diagonal on the right side. (Fig. 450)

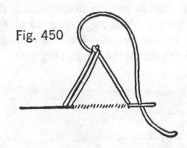

Fig. 450

Repeat the stitch to the point, and from the point to the base, until the triangle is filled with smooth rows of stitches. Finish with three or four stitches on the underside. (Fig. 451)

Fig. 451

Self Fringe

To make fringe, trim edge of fabric on the grain line. Decide on the depth of the fringe and machine-stitch along this line. Pull cross threads as far as the stitched line. (Fig. 452)

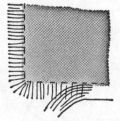

Fig. 452

Knotted Fringe

This is made after the hem has been completed. Groups of threads are pulled through the hem to form the fringe. Knot each group of threads separately close to the hem. You can decide on the number of threads you want and how close you want the fringe to be.

When all the threads are knotted, measure them, and cut the ends to even the fringe. You might want to make yourself a cardboard gauge to measure evenly. Use pearl cotton, wool, or other textured thread or yarn for the fringe. (Fig. 453)

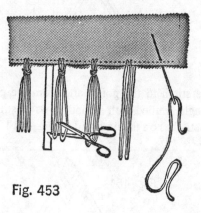

Fig. 453

Tassels

Make a cardboard gauge the length of the tassel and wind yarn around gauge to the desired thickness. Tie strands together at upper end, and cut yarn at opposite end. (Fig. 454a) Remove cardboard and wrap thread around upper end several times; knot to secure. (Fig. 454b)

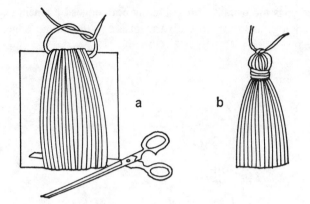

a   b   Fig. 454

Embroidered Edgings

These can be purchased by the yard, either gathered or ungathered; the latter is usually cheaper. If you decide to gather the edging yourself, buy one and a half times the area to be trimmed. If you buy the edging already gathered, buy only the amount needed, since it is measured by the finished edge of the binding. (Fig. 455)

Fig. 455

These edgings are usually stitched along both edges by machine. Gathered edgings are sewn to the garment along the bound edge. (Fig. 455a)

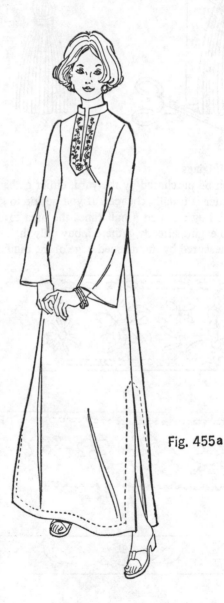

Fig. 455a

Rickrack

This is available in three sizes, baby, medium, and jumbo; in a grand assortment of colors, and sometimes with metallic threads woven in. Combinations of colors and sizes of rickrack can make interesting borders on skirts, pants, or curtains for the home. (Fig. 456)

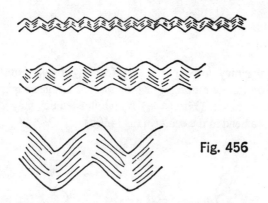

Fig. 456

To sew rickrack on by hand, take a small stitch at each point of the rickrack; the lazy-daisy stitch can be particularly effective. (Fig. 457)

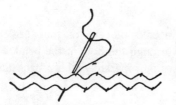

Fig. 457

Machine-stitch through the center of the rickrack to form bands or to outline a design. (Fig. 458)

 Fig. 458

Rickrack may also be stitched along the inside of a finished edge of the neckline, armhole, or pocket, so that only half the sawtooth is visible. (Fig. 459)

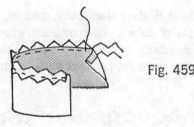

Fig. 459

Sequins

Sequins may be bought in strip form by the yard and hand-sewn to the outline of a design, or they may be applied separately to the design as shown. (Fig. 460a) Individual sequins may also be sewn on with a bead in the center. (Fig. 460b)

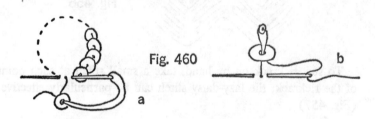

Fig. 460

a   b

Beading

Use a very fine needle—the eye of the needle must be thin enough to go easily through the hole in the bead. For plain beading, each bead is sewn on separately with a backstitch. (Fig. 461)

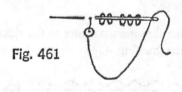

Fig. 461

A festoon of beads is made by stringing a group of beads on the thread and securing in place with a backstitch. (Fig. 462) The number of beads depends upon the size and spacing of the loops you want.

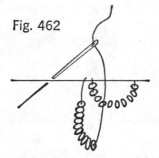

Fig. 462

Tailored Bow

A tailored bow may be made of ribbon or self fabric. Cut one long piece, three times the size of the finished bow, and one short piece for a center tab. (Fig. 463)

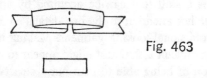

Fig. 463

Mark the center of the long strip and fold as shown, tacking the center at the underside. (Fig. 464)

Fig. 464

The short piece is wrapped around the center and tacked on the wrong side. (Fig. 465a, b)

a   Fig. 465   b

19 Tailoring

———◆———

Tailoring is a skill that can be acquired by any sewer who is willing to give her attention to the fine details so essential in turning out a professional-looking garment. Making a suit or coat is not nearly the difficult task that it might appear to be, and certainly the satisfaction of being able to turn out a smart-looking tailored garment at a fraction of its retail price is more than enough incentive to the average woman.

Patience and careful workmanship are the two basic requirements of learning to become your own tailor. The tailoring procedures themselves are not difficult; many of them are the same as those used in making any other garment.

HOW TO CHOOSE YOUR PATTERN AND MATERIAL

The things you learned about buying a pattern and choosing fabric in Chapter 1 also apply to tailored garments. For your first tailoring job, select a pattern that is simple—an unlined jacket or coat without a collar, for example.

Remember that you buy a coat or suit pattern in the same size as your dress pattern. Sufficient allowance has been made in the pattern for the clothes that are worn with these garments. Select a style that will look well made up in the material you plan to use. For instance, thick wools or rough-textured tweeds look best when made up in casual, loosely fitted clothes. The smooth-finished wools and synthetic blends, which can include gabardine, flannel,

Fig. 466

broadcloth, men's-wear worsted, and coverts, are suitable for the more fitted styles and intricate seaming details.

All fabrics should be preshrunk before you begin to work with them—look for the label on the bolt or look at the selvage edge of the fabric for printed information. If the material is not guaranteed preshrunk or if you have purchased a remnant piece, you can have it sponged at a dry cleaner's or follow the instructions in Chapter 3 for doing it yourself.

For a beginning project, select fabric that is not stretchy or loosely woven—do not choose a plaid or striped fabric for a first tailoring venture, either. With more experience, you can try the plaid suit you have always wanted.

Corduroy and velveteen are attractive in certain types of coats and jackets. Choose a pattern with few pieces and one that does not require a lot of outside stitching; these materials are more difficult to press than fine wools. While corduroy and velveteen are usually cotton-backed, they can often be used for cold-weather coats if they are properly interlined. Without an interlining they make good sports coats and suits for milder climates.

Coats, suits, and separate jackets can be made of washable cotton, denim, linen, and synthetic blends for summer wear. Choose a fabric that will be wrinkle-resistant and that requires little care, with little or no pressing. For washable tailored garments, select a pattern that is simple in construction so you will not be faced with difficult pressing problems. Remember too, all trimmings and interfacings used should have the same laundering characteristics as the outer fabric you are using.

Raincoats or capes are other garments you can make. Choose fabrics that are water-repellent, such as the vinyl leather-like fabrics, or make the coat and have the garment treated for waterproofing by the professional dry cleaner. Some of these treatments must be repeated after several cleanings, so check this with the cleaner. A raincoat can be made lined or unlined; use a seam finish that will eliminate raw edges, such as a welt or flat felled seam, in an unlined coat.

Lining Material—is generally crepe, satin, or taffeta in silk, rayon, or polyester. The material chosen should be as fine in quality as the material of the coat or suit, for a cheap-looking lining can ruin the appearance of the entire garment and a cheap lining will wear out long before the outer fabric.

For most tailored garments a lining in a matching color is the best choice. Novelty linings are sometimes used for effect: for example, a plaid wool lining in a corduroy sports jacket; or a fleece lining in a jacket or coat. An ensemble is especially attractive when the coat is lined with the same print material that is used for the dress worn beneath it. In making an outfit like this, however, remember that a coat with a printed lining will not look well with all other clothes. Lightweight coats and jackets of piqué and linen should be lined with smooth cotton. In each case make sure that the lining material is also preshrunk, for a lining that shrinks can ruin any garment.

Interlining—A heavy coat for winter wear must be interlined for additional warmth. This interlining should be one of the lightweight woolen materials made especially for the purpose. Wool interlining will give the most warmth. Putting an interlining into a coat can be a little tricky, and some home tailors prefer to avoid using two materials—lining and interlining—by using one fabric that acts as both interlining and lining. This could be satin or taffeta backed by a thin layer of foam or fleece, or Milium (a fabric backed by an aluminum coating). There is also a quilted combination of lining and interlining that is usually satin or crepe and fleece. The fabrics are machine-stitched together by square or diagonal quilting.

Interfacing and Facing—Interfacing is a must for tailored garments. You can use preshrunk unbleached muslin, tailor's canvas, nonwoven interfacing, or a fusible interfacing; all are available in various weights according to the fabric used for the garment and the desired effect to be achieved (see Chapter 5). The interfacing is stitched between the garment and the facing. It gives firmness to the lapels so they have the proper shape and roll; it is also used in the collar.

A jacket or coat pattern will include a separate pattern piece for the interfacing and for the facing. The facing is cut from the garment material and is shaped to fit the section of the garment.

Underlining—Loosely woven fabrics should be underlined with a backing fabric to give added body. See the section on underlinings in Chapter 5. Consider the weight of the underlining with the outer fabric when choosing an interfacing.

TAILORING SUPPLIES

In tailored coats and jackets, tape is used to reinforce the neck, front edges, and lapels. This is particularly important if the fabric stretches easily. Buy cotton twill tape, ⅜ to ½ inch (1 to 1.3 cm) wide, for the purpose. Preshrink the tape by immersing it thoroughly in warm water and letting it dry.

For machine stitching, use dual-duty thread in the same shade as or a shade darker than the garment fabric. For topstitching you might want to use silk buttonhole twist. All threads should be colorfast, of course.

Finish the seams and hem of an unlined jacket or coat with a binding, matching the color as nearly as possible to the fabric (see Chapter 7). Use cotton binding for washable fabrics, silk or rayon for woolens and other fabrics that will be dry-cleaned.

Buy your buttons along with your other notions so that you will be sure of the correct size when you make the buttonholes. If you are making a suit, buy the zipper for the skirt placket, as well as any hooks and eyes or snaps you may need. If you are using shoulder pads, buy them now.

Now is a good time to invest in a dress form, if you don't already own one. A dress form is a great help to the woman who sews alone and is especially useful for tailoring jobs. Assemble all the materials and equipment you need before you begin; then you will find it easier to concentrate on the interesting process of tailoring ahead of you.

MAKING A COAT OR JACKET

There are two general rules in which lie the secrets of all good tailoring.

Work carefully Whether you are cutting, fitting, or sewing, work as neatly as you can, for tailoring is largely a matter of precision workmanship.

Press as you go The careful step-by-step pressing of your garment is essential for a crisp custom-made finish. The same results can never be achieved if all pressing is left until last. Review the suggestions for professional pressing in Chapter 3; and this would be an opportune time to consider purchasing some of the pressing aids described—they will make the task easier for you.

Cutting and Fitting the Pattern—Before you do anything with the pattern itself, study the directions that came with it. Don't overlook the pattern layout! Review the information contained in Chapter 1 on the pattern layout and markings; if you are working with a very bulky fabric it is more accurate to cut on a single thickness of fabric to prevent shifting. Test the fabric you are using for the most visible and lasting means of marking; with bulky fabrics and tweeds you might find it easier to use tailor's tacks. Also review the information in Chapter 2 on altering a pattern.

Professional tailors usually work with a muslin pattern so that the garment can be fitted as smoothly as possible. It might be worth it for you to take the extra time and patience for this. Cut the muslin pattern from the paper pattern—it is not necessary to cut facings, but do cut the two sleeves. Baste the garment together; baste the sleeves into the armholes. Fit the muslin, and when all necessary alterations have been made and carefully marked, rip the pieces apart and press them. Mark the grain line on each piece from the paper pattern; lay the muslin pieces on the material and cut out the garment. Transfer all markings and changes you have made on the muslin pattern to the material.

Tailoring Steps—Organizing your work into units is as important to tailoring as it is to dressmaking; it will eliminate the unnecessary handling that gives the garment a worn-out look before it has been completed. The tailoring steps will be the same for a coat or a jacket—the difference is usually in finishing the hem.

Pin and stitch darts and seams in front section of garment.

Interfacing and Pad-stitching the Front Section—Cut the interfacing according to the pattern piece. To eliminate the bulk of darts in the interfacing, slash through the center of the dart and lap cut edges on stitching lines. Machine-zigzag or catch-stitch edges together. (Fig. 467) Baste the interfacing to the wrong side of the garment with rows of loose diagonal basting stitches. Catch only one or two threads of the outer fabric; if you have used a backing, catch only the backing fabric. Baste along the roll line of the lapel through interfacing and outer fabric.

Parallel rows of hand tacking, called pad stitching, start at the roll line and fill the lapel to the seam line. Hold the material over the hand as you stitch, so that the lapel will have the easy, unstrained roll that is a sign of fine tailoring. Make the pad stitches about ⅜ inch (1 cm) long and the rows about ⅜ inch (1 cm)

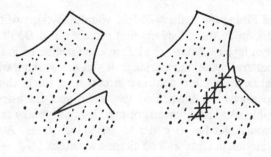

Fig. 467

apart; use thread the same color as the garment and pick up one or two threads of the outer fabric. (Fig. 468) Steam-press the lapel over a tailor's ham to give it shape.

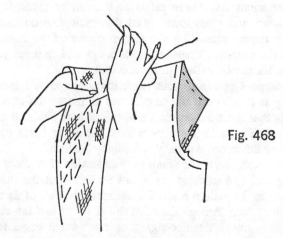

Fig. 468

Trim interfacing ¾ inch (2 cm) along front and neck edges. Pin preshrunk cotton twill tape to the edges with one edge of the tape at the ⅝ inch (1.5 cm) seam line; sew by hand along seam line and sew the other edge to the interfacing. If the lower edge of the garment is curved, shape the tape by steam-pressing and "swirling" it into a curve before applying. To stay the roll of the lapel, sew the tape along the basted line from the neck edge to the front tape. (Fig. 469)

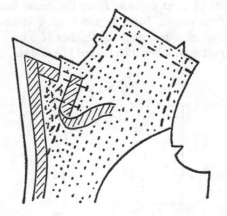

Fig. 469

If you are using a fusible interfacing, cut off the seam allowance on the interfacing before applying it to the outer fabric; follow the manufacturer's instructions for fusing the interfacing. Always test the interfacing on a swatch of your garment fabric before applying it to the garment—fusibles are not recommended for certain fabrics. Additional body can be provided to the lapel and undercollar by cutting another piece of interfacing to the triangular shape of the lapel and to the shape of the undercollar stand; fuse in place over the interfacing already applied.

Bound buttonholes are usually made in tailored garments, and they are made after the interfacing has been attached. Review the various methods for making bound buttonholes in Chapter 12 and make a sample in your fabric before attempting the buttonholes in the garment. Worked buttonholes can be made in sports jackets and blazers; these are made after the garment is completed.

If your pattern design includes pockets, they are usually made and applied to the front sections before the seams are stitched. Follow the instructions in the cut and sew guide. Review Chapter 13 for some helpful hints for making perfect pockets.

Muslin Reinforcement for the Back Unit—Stitch and press seams and darts in back. A muslin reinforcement will shape and stabilize the garment through the shoulder area. If your pattern does not include a pattern piece for a muslin reinforcement, you can easily use the back pattern piece as a guide. Place the center back seam line on the fold of the muslin. Measure and mark 7 inches (18 cm) from neck edge; measure and mark 2½ inches (6.5 cm) from underarm edge. Connect markings with a curved line and cut. (Fig. 470)

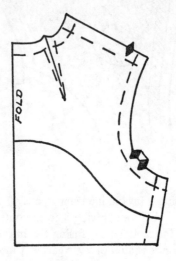

Fig. 470

If the garment you are making has seaming lines on the back, lap and pin the back and side back pattern pieces on the seam line so that the muslin reinforcement can be cut without seams.

Stitch darts in muslin (if any) and press in direction opposite to the outer fabric. Pin muslin to garment back with wrong sides together, matching centers and cut edges. Diagonal-baste in place.

Stitch shoulder seams and side seams. Trim interfacing on back section close to stitching line.

Interfacing the Undercollar—The collar of tailored garments consists of an undercollar, usually cut on the bias grain with a seam in the center back, and the upper collar. The interfacing is cut from the undercollar pattern piece. Stitch center back seam of the undercollar. Mark seam lines and roll line carefully on the interfacing. Lap interfacing pieces on seam line and machine-stitch or catch-stitch on seam line. Trim interfacing close to stitching lines.

Pin interfacing to the wrong side of the undercollar, with marked side of interfacing uppermost. Cut off outer corners of the interfac-

ing ⅛ inch (3 mm) inside seam line, to eliminate bulk when turning the corner. Diagonal-baste through center of collar. (Fig. 471)

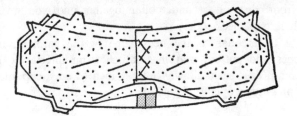

Fig. 471

Pad-stitching to Shape the Roll of the Collar—Rows of pad stitching
are used to shape and maintain the roll of the collar. Start with
a backstitch; make the diagonal stitches about ⅜ inch (1 cm)
long; use thread to match the outer fabric and catch the thread
of the outer fabric through the interfacing. Make the first row of
pad stitching on the roll line of the interfacing. Hold the collar
over the hand in the shape it will have when worn, shaping the
roll as you pad-stitch.

To pad the outer section of the collar, start at center back seam
line, and make stitches slightly larger than on the inner section
of the collar, with rows farther apart; follow the grain line of the
interfacing and work toward outer edge of collar, holding collar
over the hand. Trim interfacing on seam line. (Fig. 472) Catch-
stitch outer edges of interfacing to undercollar. Steam-press the fin-

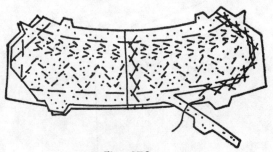

Fig. 472

ished undercollar over a tailor's ham to give it shape. (Once the pad stitching is completed, the undercollar should not lie flat since this would destroy the shape created by stitching and pressing; pin the front edges of the undercollar together until you are ready to apply it to the neck edge.)

Pin undercollar to the neck edge of the garment, matching notches and pattern markings. Stitch; trim interfacing close to stitching. Trim seam allowance to ⅜ inch (1 cm), clip into curves, and press seam open. (Fig. 473)

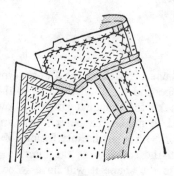

Fig. 473

Stitching Upper Collar and Facing—Stitch the back facing to the front facings at shoulder seams. Pin upper collar to the neck edge of facing with the right sides together. Stitch, trim seam allowances to ⅜ inch (1 cm), clip curves, and press seam open. (Fig. 474)

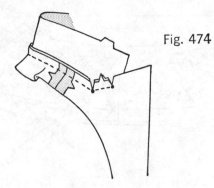

Fig. 474

Pin and baste the front facings and upper collar to the garment fronts, with right sides together; match all notches and pattern markings. The facing will be slightly larger than the garment in the lapel and upper collar area, to allow for turning the facing. This extra fullness can be eased in as you baste. (Fig. 475)

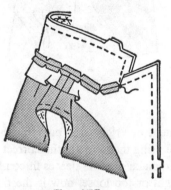

Fig. 475

Trim and grade seam allowances, reversing the grading at the roll line of the lapel. Remember when grading seams that the seam allowance closest to the outside of the garment will be the wider one. Clip into the seam allowance at any curve or point so that it will lie flat when pressed.

Turn collar and facings to right side; press, rolling seam slightly to the underside.

Pin neck seams together on outside of upper collar. Lift the facings and sew the neck seam allowances together between the shoulder seams. Catch-stitch the edge of the facing to the seams. (Fig. 476)

Setting in the Sleeves—Some tailored sleeve patterns consist of two pieces, the upper sleeve and the under sleeve; this type of sleeve makes a good fit. Stitch seams of sleeve sections, easing upper sleeve to fit the under sleeve. Press the seam open on a sleeve board or seam roll.

Machine-stitch along seam line of sleeve cap and gather to fit the armhole as directed in Chapter 10. Carefully pin and baste both sleeves into the armholes of the garment.

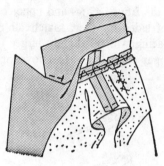

Fig. 476

Try the garment on, right side out. Pin the shoulder pads in place, if you are using them, to get the correct fit of the armholes. Lift your arms to make sure the sleeves fit comfortably. If the armholes are too tight or too loose, now is the time to make the adjustment. (NOTE: all fittings should be made over a blouse if one is to be worn with the jacket.) While you have the garment on, measure the length of the sleeves and pin up the sleeve hems. Remove the garment and machine-stitch the sleeve into the armhole. Make another row of stitching about ¼ inch (6 mm) from the first row and trim the sleeve seam to ⅜ inch (1 cm) between notches.

A slight padding is needed in the sleeve cap to give support. Cut two strips of lamb's wool, polyester fleece, or flannel 3 inches (7.5 cm) by 6 inches (15 cm). Make a 1-inch (2.5 cm) fold along one long edge; slip-stitch fold to seam at cap of sleeve, with wider part of strip toward sleeve. (Fig. 477)

Pin shoulder pads in place if they are being used—it is best to try the garment on again and position the pads from the outside. Sew pads to the shoulder seam allowances. In an unlined garment the pads should be covered with lining fabric of a matching color.

To give more body to the sleeve hem, cut a bias strip of preshrunk muslin about 2 inches (5 cm) wide. Turn under ¼ inch (6 mm) along one long edge and press; pin the folded edge of the bias strip along the hemline of the sleeve. Slip-stitch the fold loosely to the hemline; lap and catch-stitch cut ends of strip. (Fig. 478)

Turn the sleeve hem up and sew to muslin strip. If the sleeve is to be unlined, this bias strip should be the width of the hem only; finish the raw edge of the sleeve with hem binding.

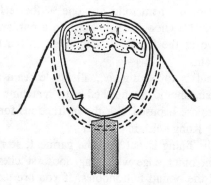

Fig. 477

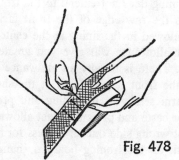

Fig. 478

Hemming—The hem of a jacket is usually turned up on the hemline given on the pattern; alterations in length should be made on the paper pattern before it is cut out. For a coat, wear a pair of shoes with the same heel height you plan to wear; put the coat on, pinclosed at center fronts, and have someone assist you in marking the hemline.

Insert a bias strip of muslin in the hem of the jacket or coat, as explained for the sleeve. The muslin strip should be at least 1 inch (2.5 cm) wider than the hem, unless the garment is unlined. Catch the free edge of the strip to the garment seams. Finish the raw edge of the hem following one of the techniques described in Chapter 11; choose a hem finish in accordance with the weight and weave of the fabric. Sew the hem to the bias muslin strip; press the hem.

If your garment is to be unlined, all inside seam allowances, including the hem, should be finished with matching binding so that no raw edges are exposed. See the instructions for the bound seam or the Hong Kong finish in Chapter 7.

Finishing—Before the lining is put into the garment, sew interfacing to front facing at outer edge with long, loose stitches; complete the underside of the bound buttonholes. If you are using worked buttonholes, make them now. Remove all basting threads. Press the entire garment, or, if possible, have a tailor press it before you put the lining in. This gives him the opportunity to apply steam easily to the outer fabric if it is necessary.

Lining the Coat or Jacket—The lining of a coat or jacket is handled in the same manner up to the point where the garment is hemmed.

Cut the lining according to the pattern pieces included in the pattern. The front lining does not extend to the front edge of the garment, but covers the raw edge of the front facing. A 1-inch (2.5 cm) pleat is allowed in the lining at the center back of the garment. This pleat allowance will give you greater freedom of shoulder movement. There is usually an allowance for a ½-inch (1.3 cm) pleat in the front lining pieces at the shoulder seams.

Stitch the underarm seams of the lining and press the seams open. Stitch darts, or baste and press the pleat allowances in place.

Place the garment wrong side out on a dress form. If you have no dress form, work on the ironing board or hang the coat on a hanger. Pin the lining to the coat, matching the underarm seams. The lining should be right side out, so that the two wrong sides of the material face each other. Pin the 1-inch (2.5 cm) pleat in place from the neck edge down the center back.

Baste the lining to the garment at both armholes; then, with long, loose basting stitches, tack it to the seams of the coat within 6 inches (15 cm) of the hem. Pin and baste lining along front facing, turning under raw edge of lining over facing.

Pin the shoulder seam of the front lining to the shoulder line of the coat, smooth out, and baste. Bring the edge of the back lining over the front section along the shoulder line. Smooth out, turn under raw edge, and slip-stitch in place. Slip-stitch the lining to the facing along the front edge and across the neck. Catch-stitch across the back pleat about 2 inches (5 cm) down from the top edge. Catch-stitch across the shoulder pleats.

Join the sleeve sections by machine and press seams open. The sleeve lining is slipped over the sleeve. Turn under the seam allowance of the lining at the armhole and slip-stitch to the coat lining. Then attach the bottom of the sleeve lining to the hem of the sleeve by slip-stitching. The lining should not be drawn tight—allow enough ease for elbow room when the arm is bent. (Fig. 479)

Turn up the hem on the lower edge of the lining and sew by hand. The hem of the lining should be about 1 inch (2.5 cm) shorter than the hem of the coat. (Fig. 480)

The side seams of the lining are fastened to the side seams of the coat with a bar tack, as illustrated, but the lining is left free at the bottom of the coat. (Fig. 481)

If you are making a jacket, the bottom edge of the lining is slip-stitched to the jacket about ½ inch (1.3 cm) above the finished hemline of the jacket. The lining forms a fold at the bottom when pressed down. This conceals the slip-stitching and at the same time prevents any strain or pull on the lining. (Fig. 482)

Interlining a Coat—For cold weather, a wool interlining is necessary in a coat. The jackets of winter suits may also be interlined. Buying a lining fabric that already contains the interlining will minimize the work involved, but in most cases fine tailoring calls for the separate interlining.

There are two techniques for applying an interlining to the garment:

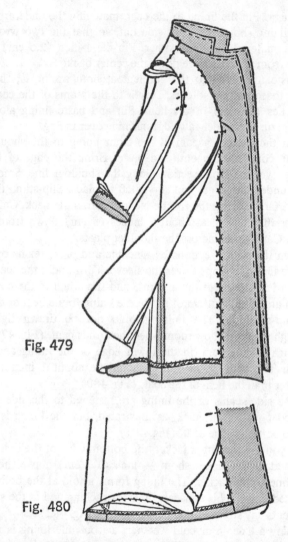

Fig. 479

Fig. 480

METHOD A: The interlining is put together separately and then put into the coat before the lining is tacked in place. Omit the pleat allowance at the center back and shoulder lines of the interlining. Slash darts and press open after they have been stitched. Overlap the seams by placing one raw edge on top of the other, matching seam lines, and catch-stitch or machine-stitch along seam

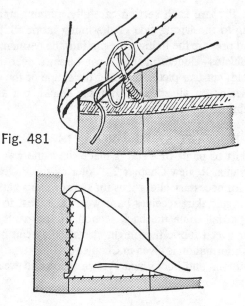

Fig. 481

Fig. 482

line. Excess fabric may be trimmed close to the stitching line to eliminate bulk.

Turn the coat inside out and place on dress form or hanger. Pin the interlining in place on the coat and sew the interlining around the armholes and under the front facing with small running stitches.

The interlining can extend about 1 inch (2.5 cm) under the facing to allow for sewing in place and then be cut off. Cut it off about 2 inches (5 cm) above the finished hemline of the coat. Tack it loosely at intervals to the side seams of the coat.

Set the interlining into the sleeves in the same way. Sleeve interlining, as a rule, does not extend all the way to the wrist. In a two-piece tailored sleeve, the interlining is usually cut for only the wider top section and then caught to the seams in the sleeve with running stitches.

METHOD B: The interlining pieces are attached to the lining pieces by basting the two fabrics together and stitching them as one unit. Prepare each section carefully, pinning and basting the interlining to the wrong side of the lining fabric. Stitch the lining seams and prepare the lining to be put into the garment.

Underarm Shields—Underarm shields can be sewn over the lining. For each shield, cut two pieces of lining the shape of the shield, allowing for seams on all edges. Cover the shield; pin and slip-stitch to the lining on the inside of the garment.

MAKING THE SUIT SKIRT OR PANTS

The skirt or pants of a suit is made the same way as any other skirt or pants. Review Chapter 2, "Altering the Pattern to Suit the Figure," for necessary alterations for skirt or pants pattern.

Since a suit skirt receives hard wear, it is best to underline or at least partially line the back section. If the pants are of lightweight or tweed fabric that might stretch, they can be underlined. Detailed information is given in Chapter 5.

Sew buttons and hooks and eyes in place and wear your outfit with pride!

20 Sewing for Children

By all means make your children's clothes. Prices asked for ready-made children's clothes can be very high and you can duplicate the designs and fabrics for about half the cost.

CHOOSING FABRIC

Pattern catalogues have a special section for children's clothes; plan your child's wardrobe as you would your own. Choose fabrics that will stand up to the activity involved—sturdy fabrics such as denim, poplin, or duck for play; corduroy, knits, cotton, blends for school; the more delicate fabrics such as organdy, eyelet, velveteen, and sheers for dress-up.

With easy-care fabrics, patterns that are easy to cut and sew, and a few short-cut construction tricks, your child can be well dressed at a minimum cost to you.

PATTERN SIZES

Patterns for children fall into six size ranges:

Babies—Patterns are designed for infants who cannot walk. There are two sizes—newborn (1–3 months) and 6 months.
Toddlers—Patterns are designed for a figure that is taller than a baby but shorter than a child. The size range is ½ to 4; an allowance is made for diapers.
Children—Patterns for children have the same waist and breast measurement as Toddler patterns; shoulders and back are wider and patterns are longer. The size range is 2 to 6X.

Boys—Patterns are designed for the boy who hasn't reached adult stature. The size range is 7 to 12.

Girls—Patterns are designed with bustline darts for the developing figure. The height ranges from 4'2" to 5'1" (1.27 to 1.55 m); the size range is 7 to 14.

Chubbie—Patterns are comparable to girl's patterns and are for the girl who weighs more than the average for age and height. The size range is 8½c to 14½c.

Buy the pattern according to the child's body measurements, not age, since children of the same age vary greatly in size. Compare the measurements with those of different sizes in the size range most suitable for your child. Breast and waist measurements should be the key to the correct pattern selection. If measurements fall between sizes, select a girl's dress pattern size closest to the breast measurement, shoulder length, and back waist length; a boy's shirt pattern size closest to the neck circumference; a boy's jacket pattern size closest to the chest measurement. Pants and skirt patterns are purchased by waist measurement. Children grow quickly, so check the measurements before you embark on any sewing project.

HOW TO TAKE MEASUREMENTS (Fig. 483)

The child should wear underwear and stand with feet together; tie a string around natural waist.

Breast or Chest—Under arms, over the fullest part of the chest in front, across shoulder blades in back.

Waist—Around the natural waistline.

Hip—Around the fullest part of the buttocks.

Back Waist Length—Measure from the prominent bone at the base of the neck to the string at the waistline.

Back Width—Across the widest part of the back.

Arm Length—From top of arm to wrist, with arm slightly bent.

Shoulder Length—From base of neck to top of arm at shoulder.

Front Waist Length—From base of neck to string at waist.

Finished Skirt Length—From waist to desired hemline.

Finished Dress Length—From center back neck to desired hemline.

Finished Pants Length—From waist to desired hemline along side.

Height—Have child stand against a wall, without shoes; measure from floor to top of head.

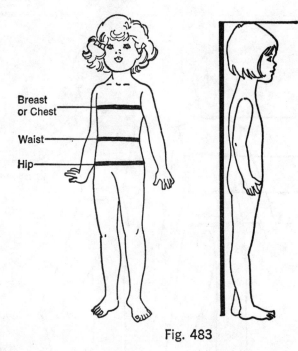

Breast or Chest

Waist

Hip

Fig. 483

For Boys Only (Fig. 484)

Neck Circumference—Around neck.

Shirt Sleeve Length—From base of neck at center back over elbow to wrist, with arm bent.

Pattern Adjustments—The pattern can be shortened or lengthened easily at the lines indicated on the pattern piece. Review the techniques for altering a pattern in Chapter 2.

Understanding Your Pattern—The cut and sew guide will give you detailed instructions on how to put the garment together. Follow the cutting layout carefully; transfer all necessary construction markings from pattern to fabric. Read the sewing instructions before starting to sew. You will find some short-cut techniques used for children's clothes that you may not be familiar with, such as sleeves that are sewn to the garment while it is flat, then the sleeve and underarm seam are stitched in one. The factory method of construction is often used in making children's clothes.

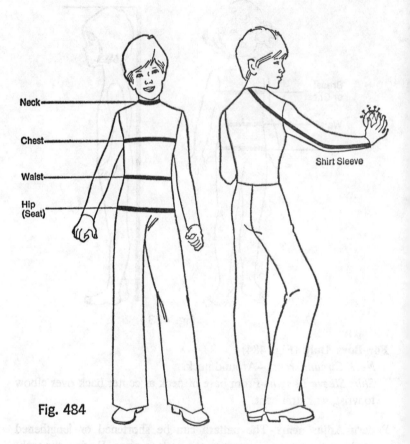

Neck

Chest

Waist

Hip
(Seat)

Shirt Sleeve

Fig. 484

SEWING TIPS

- Choose simple designs without too much detail. Decorative trim, edgings, ruffles, rickrack, or a touch of embroidery can change the look of a simple dress or jumper.
- Allow extra-wide hems so they can be let down as the child grows; or make use of the decorative tuck described in Chapter 8. Braid, ribbon, or rickrack trim can be stitched over fade lines of let-down hems. Or you may want to add a wide band as a border, in a contrasting color or print fabric.
- Adjustable straps could add an extra year of service to a skirt

or jumper; check the notions counters for decorative shoulder strap closures and buckles.

- Use flat felled seams or double-stitched seams for extra strength, particularly in playclothes and toddlers' wear.
- Reinforce buttons and sew them on firmly; be sure the buttonhole size is correct for the button, so that there will be no added strain on the buttonhole. If you want the child to learn how to dress and undress unassisted, don't use buttons that are too small for fingers that are not quite so nimble.
- Make worked buttonholes and stitch around the buttonhole twice for reinforcement on washable clothes. Use bound buttonholes only for a coat.
- Try the nylon closure Velcro, or snap tape by the yard, for sports jackets and playwear, or for the crotch seam of pants for the diaper set.
- Choose all decorative detail, buttons, and trimmings that are washable and colorfast.
- Substitute machine stitching for hand sewing wherever possible; hand finishing will pull out more easily after many launderings.
- Fusible interfacing can give a professional look with a minimum effort.
- Children love pockets for their many treasures; remember this in choosing a pattern. Or you can add a pocket or two of your own design (see Chapter 13).
- Choose skirt and pants patterns with elastic casing for quick and easy dressing, and to avoid broken zippers. The elastic casing is faster and easier to make than a waistband, too.

These suggestions should help to make sewing for your child fun and another way for you to express your creative ingenuity. Shop the better children's wear stores for ideas, look through current magazines. Children, as well as grownups, like to be well dressed and "in fashion." (Fig. 485)

Fig. 485

Fig. 485

Fig. 485

21 Sewing for Men and Boys

Every woman wants to give something special to the man in her life, and this something, whether it be a tie or a sports jacket, takes on particular meaning when it is made with tender loving care. Within the past few years, the pattern companies have made a variety of patterns available for men and boys. There is a special section within each catalogue with the latest fashions in men's wear and it is growing considerably as more women (and men too!) are taking to sewing.

If you have become adept at sewing for yourself, you should not have any problems in sewing men's wear. As with sewing for children, some techniques will be different, but now that you have learned how important it is to follow the step-by-step sewing directions carefully and accurately, you can master any technique.

PATTERN SIZES

Patterns for men are available in three size ranges: Boys, Teen-Boys, and Men.

Boys patterns are for the growing boy with a young build, about 4′0″ to 4′10″ (1.22 to 1.47 m).

Teen-Boys patterns are designed for the adolescent figure, with smaller shoulders and hips than a man. Height varies from 5′1″ to 5′8″ (1.55 to 1.73 m).

Men patterns are for the mature, adult male with average build, about 5′10″ (1.78 m).

HOW TO MEASURE

Accurate body measurements are as essential in determining the correct pattern size for men as they are for women. Take the personal body measurements over a thin shirt and pants without a belt. Tie a string at natural waist and measure as follows: (Fig. 486)

Fig. 486

Height—Stand against a wall, measure without shoes.
Neck—Around the neck, plus ½ inch (1.3 cm) for ease. This is also a ready-to-wear shirt measurement.
Chest—Around the fullest part.

Waist—At the natural waist, or string position.

Hip (*Seat*)—Around the fullest part of the hips; about 6" (15 cm) below the waist for Boys, about 7" (18 cm) below the waist for Teen-Boys, about 8" (20.5 cm) below the waist for Men.

Back Waist Length—From base of neck to string at center back.

Shoulder Length—From base of neck to top of arm.

Arm Length—With arm slightly bent, measure from shoulder bone to wrist bone, over elbow.

Shirt Sleeve Size—With arm slightly bent, measure from base of neck to wrist bone over elbow. This is a ready-to-wear measurement.

Knee—At fullest part.

Trouser Inseam—Inside leg from crotch to desired finished length.

Trouser Outseam—Outside of leg along side seam from waist to desired finished length.

Choose the correct pattern size by comparing the body measurements with those listed on the chart in the back of the pattern catalogue. Patterns include wearing ease; the amount of ease will vary with the cut and design of the garment: patterns designed "for knits only" have very little ease, the stretch and flexibility of the fabric allowing freedom of movement.

For shirts: purchase the pattern according to the neck measurement and shirt sleeve size, or ready-to-wear size.

For a jacket, coat, or vest: purchase the pattern according to the chest measurement.

For pants: purchase the pattern according to the waist measurement. If hip measurement is considerably out of proportion, select pattern according to this measurement and alter the waistline.

If the body measurements fall between two sizes, choose the small size for a thin, small-boned frame or the man who prefers a snug fit, the larger size for a husky, large-boned frame or the man who prefers his clothes to fit with more ease.

PATTERN ADJUSTMENTS

Men are quite particular about the fit of their clothes; a few adjustments made to the paper pattern before you cut into the fabric could eliminate some fitting problems. Of course, if there are major fitting problems, making a muslin first can avoid a disaster with expensive fabric. Review Chapter 2 for methods of altering a pattern.

Measurements for pants can also be taken from a pair of favorite pants that fit well. Choose pants of a similar style to those you will be making. The pattern pieces can be altered to the measurements taken. You will need:

- Waist
- Hip—at fullest part of seat
- Center back seam length
- Center front seam length
- Inseam
- Outseam

To Adjust Crotch Depth—The crotch depth is very important to the fit of pants. To determine crotch measurement, subtract the inseam measurement from the outseam measurement. Establish the crotch position on the back pattern piece by drawing a line at right angles to the grain line from the side seam to the point of the crotch. Check the measurement from the waist seam line to the drawn crotch line at the side seam. This should equal the crotch measurement. (Fig. 487)

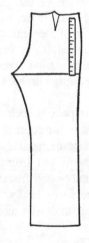

Fig. 487

If there is a difference in the two measurements, that is the amount to be shortened or lengthened. Cut the pattern on the alteration line, and adjust to correspond with the measurement.

Make the same adjustment to pattern back and front. Adjust fly and fly facing pieces to correspond.

To Adjust Outseam—First make any necessary adjustments to the crotch depth, then measure the outseam from waist seam line to lower edge along the side seam. Compare this measurement to the outseam measurement taken, remembering to allow for the depth of the hem or cuff. If there is a difference between the two measurements, that is the amount to be shortened or lengthened. Make the adjustment in the lower section of the leg on the back and front pattern pieces. (Fig. 488)

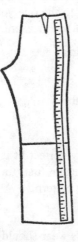

Fig. 488

To Adjust Waist—If the pants pattern was purchased according to the waist measurement, it should not be necessary to make a large adjustment. An extra-wide center back seam is allowed in the waistline of men's pants, and adjustments are easily made at the center back seam during the fitting process. Usually no adjustment is necessary on the paper pattern.

To Adjust Width at Hem—It is comparatively simple to change the shape of pants at the lower edge. Determine the amount needed at the hemline; divide the amount into fourths. Add or subtract equal amounts at the inseam and outseam on front and back pattern pieces. Draw new cutting lines, tapering from the knee to the lower edge.

To Adjust Sleeve Length on Shirts—Adjustments can be made in length at the line indicated on the pattern piece. Lengthen or shorten as necessary to compare with measurements taken.

To Adjust Jackets—Lengthening or shortening the body of a jacket and the two-piece sleeve are common adjustments. These changes should be made to the paper pattern so that sleeve and jacket vent openings are not disturbed. Remember to make adjustments to the corresponding facing, interfacing, and lining pieces as necessary.

Measurements can also be taken from a jacket that fits the man well. Use a style similar to the one you plan to make. The pattern pieces can be altered to the measurements taken. You will need:

- Center back seam length
- Back width
- Shoulder width
- Underarm sleeve length
- Front width
- Hip measurement

Of course, for a really perfect fit it is worth the time and effort to make the jacket in muslin first; then you can check the adjustments made to the paper pattern.

SUITABLE FABRICS

Fabrics used for men's wear should be sturdy, durable ones that will stand up to hard wear. Among the favorites are double knits, worsted wools and blends, flannel, cotton, denim, duck, broadcloth, leather and leather-like fabrics, suede cloth, velveteen, and fur and fur-like fabrics. Plaids, checks, and stripes are as popular as solid colors. If you have any questions about the suitability of a fabric for the design, check the back of the pattern envelope for "Suggested Fabrics," and as with women's clothes, look at the pictures on the front of the envelope to see what the designer had in mind for that particular style. A new world has opened up in the area of color and fabric design in men's wear; be guided by the type and styles the man you are sewing for feels comfortable with.

All fabrics should be preshrunk and "on grain" before you cut.

Follow the cutting layouts carefully and transfer all construction markings from the pattern to the fabric.

NOTIONS

Choose linings that are compatible with the fabric. For jackets, a lining of medium-weight taffeta, satin, rayon or acetate twill, or polyester; for pocket lining on pants, use a firm, lightweight cotton blend. Woven, non-woven, or fusible interfacings may be used. Select the interfacing according to the weight of the outer fabric. Fusible interfacings have been used in ready-to-wear men's clothing for years and are available now to the home sewer. You can achieve professional results easily and quickly, but follow the manufacturer's instructions for fusing and always test a sample of the garment fabric before you apply the interfacing. Above all, be sure that your linings and interfacings have the same care characteristics as the outer fabric.

Use dual-duty thread in a shade to match the garment fabric; for decorative topstitching, you may want to use silk buttonhole twist. Trouser zippers are available in one length, or you may purchase a 12-inch (30.5 cm) polyester coil zipper in a matching shade. The zippers are cut off at the top to fit the fly opening; the cut and sew guide will give you directions for this. There are light- and heavyweight zippers available for jackets. Use the heavy-duty pants hook and eye for waistbands; decorative hammer-on snap fasteners can be used on shirts and jackets in place of buttons.

If you are making a tailored jacket, chest pieces, shoulder pads, and sleeve heads are available in kits, can be purchased separately, or can be made by you. Your pattern will indicate the notions necessary to complete the garment.

A commercial waistband with lining and interfacing already attached is available, or you can make your own with lining fabric and suitable interfacing. You may want to spend some time looking for these commercial products that can make the job easier for you and give the professional touch.

SEAMS AND SEAM FINISHES

Review Chapter 7 for Seams and Seam Finishes. If you are making a plain seam, finish the raw edges to prevent raveling. The flat felled seam and welt seam are often used on men's clothes; no other seam finish is necessary with these. Make a sample of the seams in a swatch of the fabric you are using to get the feel of how the fabric handles.

Men's-wear patterns feature topstitching along the finished edges. To be really attractive, topstitching should be perfectly even and straight. Along the edge of the garment you could use as a guide the width of the presser foot, the seam lines etched into the throat plate of the machine, or a strip of adhesive tape placed on the throat plate the desired distance from the needle. Seam guides are available that screw on to the machine and can be adjusted to various widths; there is also a magnetic seam guide that can be used. If you are topstitching within the garment, make a line of basting to use as a guide line. Stitch just to the side of the basting line, to avoid catching the basting thread in the machine stitching. There is also a special tape that can be applied to the fabric surface and used as a stitching guide. Test the length of the stitch and tension on a scrap of your fabric—a slightly longer stitch usually looks better for topstitching.

Finish the seams of unlined jackets and coats with binding. Use either the bound seam or Hong Kong finish on seams and hems; cover shoulder pads with the same fabric.

CONSTRUCTION POINTS FOR SEWING THE CLASSIC SHIRT

Yoke—The classic shirt has a yoke across the back shoulder area for fit and durability. The yoke is usually faced with self fabric; however, if you are making a shirt of heavier-weight fabric the yoke may be faced with a lightweight lining fabric. Some shirt styles have a back pleat for additional ease through the back section; make the pleat before applying the yoke.

Pin the right side of the yoke facing to the wrong side of the shirt back, matching all notches and markings. Turn under shoulder seam allowances on yoke; press and trim to ¼ inch (6 mm). Pin the right side of the yoke to the right side of the shirt back, matching all notches and markings. Baste through the three layers.

Stitch through all thicknesses; grade seam allowances. Press yoke sections up over the seam; topstitch on right side close to the seam line. (Fig. 489)

Pin and stitch the right side of yoke facing to the wrong side of shirt front at shoulder seams. Grade seams, press toward yoke. Pin yoke over shoulder seams, edgestitch along folded shoulder edges through all layers.

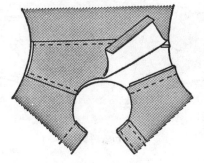

Fig. 489

Collar—A shirt collar is usually attached to a band for a good stand; the band is stitched to the neckline seam of the shirt. The collar and band must be interfaced for body and firmness; cut the interfacing from the collar and band pattern pieces.

The shape and the depth of the collar may vary, but the points of the collar should lie flat when it is worn. Collar stays could be added to help maintain the shape. These are short plastic stays, available at notions counters. A slot must be made in the undercollar and interfacing before the collar is made, if you plan to use stays. Make a buttonhole a little wider than the stay in the undercollar before applying the interfacing. Reinforce the buttonhole area with a piece of iron-on interfacing or self fabric. Baste interfacing to undercollar (trim corners of interfacing diagonally to eliminate bulk) and make two lines of stitching from the buttonhole to the point of the collar as shown, through the undercollar and interfacing. (Fig. 490) The stays can be removed when the shirt is laundered.

Collar on a Band—Trim corners of collar interfacing diagonally, ¼ inch (6 mm) inside of seam line; baste to wrong side of undercollar. (NOTE: When fusible interfacing is used on the construction of collar and band, cut off ½ inch (1.3 cm) from all edges of the interfacing before it is fused in place.)

With right sides together, pin upper collar and undercollar along unnotched edges. Stitch on seam line. For a pointed collar, take one stitch diagonally across point; for a rounded collar, stitch

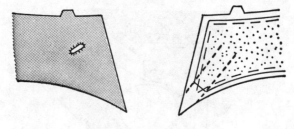

Fig. 490

slowly along curved seam line. Using a smaller stitch at ends of collar will help to reinforce points and will make stitching curved edges easier. (Fig. 491)

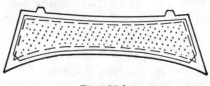

Fig. 491

Trim interfacing close to stitching line; grade seams. Turn the collar to right side. Gently push corners out. Press, rolling seam line slightly to underside of collar. Machine-baste the neck edges of collar sections together. Topstitch ¼ inch (6 mm) from finished edges, pivoting at corners of pointed collar. (Fig. 492)

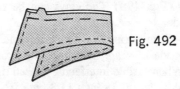

Fig. 492

Interface the wrong side of one band section. Pin right side of interfaced band to right side of upper collar, matching notches and markings. Baste. (Fig. 493)

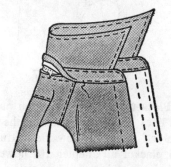

Fig. 493

Turn under seam allowance on neckline edge of band facing; press; trim seam allowances to ¼ inch (6 mm). (Fig. 494)

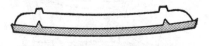

Fig. 494

Pin band facing to collar band, matching notches and pattern markings; the collar is between the two band pieces. Baste and stitch. Trim and grade seams; notch seam allowances on curved edges. Turn to right side; press.

Pin right side of interfaced band section to wrong side of neck edge of shirt, matching notches and markings. Clip shirt neck edge, if necessary. Stitch, grade seam allowances; clip curves. Press seam allowance toward band. On outside, pin folded edge of band facing over neckline seam; baste and edgestitch close to band edges. (Fig. 495)

Fig. 495

Collar and Band in One—Baste the interfacing to the wrong side of the upper collar; trim interfacing diagonally at corners. Turn under the seam allowance on neck edge of undercollar; press, and trim seam allowance. Pin undercollar and upper collar, with right sides together. Stitch around outer edges of collar. Trim and grade seam allowances; clip to stitching at corner of collar and band. (Fig. 496) Turn collar; press. Attach collar to neck edge so that inter-

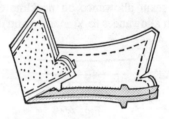

Fig. 496

faced upper collar will be on the top side. Edgestitch folded band of undercollar to neck edge. (Fig. 497)

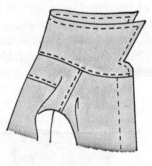

Fig. 497

Continuous Lap Placket—Is used most often on a long sleeve with a cuff. Placket lines will be indicated on the pattern; the placket is finished with self fabric. Review the instructions for making a continuous lap placket in Chapter 10; however, the stitching is done completely by machine and the finished placket is as shown. (Fig. 498)

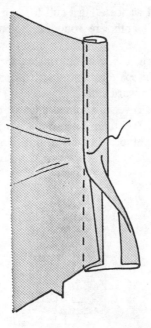

Fig. 498

Cuffs—Will be faced with self fabric and interfaced, like the collar. Baste interfacing to the wrong side of the cuff, and cut off interfacing diagonally at corners. Turn under notched edge of cuff on seam line; press, trim seam allowance to ¼ inch (6 mm).

Pin cuff facing to cuff with right sides together. Stitch along unnotched edges. (Fig. 499)

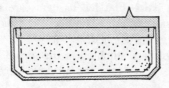

Fig. 499

Grade seam allowances. Turn cuff to right side; gently push out corners. Press. (If cuffs are rounded, notch seam allowances at curves.)

Pin and baste right side of cuff facing to wrong side of sleeve; match notches and pattern markings. Stitch; grade seam allowances; press seam toward cuff.

On outside of sleeve, pin folded edge of cuff over seam; edgestitch along fold. Topstitch ¼ inch (6 mm) from edges of cuff; make worked buttonholes in cuffs at position indicated on pattern. (Fig. 500)

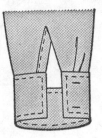

Fig. 500

On short-sleeved shirts, a mock cuff can be made entirely by machine and gives a professional finish to the shirt. Allow an extra ½ inch (1.3 cm) above the hemline of the sleeve when cutting—slash pattern and lengthen sleeve the needed amount. Mark hemline at lower edge of sleeve, and turn hem allowance to wrong side; press. Turn up hem again, encasing the raw edge. Press. Stitch ¼ inch (6 mm) from second fold through all thicknesses. You have stitched a tuck in the sleeve. (Fig. 501)

Press tuck up on right side of sleeve; insert sleeve in armhole.

Stitching Sleeve to Shirt—Flat felled seams are usually used in the construction of men's shirts. The sleeve is attached to the shirt before the side seams are stitched.

Make a row of ease stitching at the top of the sleeve, between notches. Pin the sleeve into the armhole edge, with wrong sides together, matching notches and markings. Adjust ease, baste, and stitch. Make flat felled seams. (Fig. 502)

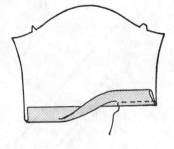

Fig. 501

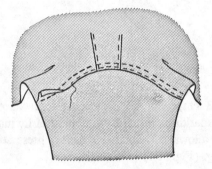

Fig. 502

Join underarm and side seams in one continuous seam, making a flat felled seam; seams should be turned toward shirt back. (Fig. 503)

CONSTRUCTION POINTS FOR SEWING MEN'S PANTS

Pants are not difficult to make but there are a few tricky areas that require some particular attention. A little extra patience devoted to these areas on your part will reward you with more than satisfactory results.

Fly-front Zipper Opening—The zipper length will be longer than the fly-front opening, but the trouser zipper is cut off at the waistline and secured by the waistband.

Mark topstitching on left front with a line of hand basting. Stitch front crotch seam from pattern marking to edge of inside leg, about

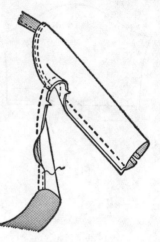

Fig. 503

½ inch (1.3 cm). Pin left fly facing to front edge, matching notches and markings. Stitch from bottom of fly marking to waist. Grade seam allowance. Open out facing; press seam allowances toward facing. (Fig. 504)

Fig. 504

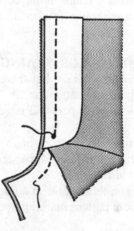

Place closed zipper face down on right side of fly facing, with the right side of the tape along the facing seam and the bottom stop of the zipper ¾ inch (2 cm) from raw edge of facing. The top of the zipper may extend beyond upper edge. Pin zipper in place, folding right zipper tape up on itself and even with the bottom stop (the zipper will not be caught in the stitching). Baste right zipper tape from bottom to top. Stitch close to the coil or chain on left tape, using the zipper foot. Make another row of stitching close to the edge of the tape. Turn facing to inside on seam line; press. (Fig. 505)

Fig. 505

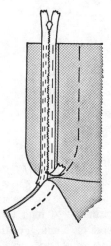

On outside of garment, pin fly facing in place and stitch from bottom to top following the basting line; do not catch right zipper tape in stitching. Tie thread ends on wrong side; remove basting. (Fig. 506)

Make fly shield of pants fabric and lining fabric. Stitch; grade seam allowances; clip curve; turn to right side, and press. To finish raw edge of shield, trim ⅜ inch (1 cm) from pants fabric. Fold lining over raw edge of pants fabric, press, and stitch close to fold. (Fig. 507)

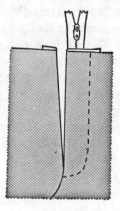

Fig. 506

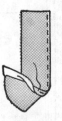

Fig. 507

On right front, press under ¼ inch (6 mm). Pin fold to free zipper tape, close to coil or chain. Position fly shield on inside of pants, matching curve of fly to curve of topstitching. Pin in place. (Fig. 508)

Turn to right side; repin right front and zipper tape to straight edge of fly shield. Open zipper; using the zipper foot, stitch through all thicknesses from top to bottom, close to the fold. Tie thread ends on wrong side.

With zipper still open, stitch across zipper tapes at waist; cut off excess zipper. (NOTE: Be sure zipper is open, so that the slider is not cut off.)

Make a bar tack by hand or machine at end of fly, catching in the shield. (Fig. 509)

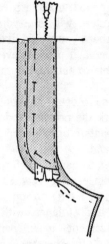

Fig. 508

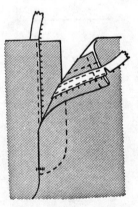

Fig. 509

Pockets—Review making a welt pocket in Chapter 13, or the instructions for patch pockets if the pants you are making have this kind of pocket.

Waistband—The waistband of men's pants is constructed in two pieces, one left and one right; a stiffener is used for a smooth, flat appearance. The center back seam is not completed until the waistband has been applied, making it easy to alter the waistline, if necessary. Your pattern will give you instructions for making the waistband, but perhaps you would like to try the following technique, using the commercial product available. You need to purchase enough to be able to cut the length of the waistband pattern pieces.

Use the pattern piece to determine the necessary length for each waistband and to mark the notches and matching points. Cut the waistband from the pants fabric, 3¼ inches (8.2 cm) wide for a 2-inch (5 cm) waistband.

Pin waistband pieces to pants; stitch on ⅝-inch (1.5 cm) seam line; grade seam allowances, and press seam toward waistband.

Press under ½ inch (1.3 cm) on top edge of lining. Place waistband between lining and stiffener, with raw edge of waistband along edge of reinforcement on stiffener. Topstitch along folded edge of lining, through all thicknesses. (Fig. 510)

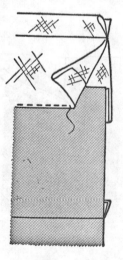

Fig. 510

Finish front ends of each waistband; trim seams, turn, and press. With waistband lining extended up, stitch the crotch seam in one continuous line, starting at the lower end of the fly opening, to the top edge of the waistband lining. Make a second row of stitching around the curve to reinforce the crotch. Trim lower curve of crotch seam. Press seam open above trimming.

To complete waistband and keep lining in place, turn lining down to wrong side and, from the right side of the garment, stitch in the crease of the waistband seam—be sure lining pleat is out of the way on the wrong side. (Fig. 511)

Fig. 511

Complete with necessary fasteners at front waistband.

PRESSING PANTS

Creases are made in the center of each leg. To locate the crease line, fold each leg piece in half lengthwise, wrong sides together and seam lines matching. Apply steam to a section of the crease; use the pounding block to set steam into the fabric.

Hang pants from the hem; special hangers are available to clamp onto the lower edge, thus avoiding creases in the leg area.

22 Accessories and Gifts to Make

———

Accessories are the finishing touch to a woman's wardrobe—the frosting on an otherwise plain cake. The most beautiful costume can look unfinished if it is not accompanied by something that gives it a chic look; it may be as simple as a colored scarf or striking necklace. The accessories you make yourself must harmonize with the outfit; be selective in the colors, fabrics, and trimmings you choose. Plan for your accessories as you plan your wardrobe; consider the design principles of proportion and line in relation to your individual figure and keep the over-all look in balance—do not overload your costume or yourself with too many extra touches.

Look in the pattern catalogues for suggestions and ideas for accessories you can make—there is a section for this category. You will find that most accessory designs come in one size and this makes them easy to use for gifts. The gift you make always receives a warmer welcome, because of the thought and time that went into its making.

If you see an accessory in a store or magazine and wish to make something similar, cut out a paper pattern and make it up in muslin. This way any adjustments or corrections in style or size can be made on the pattern to avoid mistakes later. You may find you have more design ability than you realized; besides, working out a design can be a challenge to your imagination and ingenuity.

Bags (Fig. 512)

Fig. 512

You can make bags of various sizes, from the small quilted shoulder bag to the canvas tote or duffel bag that accompanies you to the beach or on the weekend outing. Your choice of fabric can vary: canvas, denim, poplin, suede-like fabrics, vinyl, imitation leather, quilted fabrics, velveteen, corduroy, or fake fur; use linings of contrasting materials for extra color and interest. There are many different types of bone and wooden handles available at notions counters or in art needlework departments. A plain fabric may be just the place for you to try your hand at a bold monogram, embroidery design, or appliqué.

Belts (Fig. 513)

Fig. 513

You can make many exciting and unusual belts. There are only two precautions to consider: (a) make your belt in a color, style, and fabric that will look well with your dress, and (b) avoid wide, conspicuous belts unless you are tall enough to carry them off. The short woman and the plump woman can wear distinctive belts provided they keep them fairly narrow and in proportion to their figure. The tall, slender figure can wear extra-wide belts to accentuate the slim waistline area and also divide the figure.

Fig. 514

Fabrics can vary from cotton to brocade, synthetic suede, velveteen, leather or leather-like fabrics, vinyl, corduroy, or felt. You can use metal or bone buckles, or cover a buckle mold with self fabric.

Hats (Fig. 514)

You can make a sports hat to wear boating or hiking, a brimmed hat for sun or rain, a cuffed hat, or that old stand-by the beret to accent a casual costume. Use lightweight wool, jersey, felt, fake fur, poplin, duck, or vinyl for rainy-day wear. One size usually fits all, and there are styles you can make for that man of yours, too!

Shawls or Stoles (Fig. 515)

Fig. 515

These can be made with fake fur fabrics, wools, jersey, or sheer organdy or organza. Finish the edges of wool or jersey with knotted fringe or fur trim; use a self ruffle for sheer fabrics.

Vests (Fig. 516)

Fig. 516

A vest is a great top for skirts or pants, the fabric choices are limitless, and you can make a fitted style, the more casual loose version, or a short bolero type. Beading, braid, appliqué, and embroidery can be used to add decoration and a personal touch to the vest.

Scarves—can be made in various shapes—the small triangle, large square, or oblong—in remnant pieces of silk, rayon, polyester crepe, or taffeta. Hand-roll hem edges of scarves for the more expensive look. If you use taffeta, try fringing the edges for an unusual effect. The fringe should be about 1 inch (2.5 cm) deep.

Collars—can be a useful and perky accessory for a simple dress or sweater. You can make them in fabric such as piqué, organdy, embroidered eyelet, linen, taffeta, plaid or striped silks or polyester. They can be trimmed with embroidery, or edged with lace, ruffling, or bias binding.

Plan the collar to fit the neckline of the garment. If the dress has a collar and you like the shape of it, use this as a pattern. Cut the pattern in paper or muslin to the shape of the collar; add ½ inch (1.3 cm) seam allowance on all edges. If the dress does not have a collar, you can make a pattern for one, but you must be careful to measure the neckline of the garment properly.

To Make a Straight Collar   Measure the distance around the neck opening of the garment and cut the pattern with ½ inch (1.3 cm) seam allowance on all edges.

Cut two pieces of fabric according to the pattern; with right sides together, stitch along the ends and outer edge, leaving the neckline edge free. Trim seams, turn collar to right side, and press. (Fig. 517)

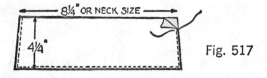

Fig. 517

Encase the neckline edge with folded bias tape, allowing the bias tape to extend 1 inch (2.5 cm) beyond each end. (Fig. 518)

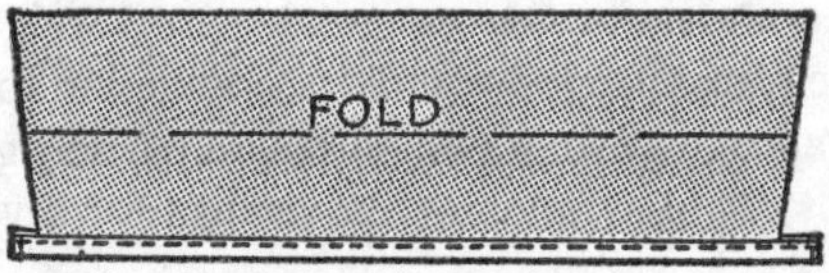

Fig. 518

Slip-stitch or snap the collar to the neckline of the garment for easy removal. (Fig. 519)

Fig. 519

To Make a Peter Pan Collar This is a little round, close-fitting collar worn at a high neckline. The detachable Peter Pan collar is made like the straight collar, but it is more difficult to cut correctly since the collar is curved to lie flat.

You can make a pattern of this shape from a Peter Pan collar you have. If you do not have a collar, measure the neckline of the garment and cut a paper pattern in the shape of a quarter circle. This pattern should measure half the neckline. Cut the collar about 3½ inches (9 cm) wide, shape front edge of the collar, and add ½ inch (1.3 cm) seam allowance on all edges. (Fig. 520a, b)

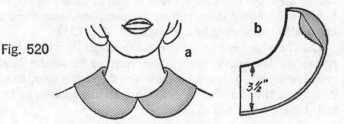

Fig. 520

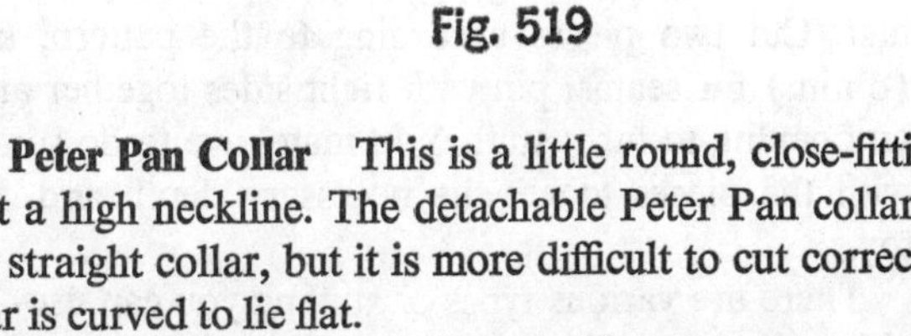

a

b

3½"

Other accessories and gifts you can make are lovely silk ties; pajamas—for yourself, men, boys, or children; lounging robes; terry cloth beach robes; aprons for outdoor barbeque parties, gardening, or household chores; or fancy pinafore cover-ups for a young girl.

Toys

Washable toys that are soft and can neither hurt the child nor damage the furniture are popular with parents as well as the child. A child never has too many toys, particularly when you can make a variety of stuffed animals and dolls at little expense. Use firmly woven fabrics—percale, broadcloth, fake fur for animals, printed cotton fabrics for clothes and trim. Make certain that all fabrics are washable and colorfast; it is wise to launder them before you cut them for toymaking. Any materials used must be able to stand hard wear.

You can simplify your task by purchasing patterns for stuffed toys, which include complete cutting and sewing instructions. The "rag" doll and teddy bear are among children's favorites, and you can easily make these.

If you want to design your own patterns, draw them on paper first. Cut two pieces according to the pattern, allowing ¼ inch (6 mm) for seams; pin with right sides together and stitch, leaving an opening to turn; stuff. You may have to do some experimenting with the pieces to get the necessary depth and dimension to the toy.

There are various types of stuffing you can use—it must be washable, of course. Try polyester, shredded foam rubber, or your old nylon stockings cut into small pieces. Toys should be stuffed firmly and evenly; this may take a little practice. Push the stuffing into the corners and complete one section at a time. Overcast the opening in the seam.

Apply the finishing touches by hand. Embroider the eyes and other features with embroidery floss or colored yarn. Pieces of felt can be used, but small fingers love to pull at these and not all felt is washable! Avoid using buttons for eyes: they may come loose and could be swallowed by a young child. (Fig. 521)

The "beanbag" is a favorite with babies and their older brothers and sisters. Use heavy cotton fabric, vinyl, or felt—make the shape round or square, or it can be cut to the shape of a pear, an apple, or a heart. It could even be made to look like a clown or an animal—turtles, frogs, and so on.

Fig. 521

Cut two pieces of the same shape; stitch ¼ inch (6 mm) from the edge, leaving an opening about 1 inch (2.5 cm) long. Fill the bag loosely with small, dried beans—not too many, as they would make the bag too heavy to throw. Stitch the opening; and you could overcast the edges with bright-colored yarn.

23 Simple Mending and Altering Techniques

———•———

The mending, darning, and sewing-buttons-tighter-before-they-pop-off can be greatly simplified by looking over all clothes before they are washed or sent to the cleaner. If worn spots are reinforced before they go through the washing machine, the hole that is about to appear can be warded off for several more launderings.

See Chapter 12 for directions for sewing on buttons, hooks and eyes, and snaps so that they will stay in place.

How to Avoid Zipper Trouble—Close all zippers before laundering or dry cleaning in order to keep the zipper from spreading and to keep the garment in shape. When a zipper has jammed, or if the raw edge of the fabric has caught in the fastener, try patiently to fix it. If the teeth of the zipper are bent or if you have pulled out a tooth from the chain, replace the zipper. Directions are included in the package, or follow the step-by-step illustrations in Chapter 12.

In replacing a zipper, be sure to buy the proper kind of zipper for the garment. Rip out the old zipper carefully. Try to re-use the same fold lines and stitching lines on the garment when stitching the new zipper.

Thread or fabric caught in a polyester coil zipper can be removed easily without damage to the zipper. Fold the zipper over itself, with right sides together, pinch the coil, and pull it apart.

Remove thread or fabric and pull the slider down to the bottom stop, then up again to reclose the zipper.

Mending Rips and Tears—Mend a rip by stitching it on the wrong side, by machine if possible; otherwise do it with small hand stitches. Stitch beyond the place where the rip began and fasten the threads securely.

Mend a tear by stitching a narrow dart on the wrong side of the material. The widest part of the dart should be at the outer edge of the cloth, where the tear began. The dart should extend 1 inch (2.5 cm) beyond the place where the tear ends. Make the point of the dart very narrow and sharp. When the dart is pressed, the mending will be scarcely noticeable.

Using Mending Tape For quick and satisfactory results in mending a tear on any except sheer fabrics, buy several packages of mending tape in various colors and widths. The tape is applied to the wrong side of the fabric and pressed on with a warm iron. Directions for applying are included in the package and the tape stays in place during washing and dry cleaning.

Knee and elbow patches in denim and corduroy are also available in a package and can be ironed on to reinforce these points of extra wear. If you are making pants or overalls for boys, apply these patches to the wrong side of the front section before stitching the seams.

Decorative embroidered appliqués and patches can be pressed on or sewn in place. They can be used with imagination to cover small holes in a garment that still has lots of wear.

Reweaving Problems—Professional reweavers make a specialty of repairing tears, moth holes, or cigarette burns in an otherwise good garment or piece of household linen. Their method is to pull out threads from a hem or some other place where they will not be missed and then knot these threads to the ends of the threads around the hole or tear. The threads are then woven into place. Repairs of this sort require skill and are usually expensive. Request an estimate of the cost before having work of this kind done; if the price is too high, perhaps you can substitute another darning technique described here.

Darning—Darning is used mostly to fill small holes or repair tears. You can darn sheets and work and playclothes by machine—it is easier, quicker, and stronger than darning by hand. Check your sewing machine manual for instructions.

To darn by hand, work on the right side of the fabric and use matching colored thread, darning cotton, or matching wool yarn for wools. Do not knot the thread; start your darning by taking several small stitches in the material about ½ inch (1.3 cm) from the hole. Turn and take another row of stitches beside the first one. Cover the hole with lengthwise threads in this manner, each row ending with several small stitches that cover at least ½ inch (1.3 cm) of the weakened area around the hole. (Fig. 522a) Cut the end of the thread after the hole has been covered. Crosswise threads are woven in and out, over and under the lengthwise threads. Extend the crosswise threads ½ inch (1.3 cm) beyond the worn edges of the hole. (Fig. 522b)

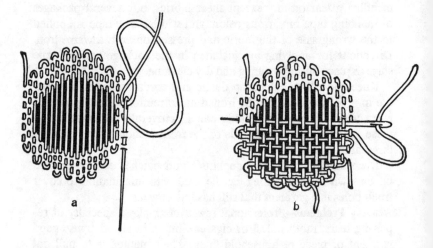

Fig. 522

Reinforcing—This is a form of darning used to give strength to a weakened spot before a hole appears. A piece of fabric is placed on the underside of the worn area and anchored with uneven basting stitches, taking a small stitch through to the right side. Trim away excess fabric when reinforcing is completed. This type of mending is not suitable for thin or sheer fabrics since it adds a certain thickness to the fabric and may be visible with sheer fabrics. (Fig. 523)

Fig. 523

Patching—To make a neat patch, trim the edges of the hole to a square or oblong shape. Clip the opening ¼ inch (6 mm) at the corners, so that the edges can be turned and will lie flat. Cut a piece of matching material about 1 inch (2.5 cm) larger than the hole on all sides, and on the same grain. If you are patching a printed fabric, cut the patch to match the print so that there will be no break in the design. Working from the right side, pin the patch to the underside of the hole. Pin or baste it in place. Use matching thread, turn under the raw edges of the hole with the point of the needle, and slip-stitch patch in place with small invisible stitches; take several stitches at each corner for reinforcement. (Fig. 524) Trim and overcast raw edges of patch on underside, if necessary.

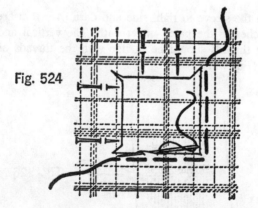

Fig. 524

Elbow Patches Suede leather patches or corduroy patches can be sewn on the elbows of men's sports jackets or sweaters. These patches are sewn on by hand, with matching thread. The suede leather patches have stitching holes punched around the outer edges. Position the patches over the elbow area; use a backstitch to sew in place.

If you prefer to darn the elbow of a good jacket or coat, turn the sleeve inside out, rip the lining at the bottom of the sleeve and roll it up out of the way while you make the repair. Cut a piece of thin, firm fabric, larger than the worn area; baste over spot on wrong side of sleeve. Using matching thread, tack with rows of diagonal basting, using loose stitches about ½ inch (1.3 cm) apart. If the fabric is worn very thin, these lines of stitching could be made closer together. (Fig. 525)

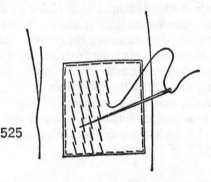

Fig. 525

Turn the sleeve to right side and darn over thin area, catching the stitches to the patch underneath. The vertical and horizontal darning threads should be in line with the threads of the sleeve fabric. (Fig. 526)

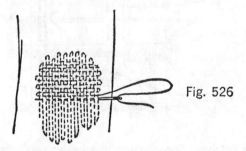

Fig. 526

Turning Collar and Cuffs—We suggest doing this only if the underside of the collar and cuffs has not worn through. Carefully rip the collar from the neckband. (The collar is set between the double thickness of the neckband.) Reverse the collar: that is, turn the worn side to the underside. Fold the collar in half, matching the points and making a crease at center back. Pin the collar into the neckband, matching center back points; pin from the center to the ends. Baste the collar in place, using the same seam allowance as in the original stitching. Stitch on inside of neckband, using the same stitch size as originally used on the shirt.

You can turn cuffs the same way you turn a collar, but since cuffs wear at the edges it is not practical to turn them unless they are double French cuffs that fold back and are held with links.

Repairing a Trouser Pocket—A small hole may wear through the corner of a pocket. If this happens, make a double row of machine stitching above the hole, following the shape of the pocket.

If the hole is too big for this simple repair, or if the lower part of the pocket is badly worn, pockets can be replaced easily with the replacement kit sold at notions counters.

MAKING ALTERATIONS IN READY-TO-WEAR CLOTHING

Women who buy their clothes ready-made usually find that they must be altered in some way, for obviously clothes turned out in mass production cannot be expected to fit an individual figure, but with a few minor alterations many of them can be made to fit properly.

Buying for Size—Since altering a finished garment is a different problem from making alterations in a garment as it is put together, it is always important to buy a dress in the size that requires a minimum of adjustment. For that reason it is wise not to acquire the habit of buying any one particular size, assuming it will always be the best fit. A size 16, for example, may fit very well in one style and badly or not at all in another. The size may also vary with the manufacturer and the amount of ease put into the garment. The price range may also affect the cut and ease allowance.

There are tricks in shopping for clothing that will help you solve many of the problems of correct fitting. If you are short-waisted, try a Half-size or perhaps a Petite size. Half-sizes are no longer limited to matronly figures but come in many attractive styles. If your figure is slender and youthful, a Junior size may be best for you. Although many of these Junior-size dresses are designed for teens, you will find many styles also that are meant to be worn by the mature woman with a slender figure. If you are tall, take advantage of the tall sizes, proportioned for those who are above average height.

A final word: when you try on a dress that you are thinking of purchasing, remember that it is easier to take in a seam here and there than to let out. Buy the size that requires a minimum of alterations—the type that can be made easily and quickly—and if there is any doubt as to whether the dress can be made to fit properly, don't buy it.

Alterations—Every manufacturer of ready-to-wear clothing has his own way of putting a garment together, and the way you make an alteration will depend upon the method used in putting that garment together.

Shortening a Skirt This is a simple alteration. First rip out the hem. If the skirt is to be shortened only slightly, leave the seam tape attached to it; if the skirt is to be shortened considerably, remove the tape and re-use it after measuring and marking the new hem.

Press the hem on the wrong side to eliminate the crease. To get an even hemline, try the dress on and re-mark the hem length. Follow the directions in Chapter 11 to finish the hem.

Lengthening a Skirt Rip the hem and press out the crease of the old hemline. If there is enough material to turn up for the new hem, measure, pin, and baste in place.

If there is not enough material for a hem, prepare a bias facing of a matching fabric or use a packaged hem facing, and complete the hem as directed in Chapter 11.

Taking In a Skirt This is normally done at the side seams only. Try skirt on and pin side seams as necessary from waist, tapering to hem. Remember to allow ease for walking and sitting. If the zipper is in the side seam, you may have to remove it to get a perfect fit. Mark new seam line on the wrong side of the skirt. You may have to remove the entire waistband, depending upon how much you are taking in. Restitch the seams, remove old stitching, press seams open; replace zipper and waistband; repair the hem if the seam was continued into the hemline.

Letting Out a Skirt The amount you can let out is determined by the width of the seam allowance and the number of darts you could let out. You will probably have to remove the zipper and waistband; be careful that you do not make the seam allowance so narrow that the seam will give with the first wearing. Sew seam binding to the seam allowance in the zipper area for additional width.

Pants These alterations described for a skirt may also be made with pants. If the pants have a cuff, the alteration can be more complicated; you will have to determine the best method according to how the cuff is applied. Review sleeve finishes with cuffs in Chapter 10 for some suggestions you might adapt to the pants. If you are shortening the pants, rip out the hemline and turn up the hem to the desired finished length; measure and cut the hem allowance to a depth of 2 inches (5 cm). Do not "turn up" the the width of the hem or leave a hem allowance of 5 or 6 inches (12.5 to 15 cm) at the bottom of the pants leg—this only adds bulk and looks untidy.

NOTE: Permanent-press fabrics can be shortened easily, but not lengthened; taken in, but not let out. The permanent crease line of the hem or seam cannot be removed.

24 Taking Care of Your Clothes

You may make or buy the most beautiful of clothes, but if you treat them carelessly, you still won't look your best wearing them. For that reason it is important to make the care of your clothes a regular part of your routine.

You have seen many articles in newspapers and magazines advising you to mend every little rip and tear, check every snap, wash separate collars and cuffs—all the very instant after you remove your dress. Of course, if you change your dress at four o'clock in the afternoon and have nothing else to do before dinner, you might be able to follow those directions. But you can't if you are a busy homemaker or career woman—or both—who has barely enough time for a quick change of clothes before going out for an evening. That "fix every snap every day" advice was geared to a more tranquil life. Our advice is to devote one night a week getting all your clothes and accessories in order. This might be the same night you set aside for other grooming routines. If you are going to be well dressed, your clothes must be in order.

POINTERS FOR DAILY CARE
The following are good habits to form:

- Hang your dress, coat, or suit on a hanger as soon as you remove it. If possible, avoid using thin wire hangers as they may leave stretch marks in the shoulders or sleeves of your garment. It is best to use a wooden, plastic, or padded hanger that is fairly wide. For a garment made of delicate lace or chiffon, use a hanger that is completely padded. Such hangers are available with cotton or foam rubber padding, covered with velvet or other fabric. You can easily make padded hangers, if you desire.

- Air your sweaters and knitted garments, then store them flat in a drawer or chest. Do not hang them up.
- Keep the door of your clothes closet open at night so that your clothes will have a chance to air.
- Wash stockings daily. Fibers are weakened if stockings are allowed to accumulate for the family wash.
- Air shoes worn during the day before putting them away. Cover all shoes not in everyday use. Have run-over heels repaired at once.
- Smooth leather gloves out flat and put them in a drawer or box. Keep gloves clean; many leather gloves can be hand-washed in Woolite.
- Keep hats brushed and in a hat box when not worn.

PRESSING

Pressing is an important step both in making your clothes and in caring for them. Pressing the seams while the garment is being made will help to give the finished garment a professionally made look, as we discussed in Chapter 3. Pressing your clothes regularly will help you look well dressed and will also add to the over-all life of the garment.

Pressing should never be a last resort. There are men and women who wear clothes day in and day out, and when the garment (usually a woolen suit or coat) is hopelessly baggy and stretched at the elbows, knees, and seat, they rush it to the cleaner; and the cleaner is blamed if the garment does not look like new when it is returned.

Because different textile fabrics require separate treatment in pressing, review the information contained in Chapter 1 on "What You Should Know About Fabric."

Care labels are sewn into the garment; follow the manufacturer's instructions.

Pressing jobs will be made easier with a combination steam-dry iron that has a good thermostat and settings marked for various fibers.

MENDING, DARNING, AND PATCHING

Keeping your clothes and accessories as well as the clothes of the family in good repair is just as necessary as laundering, cleaning, and pressing them. You will find directions for wardrobe mending, darning, and patching in Chapter 23.

REMOVING STAINS

Stains on garments are always a problem. To remove them at home sometimes requires a little knowledge of chemistry, at least enough to know what type of cleaning agent and what methods of cleaning are most effective for the various types of stains. With the aid of a cleaning pad of some absorbent material and clean, lint-free cloths, you will be able to remove many of the common stains yourself. Others are better left to a professional cleaner.

General Directions for Stain Removal—Treat all stains as soon as possible after they occur. When a stain is allowed to remain on the piece of material, it may penetrate the fibers of the cloth and become much more difficult to remove.

Always test the cleaning agent in an inconspicuous area, preferably an inside seam, before attempting to remove the stain. Some cleaning agents will leave a ring or mark.

Treat stains before laundering; all stained articles should be set aside and the stains removed before they are put into the wash. The hot water used for laundering will set the stain.

If you do not know what the stain is, or feel you cannot remove it yourself, send the garment to a reputable dry cleaner. You can help the cleaner do his job well if you tell him the nature of the stain, that is, grease, tea, and so on. *Warning!* When using any dry-cleaning fluid in the house, open the window to get enough air to counteract any fumes from the cleaning agent. Be sure there is no lighted gas range or lighted cigarette in the room. Use great caution regardless of the mildness of the cleaning fluid and the "safety" assurance on the label.

Specific Instructions for Stain Removal—Below are given the most common causes of stains and the most satisfactory way to remove them:

Chewing Gum Scrape off as much as possible. Dampen a clean white cloth with the cleaning fluid and apply with a circular rubbing motion. If directions are included on the container, follow those.

Coffee   Use cool water. Soak the stain immediately, wash in a mild detergent, rinse thoroughly. If the garment is not washable, sponge with cleaning fluid.

Egg   Try clean, cold water first. If that does not remove the stain, try soap and cool water. Hot water hardens egg and may set the stain. The same treatment applies to meat, fish, and cheese, except cream cheese.

Fat   *See* Oil. Same treatment. Fats include cream cheese, butter, cream, mayonnaise.

Fruit   Use cold water. The trick here, as with most stains, is to act at once. A stain that has a chance to dry is much more difficult to remove than a fresh stain. If the fabric is washable, soak the stain in cool water; then apply a household bleach. If the garment must be cleaned, sponge the stain with cool water, apply a soapless shampoo, and allow to stand for several hours. Then apply a few drops of white vinegar.

Grease   *See* Oil. Same treatment.

Ink   Permanent ink is difficult to remove. A chlorine bleaching compound may be used safely only on white material, for it will remove the color on the fabric at the same time that it removes the ink. These compounds have a tendency to weaken fibers of the material, so the stained spot should never be soaked in a bleaching agent for more than ten minutes. If the material is colored and not washable, you may try a solution of denatured alcohol and water, but you would probably be wiser to take the stained garment to the dry cleaner. A patented rust remover is also useful with the removal of ink stains.

Washable ink can be removed by soaking the stained portion of the cloth in cold water for fifteen minutes before washing in a mild detergent and rinsing well.

Lipstick   Place the wrong side of the stained area on an absorbent towel. Pour cleaning fluid slowly through the stain until bleeding stops. Dry and launder with detergent in hot water.

Mildew   Mildew is a fungus growth. It is sometimes caused by leaving dampened clothes unironed, but in a damp climate it may attack any material not exposed to the air. New or slight stains can sometimes be removed by washing and drying in the sun. Old stains, however, can seldom be taken out completely.

Nail Polish If the stain is on cotton, polish remover may be applied, but this cleaning agent cannot be used safely on acetate fabrics. For these fabrics, send garment to the cleaner at once.

Oil Oil or grease stains can sometimes be removed by placing the stained spot between two clean blotters and pressing with a warm iron. For a large spot, try cleaning fluid. This treatment is for clear oils, such as sewing machine oil. A stain from a heavy, dark oil should be given to a professional cleaner, unless it is on washable material. For washables, the treatment is hot water and detergent.

Rust For white cotton or linen, wash and bleach in the sun, or in a small amount of chlorine bleaching compound. There are also satisfactory patented rust removers—follow the manufacturer's directions.

Tar Same treatment as for chewing gum. If it is a large stain, or on a nonwashable fabric, better send the garment to the cleaner.

Water Spots If a material is so delicate that it water-spots, the best treatment is to send the garment to a cleaner; or you can test a small piece of the fabric clipped from an inside seam, to see if it washes without shrinking or loss of color. If washing seems to be safe, put the entire garment into clean, cool water. For velvet, velveteens, and corduroys, water spots can be removed by steaming the garment over the spout of a tea kettle filled with boiling water, or hanging the garment in a closed bathroom filled with steaming hot water.

RECYCLING CLOTHES

A woman who is adept at remodeling her clothes will get a great deal of satisfaction out of this type of sewing. Not only is there a saving of actual cash, but there is also a sense of accomplishment in having increased the life of a garment. You will certainly find it worth your while to go through your closets to see if there are any clothes that might be recut, retrimmed, or even combined with others or other fabrics to make a new outfit.

What Is Worth Making Over?—To be sure that your time and effort will be used to the best advantage, examine the things you want to make over. Hold them up to the light to see if the fabric is in good condition. Woolens attract moths and you may discover pinpoint holes. You may find some small tears; however, if there is still enough good material, clothes with slight damage can always be salvaged. Some materials can be turned and used on the wrong side. In many cases a new pocket or a touch of embroidery can be added to cover up a place that has a tiny hole or tear, if the rest of the material is sturdy enough to give good wear.

Selecting Patterns—When you are recycling a garment it is essential to get a pattern that is not too complicated and does not call for large pieces of material. For instance, if you are going to remake a two-piece dress that has a narrow skirt, do not choose a pattern with a princess line or wide flared skirt. The same principle applies if you are making over a jacket with set-in fitted sleeves—do not choose a pattern with a raglan shoulder line. The pattern you buy must not include any pieces larger than the pieces of your original garment. Of course, there may be a place or two where you will have to do a little inconspicuous piecing, or you can add new material of a contrasting color.

Preparing Material—Garments should be dry-cleaned or washed before you start to rip them apart. It is always more pleasant to work with clean material.

Use a seam ripper or small scissors to open the seams. Clip the threads at short intervals and pull gently apart. Used material may not be strong enough to stand quick ripping of seams, so do it carefully.

When the garment is ripped apart, it should be pressed. If the material has a definite right and wrong side, mark the wrong side of each piece to avoid a mix-up later when you are cutting. Also mark the straight grain on the right side of the material to aid you in placing the new pattern.

Piecing Insufficient Material—If it is necessary to piece material that is not large enough, do this in inconspicuous places. The piecings will not be noticeable if you make sure that the materials joined are on the same grain; that the design, if any, matches; and that the seams are flat and have not been stretched in stitching.

Sometimes it is better to use contrasting material for recycling. Choose a fabric that looks well with the old fabric you are using.

Cutting—Now that the material has been cleaned, ripped apart, and pressed, spread it out right side up. Place the pattern pieces on the fabric, making sure that each is placed on the straight grain. Then, before you do any cutting, check again to see if and where you will need to piece. It is better to take the time to do this before you cut than to discover, too late, a short piece you overlooked.

Suggestions for Make-overs—Your clothes closet is probably conceal-
ing a variety of clothes you can use for some clever recycling job;
all you need is imagination and patience.

- Remodel a man's jacket into a vest. Try to make use of the buttons and buttonholes, thus saving a few construction steps. Take
the jacket apart at all seams; remove the lining and shoulder
pads. Press pieces flat, and locate the straight grain. Use the lining of the jacket to line the vest, if it is in good condition.
- A dress or jumper that is too short can be cut to tunic length.
The finished length of the tunic should be measured to the end
of your fingertips; allow 2 inches (5 cm) for the hem. Wear the
tunic with a blouse, over pants.
- If you are tired of that basic A-line dress, remove the sleeves,
finish the armhole with a facing, and wear it as a jumper. Or
replace the sleeves with a new set of another fabric or color—
full bishop sleeves in chiffon will give an entirely new look.
- A full circular or flared skirt could be recut into a slim-line silhouette or a skirt for a child.
- A man's shirt with worn collar and cuffs can find new life as
an apron or a pinafore for a small child. Remove the sleeves
and collar, and open out the shoulder seams so that the shirt
is flat. Make use of the hem along the bottom edge, and gather
the top to fit into a waistband with ties. You can use odds and
ends of rickrack, braid, or other decorative trims for additional
color.
- You could probably get a child's coat out of the material in a
man's or woman's coat; or remake your old-style coat into a
shorter-length jacket. Choose a pattern with the same construction lines as the coat. The edges could be finished with decorative
fold-over braid in a contrasting color.
- Old ties can be cut into odd-shaped pieces for patchwork. You
can make belts, pillows, or eyeglass cases for gift giving.
- If you are handy with knitting needles, you can replace the worn-
out sleeves in a woolen blouse or jacket with new knitted sleeves.
The textural difference in the fabrics will give additional interest.

25 Sewing for the Home

———◆———

Sewing is a pleasant occupation that can be put to many uses. Curtains, draperies, and slipcovers can do much to add to the beauty of your home and to reflect the warmth and personality of you and your family. Sewing these is a major part of decorating the home and should be planned for carefully.

FABRIC SUGGESTIONS

The world of fabrics is a fascinating and wonderful array of beautiful colors, unusual weaves and textures, charming prints, wild and bold plaids, brilliant stripes. From this you must choose the type of fabric that is most suitable to you and your needs.

Colors, texture, and the design of the fabric will contribute to the over-all appearance of the room. Bright colors will tend to make a room look smaller; neutral and pastel shades add spaciousness. Textured fabrics add interest to most decorating schemes. Rich silks, damasks, and velvets lend a formal air; homespun weaves and plain-surfaced fabrics are more informal. Choose patterned fabrics carefully, always in proportion to the size of the room, the furnishings, and the particular period or decorating style.

Fabrics must be handled for drapability—hold them up to the light to see what effect the sun shining through will have on the design or texture of the fabric. Before making a final purchase, take home fabric swatches, compare them with your furnishings, and ask yourself these questions:

• Is the fabric suitable to the decorating style of the room?

- Is the design in proportion to the room and its furnishings?
- Will the design be difficult to match?
- Is the fabric easy to care for—will it require dry cleaning or can it be laundered?

DECORATING THE WINDOWS

Windows are primarily designed as the architectural means of affording light, air, and a view to the room. As you well know, windows come in many shapes and sizes, yet there are basic ways to cover windows and from these you can elaborate and dress up your windows to suit your individual taste and requirements. This is much like the simple dress that is the basis of a woman's wardrobe —it can be dressed up or down to fit the need or occasion. (Figs. 527–531)

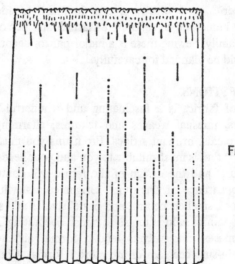

Fig. 527

Needless to say, we don't always have the type of window we would like in each room, nor in just the right place in the room, and sometimes a window can be an eyesore. But with a little thought and ingenuity, any problem window can be decorated with interest.

Add height to a window by mounting the curtain rod above the window; add width by extending the rods beyond the window.

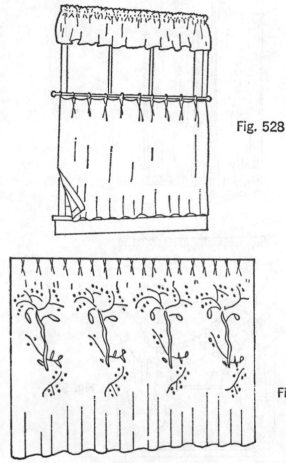

Fig. 528

Fig. 529

Choose a pattern to help create an optical illusion—a vertical stripe or pattern will carry the eye up and down, thus giving an illusion of height; while horizontal designs carry the eye across, giving an illusion of width.

Window Hardware—A wide variety of hardware is available, designed and engineered specifically to solve most window problems and to give your windows an added look of elegance. The choice of the correct rod and accessories will ensure the best results for the finished window treatment.

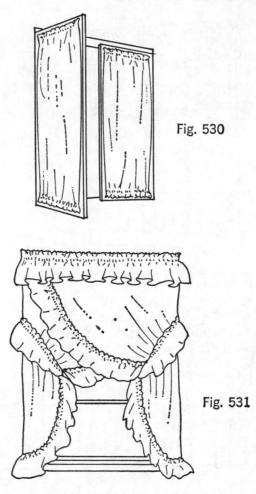

Fig. 530

Fig. 531

Basically, hardware is meant to be concealed, but the beautiful rods available today are designed to add beauty to your window treatment. Take a trip into the drapery hardware section of a department store and look at the display of the various rods and accessories available to you before making a final decision on your window treatment. You can also get some excellent ideas from curtains and draperies on display—ideas that you can use in creating your own decorating schemes.

Measuring for Curtains and Draperies—An important note to remember when planning your window treatment: curtains may come to the windowsill, to the apron of the window, to the floor, or to the top of a baseboard heating unit, but never an in-between point. The rods can be mounted on the window frame, inside the casing, or above the window frame. Use a yardstick or steel tape for all measurements. (Fig. 532)

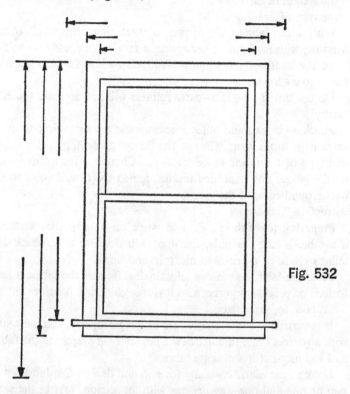

Fig. 532

Mount the curtain rods and measure each window from the top of the rod to the desired length—this is the *finished length* of the curtain or drapery.

For the *finished width* of the curtain, measure the rod plus the overlap, if any.

Yardage   To determine the necessary length of one panel, add the top and bottom hem allowances to the finished curtain length. The hem allowances vary with the style of the curtain, so check the specific requirements for the type of curtain you have decided to make. Fabrics with a design or pattern will require extra yardage for matching. Allow one design repeat for each drapery length.

The width requirement for curtains and draperies is determined by:
• the width of the window;
• the amount of fullness desired;
• the weight of the fabric;
• the type of heading used.

With sheer fabrics, allow two to three times the width of the window; with medium or heavyweight fabrics, one and one half to twice the width of the window. Add allowances for side hems or seams to each panel.

Do not skimp on width—extra fullness will add an extra touch of luxury!

Purchase thread and other accessories at the same time to avoid extra trips to the store. Choose the thread according to the weight and type of the fabric to be sewn—see Chapter 3 for a thread and needle guide. For patterned fabrics, match the thread color to the background color of the fabric.

Construction Techniques

Preparing the Fabric   Plan to work on a large, flat surface—if a table is not available, the floor will do. Use a yardstick and tailor's chalk or a pencil to measure and mark.

Press the fabric to remove all wrinkles. Be sure the fabric is Sanforized or preshrunk; otherwise it is best to shrink it before cutting —this goes for linings too!

If the curtains and draperies are to hang properly, you must start with a perfect grain line. Review Chapter 3 on preparing the fabric and techniques for shrinking fabrics.

Look at the fabric carefully for nap and design. Cut fabrics with nap or pile and one-way designs with all sections laid in the same direction. Plan patterned fabrics for a pleasing effect. If it is impossible to have a complete design at both the top and bottom of a drapery length, it is best to have the incomplete design at the bottom of long curtains where it is less conspicuous; with short curtains, plan the incomplete design at the top since the bottom repeat is more noticeable. All repeats should be at the same level on every drapery hanging in the room. The repeat is determined by measuring lengthwise from a particular area in the design to the point where it occurs again.

When cutting additional panels, be sure the design runs in the same direction and the patterns match carefully on each panel.

Seams A longer stitch length, 8 to 10 stitches per inch (2.5 cm), is preferred for curtains and draperies to avoid puckered seams. Always test your fabric for pressure, tension, and stitch length.

To join panels for multiple-width curtains or draperies, use a narrow French seam with sheer or unlined draperies. For curtains or draperies that are to be lined, make a plain seam. Review the information in Chapter 7 on seams and seam finishes.

Hems The hems on curtains and draperies can be stitched by hand or machine.

Side hems The side hems are 1-inch (2.5 cm) finished width. With sheer fabrics, double hems are preferred.

Single side hem Allow 1½ inches (3.8 cm) for each side hem. Turn edge under ½ inch (1.3 cm), turn hem 1 inch (2.5 cm), pin, and stitch hem in place. Press. (Fig. 533)

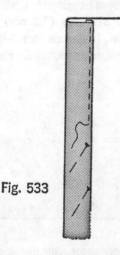

Fig. 533

Double side hem Allow 2 inches (5 cm) for each side hem. Turn under 1 inch (2.5 cm) and press. Make another 1-inch (2.5 cm) fold, pin, and stitch. Press. (Fig. 534)

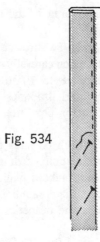

Fig. 534

Bottom hems   A double hem is preferred at the bottom because the additional weight adds to the hang of the drapery and allows for a change of length if shrinkage occurs. The hems in floor-length draperies can be basted to make any necessary adjustment in length easier after the drape has been hanging for a while.

Double hem   Make a 3-inch (7.5 cm) fold along bottom edge of drapery and press. Make another 3-inch (7.5 cm) fold, pin, and stitch in place by hand or machine. (Fig. 535)

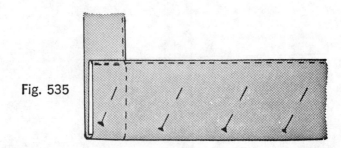

Fig. 535

Weights   Draperies and sheer curtains hang more gracefully and evenly with weighting at the bottom edge. A covered beading-type weight can be used along the full hem of the curtain. It is placed inside the bottom fold of the hem and secured by hand at

4- to 5-inch (10 to 12.5 cm) intervals along the fold line. (Fig. 536)

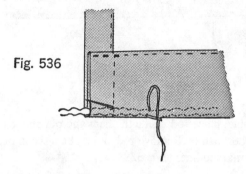

Fig. 536

Individual lead weights are covered with drapery fabric and sewn or pinned into the hem at each side hem and at each panel seam. (Fig. 537)

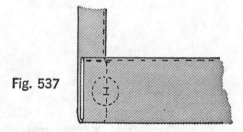

Fig. 537

Weights should be removed for laundering.

Top hems   The top hem of curtain or drapery also serves as the decorative heading.

Plain casing with heading

(A) SINGLE HEM   Make a 3-inch (7.5 cm) fold along top edge to underside and press. Turn raw edge under ½ inch (1.3 cm) and stitch along edge. (Fig. 538) To mark for the necessary width

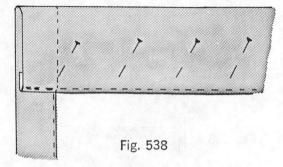

Fig. 538

of the casing, place rod inside the hem and pin above rod, allowing ease for rod to slide. Remove rod and make a second row of stitching along marked line. (Fig. 539)

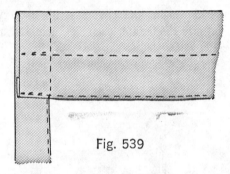

Fig. 539

(B) DOUBLE HEM   Make a 3-inch (7.5 cm) fold along top edge and press. Make another 3-inch (7.5 cm) fold, pin, and stitch along edge. Mark and stitch for casing as above.

Pleated headings   A stiffening fabric such as buckram or a nonwoven interfacing must be used in the top hem so that the pleats stand erect; it is available by the yard in 3- and 4-inch (7.5 and 10 cm) widths. Place stiffening to wrong side of the drapery, ½ inch (1.3 cm) below the top raw edge and ½ inch (1.3 cm) in from the fold of the side hems. Stitch lower edge of stiffening, fold top edge of fabric over stiffening, and press. (Fig. 540) Fold top hem down

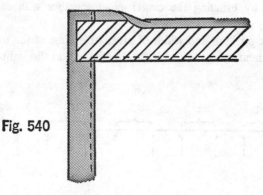

Fig. 540

again along edge of stiffening. Pin and stitch across bottom of heading. (Fig. 541)

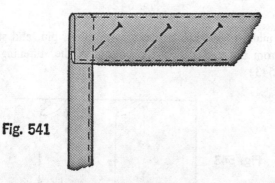

Fig. 541

To make the pleats Plan pleats in groups of uneven numbers —five, seven, nine, or more, depending upon the number necessary to take up the fullness. To determine spacing and amount to be taken up in pleats, measure the rod space to be covered (include the return and center overlap for draw draperies) and subtract this amount from the width of the hemmed drapery. The remainder is to be distributed evenly in pleats.

The first pleat should be placed about 3½ inches (9 cm) from the outer edge of the drapery, or the measurement of the return on the rod. The second pleat will be placed 3½ inches (9 cm) from the inside edge, to allow for overlap. Locate the third pleat at the center point between pleats one and two; pleats four and five are located by bringing the center pleat together with each outside pleat.

Mark position and width of pleat with pins, at the top and bottom of hem. (Fig. 542) Pleats are stitched on the right side of the fabric.

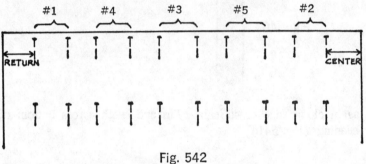

Fig. 542

To make pleats, bring markings together, pin, and stitch each fold from the top edge to the bottom of the stiffening material. (Fig. 543)

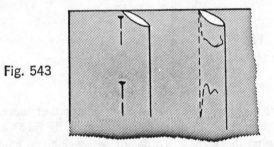

Fig. 543

Pinch pleat (Fig. 544)   Pinch the edge of the fold and push

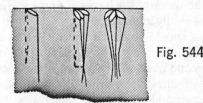

Fig. 544

back firmly to stitching line, to set "pinched" pleat in center of three equal pleats. Stitch across lower edge of heading.

Box pleat (Fig. 545) Spread large pleat an equal distance

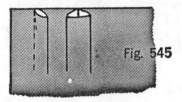

Fig. 545

each side of the stitching line and press flat. Stitch across lower edge of heading or tack by hand at top of pleat. The spacing between each pleat should be equal to the width of the pleat.

Cartridge pleats (Fig. 546) Insert cotton or a roll of non-

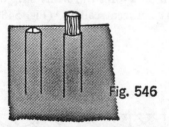

Fig. 546

woven interfacing in the fold to give a rounded shape to the pleat.

Pleater tape Professional-looking pleats can be made by using pleater tape and hooks. The amount of tape purchased should be two and one-half times the length of the rod plus returns and overlap. No additional stiffening is necessary when pleater tape is used. Fold ½ inch (1.3 cm) along top edge to wrong side, pin, and stitch tape to the top edge, extending tape ½ inch (1.3 cm) beyond finished side hems. Turn under edge of tape at side hems and sew in place. Stitch bottom edge of tape to drapery. Pleats are formed by inserting hooks in slotted pockets. (Fig. 547)

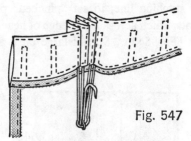

Fig. 547

Scalloped headings Shaped headings require a stiffening of organdy, buckram, or a non-woven interfacing. The number of scallops, the depth, and the spacing should be planned in proportion to the length and width of the curtain. Experiment to find the size that is right for your curtain—an average scallop is about 6 inches (15 cm) wide and 3 inches (7.5 cm) deep.

Make a pattern on a 4-inch (10 cm) strip of interfacing; allow ½ inch (1.3 cm) between scallops. (Fig. 548) The top hem al-

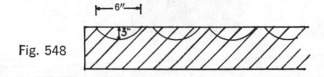

Fig. 548

lowance should be the depth of the scallop plus 1¼ inches (3.2 cm) for finishing. Stitch hems in bottom and sides of curtain. Fold top hem down to right side of fabric and pin. Center interfacing strip on fabric with points touching fold and pin in place. Stitch along scallop markings. Trim scallop to ¼ inch (6 mm) from stitching line. Clip seam allowance. (Fig. 549) Turn facing to un-

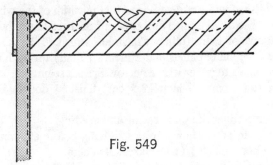

Fig. 549

derside and press flat along edge of scallop. Turn raw edge of facing under and stitch. (Fig. 550) Attach loops, rings, or clips to points of scallops.

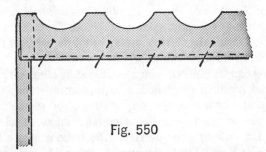

Fig. 550

Other decorative and shaped headings can be made in the same manner. Plan and prepare a pattern first.

Shirred Curtains—Or glass curtains are one of the simplest and easiest curtains to make. Sheer fabrics such as batiste, Dacron, ninon, organdy, marquisette, dotted Swiss, or nylon or polyester blends are used. The top is finished with a simple casing and heading; the curtains hang next to the window glass and may be used alone or with overdraperies.

TO MAKE: To the *finished length*

add top hem allowance: 3 inches (7.5 cm) for single hem
                          6 inches (15 cm) for double hem, and

add bottom hem allowance: 3½ inches (9 cm) for single hem
                          6 inches for double hem

The *finished width* is determined by the width of the window and the fabric used. Allow two and one-half to three times the width of the window for extra fullness; include ½-inch (1.3 cm) seam allowance for joining panels and 2 inches (5 cm) for each side hem.

* Stitch panels together with a narrow French seam.
* Stitch side hems (1-inch [2.5 cm] finished double hem) and press.
* Finish top edge with plain casing and heading.
* Pin bottom hem; allow curtains to hang before stitching hem.
* Adjust bottom hem, if necessary; stitch hem.
* Insert beading-type weighting in bottom of hem.

Café Curtains—Café curtains can be used successfully in any room of the house and with most furnishings, particularly early American and provincial. The fabric range is unlimited and the various ways to use cafés can set your imagination awhirl. Try two or more tiers —either of the same or varying lengths. Combine café curtains with long draperies—or a short valance. The rods for café curtains can be mounted inside the window casing or on the window frame, depending upon the effect you want.

The top can be finished with a scalloped heading, formal pleats, casing and heading, or plain hem with decorative clip-on hooks.

TO MAKE: For *length,* measure from the rod to the point your curtains are to reach. For tiered curtains allow at least 2 to 3 inches (5 to 7.5 cm) for overlap. Add bottom hem allowance— 3½ inches (9 cm) for single hem, 6 inches (15 cm) for double hem—plus the necessary amount for the top finish, depending upon the heading style you choose.

For *width,* allow twice the finished width of the curtain plus ½-inch (1.3 cm) seam allowance for joining panels and 1½ inches (3.8 cm) for each single side hem, 2 inches (5 cm) for each double side hem.

* Stitch panels together with a narrow French seam.
* Stitch side hems and press.
* Finish bottom hem.
* Finish top edge with decorative heading of your choice.

Ruffled Curtains—The curtain with ruffled edges is a true favorite for the informal style. The panels may meet at the center or overlap in a full crisscross effect and tie back to the window frame. Fabrics such as organdy, lawn, percale, broadcloth, marquisette, and polyester are used.

TO MAKE: In determining the *finished length* of this type of curtain, consider the width of the bottom ruffle as part of the length measurement. Measure from the top of the rod and add 3 inches (7.5 cm) for top casing and heading and ¼ inch (6 mm) for bottom hem.

For the *width,* allow at least two and one-half times the finished width, three to four times more if the curtains are to crisscross; add ½-inch (1.3 cm) seam allowance for joining panels, 1 inch (2.5 cm) for side hem, and ¼ inch (6 mm) at center edge.

The width of the ruffle will vary with your individual taste, but the ruffling should be very full, so allow two or three times the finished length and width of the curtain. Cut the fabric for the ruffling strip on the lengthwise or crosswise grain. Join the ruffling strips with a narrow French seam; finish both raw edges of the ruffle with a narrow hem.

To Make the Ruffles   For even gathers or pleats, use the ruffler attachment. Test for fullness, using a strip of the same fabric. Adjust the attachment to obtain the desired fullness—follow the directions in the sewing machine manual for adjustments. Review Chapter 15. (Fig. 551)

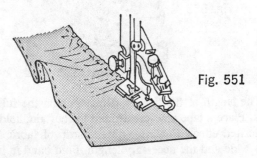

Fig. 551

To Attach Ruffle with Heading   Finish bottom and center edges of curtain with a narrow hem, ⅛ inch (3 mm) wide. Pin ruffle to the right side of the curtain along hemline; ease extra fullness in ruffle at the corners. Stitch on gathering line of ruffle. (Fig. 552)

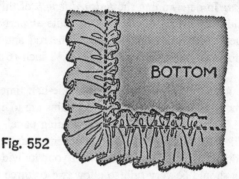

Fig. 552

To Finish Curtain Finish side edges with a ½-inch (1.3 cm) double hem. Finish top edge with a casing and heading.

Curtain with a Ruffled Valance—The length of the ruffled valance must be the same width as the curtain. Finish the ends of the ruffled valance with narrow hems. Pin and stitch ruffle to top of curtain, matching stitching lines. (Fig. 553)

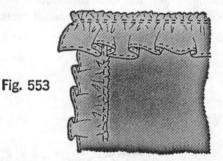

Fig. 553

Tiebacks—The length of the tieback depends upon the fullness to be held back. Place a tape measure around the curtain, holding it back for the desired effect. Cut a lengthwise strip of fabric 2½ inches (6.5 cm) wide and the necessary length. Fold band in half lengthwise, turn raw edges under ¼ inch (6 mm), and press; turn ends under ¼ inch (6 mm) and press. Insert ruffle in band and topstitch. Slip-stitch ends of band. (Fig. 554)

Fig. 554

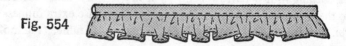

Draperies—Lined and Unlined—Draperies may be lined or unlined, depending upon the effect you wish to achieve. Some drapery fabrics will look best without linings to allow the light to bring out the design interest or texture of the fabric. The unlined drapery will give a more informal treatment to the window.

A lined drapery hangs gracefully and gives long wear. The lining will help to filter the direct sunlight and will absorb dirt and dust. White or neutral beige sateen, or polished cotton, is the fabric generally used to line draperies.

Unlined Draperies

TO MAKE: To the *finished length*

add top hem allowance: 3½ inches (9 cm) with 3-inch (7.5 cm) stiffening

4½ inches (11.5 cm) with 4-inch (10 cm) stiffening

add bottom hem allowance: 3½ inches (9 cm) for single hem

6 inches (15 cm) for double hem

NOTE: When pleater tape is used, allow only ½ inch (1.3 cm) at top edge for attaching tape.

For *width,* allow two to three times the finished width, depending upon the weight of the drapery fabric, and

add 1½ inches (3.8 cm) for each single side hem, 2 inches (5 cm) for each double hem;

add ½ inch (1.3 cm) for joining panels of multiple-width draperies.

• Join panels with a narrow French seam.
• Insert stiffening along top edge of drapery as directed under "Pleated Headings."
• Stitch and press side hems.
• Pleat drapery according to the particular heading desired.
• Pin and baste hem along bottom edge of drapery; allow curtain to hang before stitching hem, to adjust length, if necessary.
• Insert weighting in hem.

Lined Draperies   The initial steps in making lined draperies are the same as those for unlined draperies.

TO MAKE: To the *finished length*

add top hem allowance: ½ inch (1.3 cm), and

add bottom hem allowance: 3½ inches (9 cm) for single hem

6 inches (15 cm) for double hem

For *width,* allow two to two and one-half times the finished width, for draw draperies. With side draperies, one or two widths of fabric are usually sufficient at each side of the window. Add 1½ inches (3.8 cm) for each side hem, and add ½-inch (1.3 cm) seam allowance for joining panels of multiple-width draperies.

- Join panels with a plain seam; press seams open.
- Pin and baste bottom hem in lining fabric.

Preparing the Lining—Cut the lining 2 inches shorter and 3 inches narrower than the drapery fabric. The lining seams must correspond with drapery seams on multiple-width draperies.

- Join panels of lining with a plain seam; press seams open.
- Pin and baste bottom hem in lining fabric.

To Join Drapery to Lining

- Place right sides of drapery fabric and lining together with tops and right edges even; pin and stitch along right side ½ inch (1.3 cm) from edge. (Fig. 555)

Fig. 555

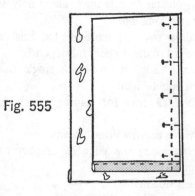

- Pin and stitch left edges of fabric and lining together in the same manner. Because the lining is narrower than the drapery, the drapery fabric will bell out. (Fig. 556)
- Press seams open.
- Center lining over drapery carefully, so that the drapery extends evenly at each side; on multiple-width draperies, match drapery panel seams to corresponding lining panel seams.
- Pin and stitch drapery and lining together at top edge, ½ inch (1.3 cm) from raw edge. (Fig. 557)

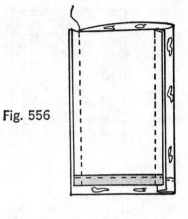

Fig. 556

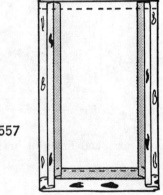

Fig. 557

- Pin strip of stiffening across top of drapery, and stitch in place on ½-inch (1.3 cm) seam line. (Fig. 558)
- Lining and drapery are stitched together at top and along sides. Turn the drapery to the right side; center lining over drapery. (Fig. 559)

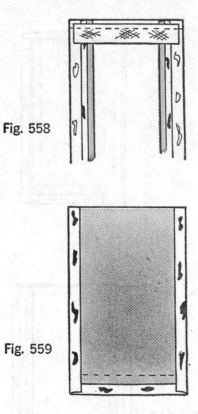

Fig. 558

Fig. 559

• Stitch through drapery and lining at lower edge of stiffening. (Fig. 560)

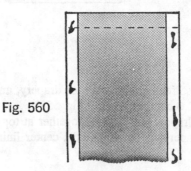

Fig. 560

- Pleat drapery according to the particular heading desired.
- Insert weights in hem of drapery fabric at seams and side hems; slip-stitch side hem at lower corner of drapery.

Finally, press the drapery completely, insert drapery hooks, and hang on rod. For a professional-looking job, draperies should hang in perfect folds. Here's a good trick, whether you are hanging your new draperies or rehanging draperies that have been returned from the cleaner.

Start at the top of the drapery and finger each pleat down a foot or so, and pin in place. Work downward, shaping pleats in this manner. Leave the draperies pinned for a day or two and you will have even folds that stay in place.

To keep the outside edge of the curtain taut against the wall, sew a plastic ring to the wrong side of the bottom hem. Insert a cup hook in the baseboard or wall in line with the ring on hem. Slip ring on hook.

Valances—A *valance* is a short piece of fabric used at the top of a window—it may be gathered or pleated. It is an ideal camouflage for drapery hardware, works wonders to add height to the small window or shorten the extra-tall window, and can unify two or three separated windows into a pleasing group.

A *cornice* will give the same effect as a valance, but it is usually made of wood or another firm material. It can be painted to match the woodwork or covered with fabric or wallpaper.

A *swag* is a draped valance that falls in more formal folds, usually with a cascade at each side.

Any of these treatments will achieve the same effect, so that your choice and the décor of the room should be the deciding factors. For the most pleasing effect, the depth of the valance must be planned in proportion to the height of the windows and the length of the curtains. The deepest point of the valance should be about one-eighth the length of the draperies. A valance that is not in the proper proportion can easily distort the window design.

A valance board can be made of wood to fit across the top of the window frame and the various types of valances can be mounted to it. Or you might plan to hang the valance like the curtain on a combination curtain and valance rod.

The Gathered Valance (Fig. 561)   This is one of the simplest

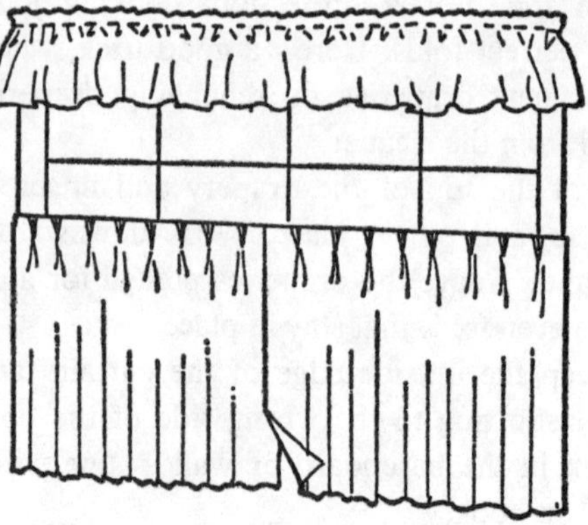

Fig. 561

but most effective valances. It can be used with full-length shirred curtains or as a perky top to the simple café curtains. Use sheer or lightweight fabrics.

TO MAKE: To the *finished depth*

add top hem allowance: 3 inches (7.5 cm) for single hem
                          6 inches (15 cm) for double hem, and
add bottom hem allowance: 3½ inches (9 cm) for single hem
                          6 inches (15 cm) for double hem

The *finished width* is determined by the width of the window (or window area to be covered) and the fabric used. Allow two and one-half to three times the width of the window for extra fullness; include ½-inch (1.3 cm) seam allowance for joining strips and 2 inches (5 cm) for each side hem. Cut fabric for valance on crosswise grain.

• Stitch strips together with a narrow French seam.
• Stitch side hems (1-inch [2.5 cm] finished double hem) and press.
• Finish top edge with plain casing and heading.
• Pin and stitch bottom hem.

The Pleated Valance (Fig. 562)   For a tailored, more formal

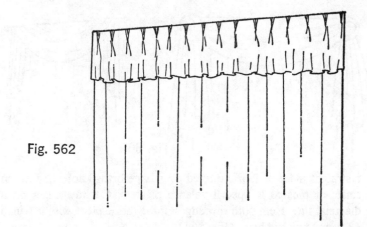

Fig. 562

effect, the pleated valance is used with draperies or with draperies and shirred curtains. Any type of pleated heading is appropriate, but should match the pleating used on the draperies if it is a combination. The valance may be lined or unlined, depending upon the weight and type of fabric.

TO MAKE: To the *finished depth*

  add top hem allowance: 3½ inches (9 cm) with 3-inch (7.5 cm) stiffening

add bottom hem allowance: 3½ inches (9 cm) for single hem

           6 inches (15 cm) for double hem

For *width* allow two or three times the finished width of the window (or window area to be covered); add 1½ inches (3.8 cm) for each single side hem or 2 inches (5 cm) for each double side hem, and add ½ inch (1.3 cm) for joining strips.

• Join strips with a narrow French seam.
• Insert stiffening along top edge of valance as directed under "Pleated Heading."
• Stitch and press side hems.
• Pleat valance according to particular heading desired.

 NOTE: If valance is to be lined, attach lining to wrong side by hand before pleating.

• Pin and stitch hem along bottom edge.

The Swag (Fig. 563a, b) Simple swags can be created with

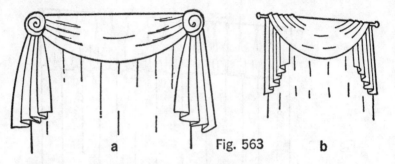

a   Fig. 563   b

a straight piece of fabric draped over large brass knobs or festoon rings, or pleated in special valance pleaters. Cut raw edges on a diagonal line. Hem both raw edges of the fabric piece with a 1-inch (2.5 cm) finished hem. (Fig. 564)

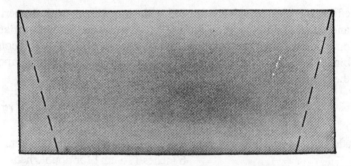

Fig. 564

For the very elegant and formal swag and cascade (Fig. 565)

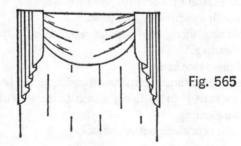

Fig. 565

experiment with muslin for the desired effect, getting the correct length and depth of the swag before cutting into the fabric. The swag and cascade are tacked to a valance board.

TO MAKE: Cut the fabric on the crosswise grain. The top edge should be the length of the valance board; the bottom edge should be at least 12 inches (30.5 cm) wider than the top. Make a 1-inch (2.5 cm) finished hem along bottom edge. Divide the sides into even spaces, which are to form the folds of the swag. (Fig. 566) Pin and stitch pleats in place. (Fig. 567) Tack to valance board.

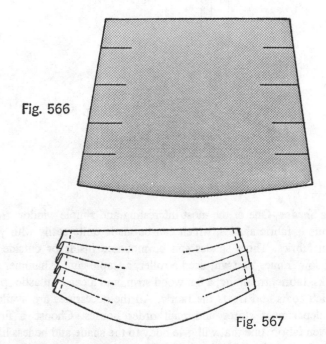

Fig. 566

Fig. 567

For the cascade, allow for the return side hems and bottom hem, and pleat according to the amount of fullness desired. Three or four pleats are usually sufficient. (Fig. 568) Tack in place on valance board.

The swag can also be hung over a round rod of wood or brass. Make the swag in separate sections and attach over the rod with snap tape. (Fig. 569)

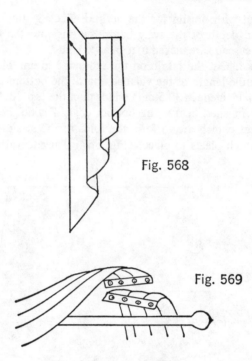

Fig. 568

Fig. 569

Fabric Shades—One of the most interesting and simple window treatments is fabric shades, which can be made quite easily with your own fabrics. These shades can be mounted inside or outside the window frame. You will need a roller, a staple gun or hammer and tacks, fabric, trimming, a flat wood strip, and a can of plastic spray, which coats and treats the fabric. All the necessities are available at department stores and mail order houses. Choose a firmly woven fabric, one that will give body to the shade and be less likely to wrinkle. (Fig. 570)

TO MAKE: Cut the fabric to the width of the roller plus 3 inches (7.5 cm) for side hems, and 15 inches (38 cm) longer than the window length.

- Stitch side hems (1 inch [2.5 cm] finished hem).
- Make a 2-inch (5 cm) channel for the wooden rod strip on the front of the shade about 6 inches (15 cm) from the bottom edge. (Fig. 571)

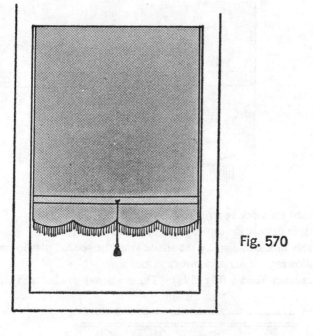

Fig. 570

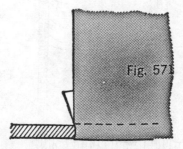

Fig. 571

- The bottom of the shade may be finished with straight, scalloped, or decoratively shaped edge; add a novelty trim to finish the edge that blends or contrasts with the fabric of the shade. (Fig. 572)

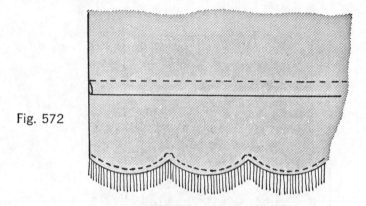

Fig. 572

- Insert the wooden strip in the rod channel.
- Staple or tack the top edge of the shade to the roller.
- Press fabric and spray the shade with the special plastic coating, following the manufacturer's directions.

Austrian Shades (Fig. 573)   These shirred shades with fringed,

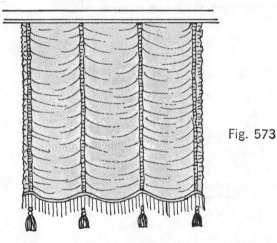

Fig. 573

scalloped bottoms are enjoying a revival. They are made either in luxurious fabrics for formal rooms or in simple materials for informal interiors. The shade may be used by itself as the complete window decoration, or in conjunction with draperies and valance;

however, the shade itself has an importance that should not be diminished by the addition of a fancy drapery or valance.

Before you buy the material for the shade, measure the window from top to sill. Allow two to three times that length for your fabric, depending on the shirring you want when the shade is let down to the windowsill. Measure the width of the window from side to side, and allow 3 inches (7.5 cm) for the side hems, plus 2 to 4 inches (5 to 10 cm) extra for the scalloped area. The more material you allow for this area, the deeper your scallops will be.

When you purchase the material, get the special shirring tape that has cords woven in and rings sewn onto it. You will need a tape for each side of the shade plus one length of tape for each scallop. Also buy traverse cord for pulling the shade up and down, fringe to match the color of the shade or to harmonize with it, and tassels (these are optional) for the bottom end of each shirring tape. Your final purchase should be a round ⅜-inch (1 cm) rod of metal or wood, the measured width of the window, to weight the shade at the bottom.

TO MAKE: First make a tubing to cover the rod from a strip of the shade material. Cut the strip 2 inches (5 cm) longer than the rod, seam it, then turn it over to the right side and slide the rod in. Slip-stitch the ends so that the rod will not slide out.

Fold and press 1½ inches (3.8 cm) to the wrong side on each side edge. Pin and stitch the shirring tape 1 inch (2.5 cm) from the edge of each side. Measure the width you desire for each scallop, generally 10 to 12 inches (25.5 to 30.5 cm), and mark lightly with chalk the places where the tapes are to go. These markings will be the guides for keeping the tapes straight. Stitch the strips of tape; be sure that all the rings in the tapes are parallel. After the tape is stitched down, tie the woven-in cord ends at the top and bottom of each tape with a temporary knot. Turn up the bottom edge of the shade ⅜ inch (1 cm) to the right side and press. Pin and stitch the fringe over the hem on the right side. (Fig. 574)

At the top of the shade, pull the tape cords up evenly, until the shades are the desired length. Tie and knot cord ends securely. The shade is wider than the window because of the extra fabric allowed for scallops. Make a hand running stitch ½ inch (1.3 cm) below the top edge of the shade, and pull the thread until you have gathered the material to the exact width to fit the window. Turn down the top edge on the gathering line and hem in place. Over

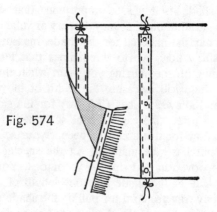

Fig. 574

this, pin a sturdy 1- to 1½-inch (2.5 to 3.8 cm) twill tape and stitch it flat on both edges. (Fig. 575)

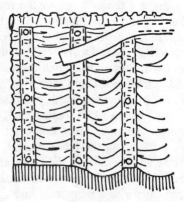

Fig. 575

Fit the covered rod at the bottom of the shade and tack the rod covering firmly to the tape. Cut long lengths of the traverse cord and tie ends securely to the rod at the center of each tape. Slide the traverse cords from the rod up through the rings, which are part of the tape. (Fig. 576)

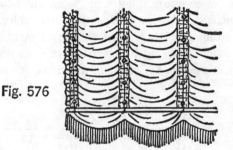

Fig. 576

TO HANG the shade, you need to attach a flat board, 1 inch (2.5 cm) thick, to the top of the window frame. Before attaching this board, insert small eye screws in its back, in line with the tapes. Attach the shade to the top of the board by tacking through the taped edge at the top of the shade, or by snaps. If you use snaps, invest in the upholstery "gripper tape" and sew one half of the gripper tape to the underside of the top hem and nail the companion part of the tape to the board. The shade can be easily removed for cleaning with this method.

When the board is fixed to the window, and the shade is attached to the board, draw the traverse cords through the screws to one side. Adjust these cords until you can raise and lower the shade evenly. Then knot the cords together and finish with a tassel. (Fig. 577)

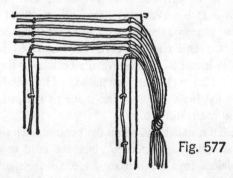

Fig. 577

Roman Shades The Roman shade, a modernized version of the Austrian shade, without the scallops, is an interesting way to dress the windows of an informal home or studio. The fabric that works out most effectively for the shade is of a solid color, smooth texture, and medium weight. Contrasting braid makes an excellent trim. The shade shows up best when there is no drapery or curtain to detract from its decorative or functional quality. (Fig. 578)

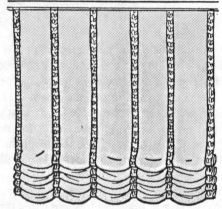

Fig. 578

Measure the length of the window from top to sill; allow 5 to 6 inches (12.5 to 15 cm) for hems at the top and bottom of the shade. Allow 3 inches (7.5 cm) across the width of the window for side hems. When buying your material get the necessary length of shirring tape and traverse cord (as described for Austrian shade), the ⅜-inch (1 cm) rod for the bottom of the shade, and the flat 1-inch (2.5 cm) board for the top of the window. In addition, buy the flat braid to go on the shade as trim, in either a design or a solid contrasting color.

TO MAKE: Turn under and stitch the hems at each side. Measure the widths at which you want to place the cord tapes, and sew them as explained for the Austrian shade. On the right side, stitch the trimming braid directly over the area where the cord tapes are stitched, covering the machine stitching of the cord tapes. (Fig. 579)

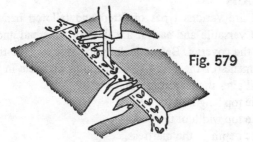

Fig. 579

Turn up and stitch the bottom hem. Make an extra stitching to provide a tubing through which the rod is inserted. (Fig. 580)

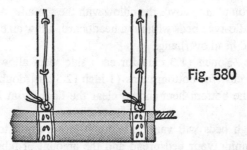

Fig. 580

The hem should be as close to the rings on the tape as possible, so that there will not be an empty gap between the bottom rings and the bottom of the shade. (If you want a fringe or decoration along the bottom of the shade, machine-stitch it on the right side ½ inch [1.3 cm] above the bottom edge, before inserting the rod.)

Cut long lengths of the traverse cord, and tie the ends to the bottom rings of the cord tape. Draw the cords through the rings. If you prefer narrower folds when the shade is drawn up than the cord tape allows, sew extra rings on the tape, spacing them halfway between the existing rings.

Turn under ½ inch (1.3 cm) to the wrong side at top edge of shade; sew plain twill tape or the gripper tape along top edge. Attach the shade to the board in the same way as directed for the Austrian shade. Follow the same directions for stringing and adjusting the traverse cords through the board screws.

BEDSPREADS

There are various types of fitted and tailored bedspreads, but the most versatile and easiest are the throw spread and its shorter version, the coverlet. Before making the spread, take the following measurements of the bed with sheets and blankets in place, since these will alter the measurements:

a. The top length of the bed.
b. The top width of the bed.
c. The depth of the mattress.
d. The length from the top of the mattress to the floor (called the side overhang and the foot overhang).
e. The top of the box spring to the floor.

Add 30 inches (76 cm) for pillow tuck-in allowance to the top length if you plan to cover the pillow with the spread.

For studio-type beds without a headboard, allow an even amount at foot and head overhang.

Include ½ inch (1.3 cm) for each side seam allowance and 2 inches (5 cm) for bottom hems (1 inch [2.5 cm] double hem, finished). The bottom hem should clear the floor by at least 1 inch (2.5 cm).

Although beds will vary in width it is necessary to remember when planning your bedspread and the amount of fabric required that a full width of fabric is placed down the center of the bed. The piecing for additional width is done evenly on each side section of the spread. (Fig. 581)

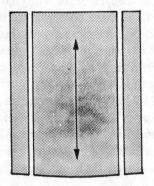

Fig. 581

To Make a Throw Spread

For Length   To the top length, add foot overhang, head tuck-in allowance (30 inches [76 cm]) plus top and bottom hems.

For Width   To the top width, add side overhangs, side seam allowances, and side hems.

Use 36-inch (90 cm) fabric for twin- or cot-size beds; 48- to 50-inch (122 to 127 cm) fabric is preferable for three-quarter and full-size beds.

* Cut one length of fabric, the full width, for the center section of the spread.
* Cut two side sections of equal length and the necessary width.
* Join side sections to the center section. These panel seams may be corded or trimmed with novelty braid, fringe, or decorative bands of fabric over the seams. Use a French seam to avoid raw edges unless the spread is to be completely lined.
* Corners of the throw spread may be pointed or rounded as you prefer. Hem the edges and finish with cording or tassel fringe. (Fig. 582a, b)

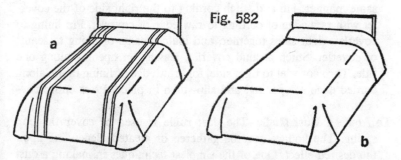

Fig. 582

To Make the Coverlet—The coverlet is made to cover the top mattress and overhang the box spring by 2 to 3 inches (5 to 7.5 cm). A separate dust ruffle is used over the box spring.

For Length   To the top length, add the depth of the mattress, overlap on each end, top and bottom hems, plus head tuck-in allowance if pillow is to be covered.

For Width   To the top width, add the depth of the mattress, side hems, side seam allowances, and overlap on each side.

* Cut one length of fabric, the full width, for the center section of the spread.
* Cut two side sections of equal length and the necessary width.

- Join the side sections to the center section; cord panel seams or use decorative braid or trim; use a French seam if coverlet is to be unlined.
- The corners of the coverlet may be pointed or rounded; hem all edges, and finish with cording or trim. (Fig. 583a, b)

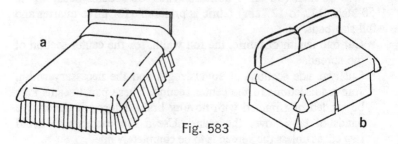

Fig. 583

For Lining If the coverlet is to be lined, join side sections to the center panel with a plain seam and press seam open. Cut lining sections to correspond with coverlet. Join lining sections in same manner. Pin and stitch cording to the right side of the coverlet with raw edge of cording to raw edge of coverlet. Pin lining to coverlet, right sides together, and match seams of lining to seams of coverlet. Stitch around coverlet, leaving an opening along one side. Turn coverlet to right side, fold raw edge of lining fabric along corded edge at opening, and slip-stitch in place. Press entire coverlet.

To Make a Dust Ruffle—The dust ruffle is used to cover the box spring. The flounce may be gathered or pleated, depending upon the desired effect. One of the simplest techniques in making a dust ruffle is to attach the flounce to a piece of muslin to fit the entire top of the box spring plus ½-inch (1.3 cm) seam allowance on all edges. If the bed has a headboard and you are making only three sides to the dust ruffle, add 2 inches (5 cm) to the length of the muslin piece.

TO MAKE: The *length* is determined by the type of flounce used. A gathered flounce should be one and one-half to two times the measured length and width of the box spring. A pleated flounce must be planned according to the spacing of pleats, the depth of the pleats, and the number of pleats required. Make the dust ruffle in three separate sections: two side sections to equal the length of the box spring, and one end section to equal the width of the box spring. For studio-type beds without headboard, make the dust ruffle in four sections, two side sections and two end sections, so that the bed looks "finished" from all angles.

The *depth*—to the measurement from the top of the box spring to the floor, add 2 inches (5 cm) for a hem, plus ½-inch (1.3 cm) seam allowance.

- Stitch lengths of fabric together with ½-inch (1.3 cm) seams to form the section.
- Hem bottom edge (1-inch [2.5 cm] finished hem).
- Finish side edges of each section with a ½-inch (1.3 cm) hem.
- For a gathered dust ruffle, gather top edge of each section with the gathering foot or machine ruffler; pin and stitch each section to muslin piece. (Fig. 584)

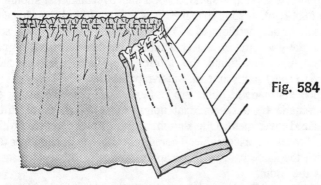

Fig. 584

- For a pleated dust ruffle, pin pleats in each section of the flounce and stitch across top of pleats to secure them; pin and stitch flounce to muslin piece. (Fig. 585)

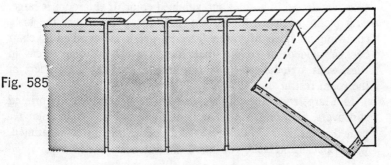

Fig. 585

The dust ruffle is placed between the box spring and the mattress.

SLIPCOVERS

Slipcovers bring new life to a hard-used room. They can make a room appear cooler for the summer season. They can make pieces of furniture compatible that ordinarily would not look well together. When you are redecorating your home, slipcovers are among your best allies. Today's slipcover is a fresh, new covering that will add charm, warmth, and brightness to the room and "fit" the furniture like upholstery.

Suitable Fabrics—There is a large selection of fabrics suitable for slipcovers. Fabrics of linen, chintz, cretonne, sailcloth, denim, ticking, and novelty-weave cottons are available in printed, plain, or plaid patterns. Whatever the name, a good slipcover material should be fairly dust-tight. It should also be firm enough to hold its shape on the chair or sofa without excess wrinkling and closely woven so it is less likely to stretch. Select a fabric that is Sanforized or preshrunk. Also investigate the fabrics that have been specially treated to resist stains and are water-repellent.

Slipcovers made at home are less expensive than those that are custom-made by a commercial upholsterer, but they are still a good-sized investment. One reason is the yardage required, which in most cases is considerable. Therefore, choose your slipcover fabric with the same care as the drapery fabrics or other accessories within the room.

Suitable Color and Design—A piece of furniture should be slipcovered as you would dress a woman—to bring out the good points and to conceal those not so good. If a chair is too large in a small room, the slipcover should be of a plain material or one with an inconspicuous design in a quiet and subdued color. If the room is large, with plenty of space for all the furniture, you can use the lush, sprawling bouquets of flowers large enough to cover an entire chair back—provided, of course, that you have enough quiet areas in rugs, walls, or other pieces of furniture to keep the atmosphere of the room restful.

In a large room the sofa and one chair might have gaily printed slipcovers, with only the second chair covered in a solid color repeated in the print. In this case the draperies might well be printed, with tiebacks and facings of the solid color.

In a small room the sofa might have a plain cover, since it is the largest piece. One chair might also be covered in a plain material and the second chair in a figured or flowered material. Make draperies to match either the plain or the figured material.

Amount of Material Required—To estimate the amount of fabric needed for a slipcover, measure the chair carefully, following the construction lines of the chair or the seam lines of the upholstery. Measure the length and width of each part of the chair at its largest point and add 1 inch (2.5 cm) for seam allowance on all sides, plus 5-inch (12.5 cm) tuck-in allowance across back of seat, on each side of seat, and where arms join the back section (the areas of the chair that are separated from each other). Add the length measurements of all sections and divide by 36 inches to estimate the number of yards necessary (or by 100 to convert from centimeters to meters). The fabric width and type of bottom finish must also be considered when determining fabric requirements. Try to choose a fabric that will fit the widest part of the chair without seaming. For the skirt, measure the distance around the chair, allowing at least two or three times the measurement, depending upon the type of skirt you choose. Allow 1 to 1½ yards (0.95 to 1.40 m) extra for placement of a floral design or matching stripe and plaid designs. Measure all the seams that are to be finished with cording or fringe to estimate the necessary amount of trimming.

Cutting Fabric and Pin-fitting to Chair—Be willing to fit and pin and refit if necessary, to get a well-tailored, professional look to your slipcover. Remember that you are working with an inanimate object, which will not mind standing long hours for a fitting—it is standing anyway! If you feel unsure of yourself, take the extra time to pin-fit a muslin pattern. This will build your confidence and serve as a permanent pattern for future covers—even professionals do this for a new design or idea. A muslin pattern can also help in the planning and placing of the design repeat—but so many of us are anxious to cut right into that fabric.

For a slipcover that fits well, wears well, and retains its shape, it is necessary to cut on the true grain of the fabric. The lengthwise grain should run from the top to the bottom of the chair; the crosswise grain should run across the chair. Place the fabric over the chair to determine the most advantageous placement of the design motif. Center a large motif on the back (front and back), on the cushion or seat, on the arms and sides. Center the pattern on both sides of the cushion so it can be reversed for extra wear. Needless to say, plain fabrics or those with an allover design can be placed and cut more easily. Striped and plaid fabrics require matching all seams.

Cut pieces of fabric to correspond with the measurements for each section of the chair; include a 1-inch (2.5 cm) seam allowance and 5-inch (12.5 cm) tuck-in allowance where necessary. Pin each fabric section to the chair, with the right side of the fabric up to ensure the fit and placement of design. The seam line on the slipcover must follow the construction lines of the chair.

Since each chair varies so in shape and style, we can only set forth the procedure for making a slipcover; you must adapt these steps to your individual problem.

STEP 1: *Inside Back* (Fig. 586)

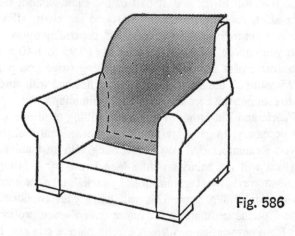

Fig. 586

Remove the cushion from the chair. Place the fabric over the inside back, centering the design. Pin from center out to seam lines. Smooth fabric so there is a 5-inch (12.5 cm) tuck-in allowance at the base where the back joins the seat. Allow 1-inch (2.5 cm) seam allowance at the sides. Shape fabric to conform with the curve of the arm, notch seam allowance as necessary to keep fabric smooth. Trim excess fabric, allowing 1-inch (2.5 cm) seam and 5-inch (12.5 cm) tuck-in at base.

STEP 2: *Seat* (Fig. 587)

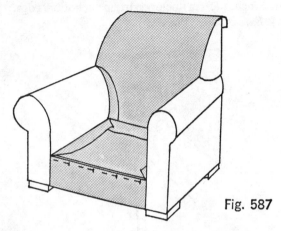

Fig. 587

a. Place fabric over seat; match to back piece. Smooth and pin fabric from center to sides. Allow 5 inches (12.5 cm) for tuck-in at back and each side edge of seat.
b. Place a piece of fabric across the front panel of chair, center design, and pin from center to sides. Allow 1-inch (2.5 cm) seam allowance at top and side edges. Allow 2 inches (5 cm) below skirt line at bottom edge.

STEP 3: *Outside Back* (Fig. 588)

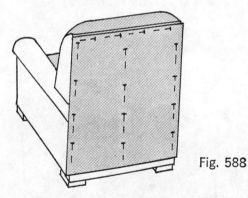

Fig. 588

Place the fabric on the chair back, centering the pattern. Pin along the top and sides, leaving a 1-inch (2.5 cm) seam allowance.

Smooth as you pin and follow curve or shape of chair for proper fit. Allow 2 inches (5 cm) below skirt line at bottom edge.

STEP 4: *Side Boxing* (Fig. 589)

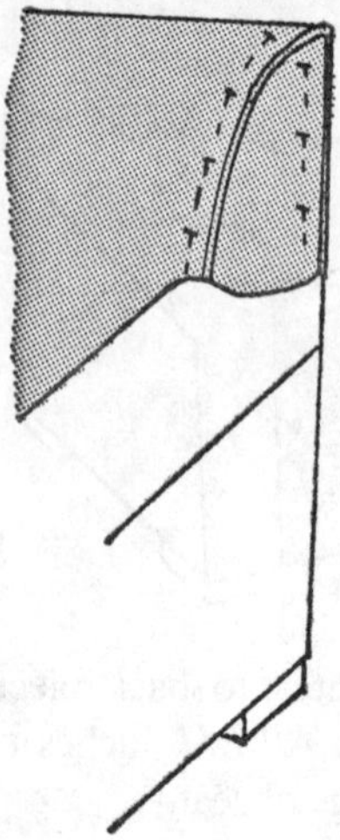

Fig. 589

Pin side back pieces (above arms) to inside and outside back along seam lines; center design. Allow 1-inch (2.5 cm) seam allowance. Join in an even line with the part of inside back that comes over the curve of the arm.

STEP 5: *Inside and Top of Arms* (Fig. 590)

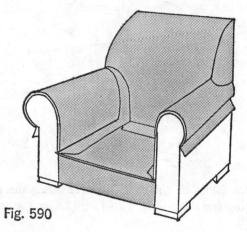

Fig. 590

Place fabric on inside top of arm, center design, smooth, and pin from center to front seam. Allow 5-inch (12.5 cm) tuck-in along bottom of inside arm. Pin to curve of back piece as in Step 1 and notch curve carefully. Trim away excess fabric at curve; allow 1 inch (2.5 cm) for seams and retaining the 5-inch (12.5 cm) tuck-in at base. Remove from chair and cut a second piece to match. Pin both pieces in place on chair.

STEP 6: *Front Arm* (Fig. 591)

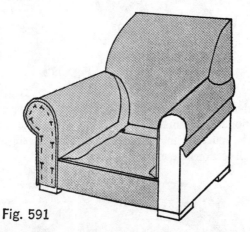

Fig. 591

Place fabric to front arm section. Center design and pin to seam line; carefully trim around curve at front of arm. Allow 1-inch (2.5 cm) seam allowance. Remove from chair and cut a second piece to match. Pin both pieces in place on chair.

STEP 7: *Outside Arm* (Fig. 592)

Place fabric to outside arm back, center design, and pin from center out. Smooth fabric under curve of arm and pin to seam line at top edge and at front and side seam lines. Allow 1-inch (2.5 cm) seam allowance. Allow 2 inches (5 cm) below skirt line at bottom edge. Remove from chair and cut a second piece, in reverse, for other arm. Pin both sections in place on chair.

All pieces are pinned in place on the chair, except at the tuck-ins. Check each section carefully—this is the time to make obvious corrections in grain and fit. Trim all seam allowances (except at tuck-ins) to an even 1 inch (2.5 cm).

TO MARK: While the slipcover is pinned so neatly on the chair, turn back seam allowances and mark all seam lines on the wrong

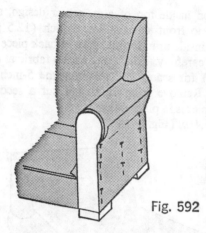

Fig. 592

side with chalk or pencil, marking over pins. At shaped sections, make additional cross marks 1 inch (2.5 cm) apart to indicate where pieces must be matched. Do not remove slipcover from chair until all sections are marked. (Fig. 593)

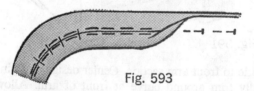

Fig. 593

Details for Construction

Seams A welt or corded seam is most often used on slipcovers. The cording may be either the same as the slipcover fabric (self welt) or a contrast, which can be purchased by the yard. Measure all seams to be finished with cording to determine the amount necessary. The average-size chair with a cushion requires about 10 to 12 yards (9.15 to 11 m); an armchair or wing chair requires 12 to 14 yards (11 to 13 m); a three-cushion sofa requires approximately 25 yards (23 m). If you are planning to match the cording to the slipcover fabric, remember that 1 yard (0.95 m) of 36-inch (91.5 cm) wide fabric will cut approximately 24 yards (22 m) of bias strips. Review Chapter 16 for preparing the cording.

NOTE: Do not try to stitch the cording and fabric section together in one operation. The cording must follow the seam line to give a neat appearance to the cover. If you think you can save time by eliminating steps, you might find yourself ripping seams. The cording can easily slip out of position between the two sections of fabric. This extra row of stitching adds strength to the seams. Review Chapter 7.

Seam Finishes Trim all inside seams evenly and overcast fabric edges together by machine or hand to prevent fraying.

Another finish is to encase the seam edges in double-fold bias tape. Use a 1-inch (2.5 cm) tape, press in half, and insert seam. Stitch along bottom edge of bias tape.

Stitching the Slipcover To sew the slipcover, complete one section at a time. The back section includes the inside back, side boxing, and outside back. The arm section includes the inside top arm, front arm, and outside arm. The seat section includes the seat and front panel. Remove the pieces to be worked on, straighten pinned seams, and correct markings if necessary. Apply cording to marked seam line before stitching fabric sections together. Place each section, as completed, on chair to check fitting. There is still time to make minor adjustments! Leave one side seam open the length of the zipper on outside back of cover. The zipper is inserted after the skirt has been stitched in place.

Joining the Finished Sections Stitch each arm section to back section along inside seam; continue stitching through tuck-in allowance.

Stitch seat section to arm section; continue stitching through tuck-in allowance.

Stitch back tuck-in allowance of seat section to inside back tuck-in allowance.

Skirts and Skirt Finishes The bottom finish of your slipcover may vary from a simple gathered skirt, to a box-pleated or group-pleated skirt, or a more tailored version with an inverted pleat at each corner. The finished skirt is usually 7 to 8 inches (18 to 20.5 cm) in depth and should clear the floor by 1 inch (2.5 cm). Measure from the skirt line on the slipcover to the floor; add 1 inch (2.5 cm) for seam, plus 1¼ inches (3.2 cm) for bottom hem.

The strips of fabric for the skirt are cut on the crosswise grain of the fabric. The amount of fabric is determined by the type of skirt.

For a gathered skirt (Fig. 594) Allow one and one-half to twice the distance around the chair at skirt line for fullness.

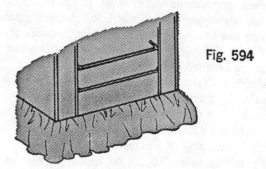

Fig. 594

For boxed pleats (Fig. 595)   Allow two to three times the circumference of the chair, depending upon the size and spacing of the pleat.

Fig. 595

For group pleats (Fig. 596)   This will take a little more com-

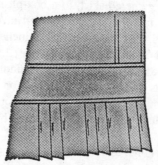

Fig. 596

puting. Decide on the number of pleats to the group, and the number of groups necessary. Multiply the amount of fabric taken up in pleats by the number of pleats and add to the circumference of the chair. Allow a few extra inches for seams and ease in joining.

For an inverted pleat (Fig. 597) If you are using a design

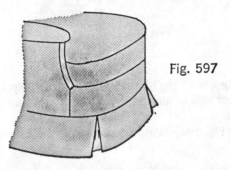

Fig. 597

that was centered on the slipcover, center the design on each skirt panel. There should be a pleat at each corner. To the circumference of the chair, add the amount necessary for four pleats, plus seams and ease in joining. Each 3-inch (7.5 cm) inverted pleat requires 12 inches (30.5 cm) of fabric.

Stitch cording or decorative trim along skirt line on bottom of slipcover with the finished edge of trim up. Make a 1-inch (2.5 cm) finished hem along bottom edge of skirt. Pin and stitch skirt to slipcover with right sides of fabric together.

The skirt may also be joined to the slipcover with a plain seam; eliminate cording or trim on skirt line.

Inserting the Zipper Be sure to use a slipcover zipper. These come in various lengths from 24 to 36 inches (61 to 91.5 cm) and have a wider tape and heavy-duty chain construction. The zipper application is the final step in making the slipcover. The zipper extends through the skirt to about 1 inch (2.5 cm) from the bottom edge of the skirt.

STEP 1: To prepare the opening, trim seams to an even 1 inch (2.5 cm). Turn in seam allowance on side of placket that is not corded (back piece) and press.

STEP 2 (Fig. 598): Pin corded edge to the zipper tape so that

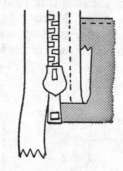

Fig. 598

the stitching line of the cording is close to the zipper teeth. Fold
end of zipper tape to underside. Baste and stitch, using the adjustable zipper foot.

STEP 3 (Fig. 599): Pin folded edge of placket over zipper tape

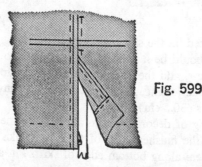

Fig. 599

so that the edge of the fabric meets the corded seam line. Match
skirt seam on slipcover. Fold under edge of zipper tape. Baste,
and stitch across the end and down the side of the zipper to give
the appearance of a lapped application.

Gripper tape, which is available by the yard, may also be used
for the placket. Prepare the placket as above. Pin the ball side
of tape to the seam allowance on side of placket that is not corded.
Stitch tape flat on both edges. Pin socket side of tape to corded
seam edge; match the ball and sockets of tape.

Stitch along both edges of tape.

Press entire slipcover and place on chair.

Covering the Cushions—Place the right side of the fabric on the
cushion and center the design in relation to the chair back. Fit

fabric smoothly over cushion, pinning from center to outer edges. (Fig. 600) Mark seam line along outer edges of cushion. Remove

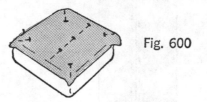

Fig. 600

fabric from cushion; trim to ½-inch (1.3 cm) seam allowance beyond marked line.

Cut underside of cushion to correspond, so that the cushion can be reversed. To do this, place right side of cut section to right side of fabric with the design matching, and cut, using the first section as a guide.

Pin and stitch cording to the edges of the top and bottom sections, following marked seam line.

Boxing Strip The boxing strip is cut in two sections on the crosswise grain of the fabric. The zipper must be long enough so that the cushion can be inserted into the cover easily.

The front section is cut long enough to go across the front of the cushion and to the center of each side, and the measured width of the cushion plus 1 inch (2.5 cm) for seams. The design should be centered on the front of the strip.

The back section is cut the same length as the front section and 1½ inches (3.8 cm) wider. Cut the strip in half lengthwise. Pin and baste lengthwise edges together with a ¾-inch (2 cm) seam. Press seam open. Pin and baste zipper in place over seam line. (Fig. 601) On the right side, stitch around zipper, about ¼ inch (6 mm) from seam line. (Fig. 602)

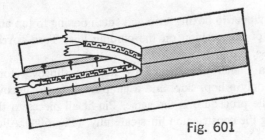

Fig. 601

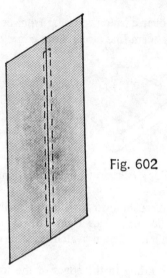

Fig. 602

Pin front and back boxing sections in place on cushion, with right sides together; mark seam lines. (Fig. 603) Stitch and press seams open.

Fig. 603

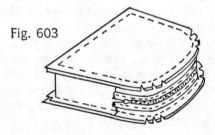

Open zipper in boxing strip and stitch boxing to top and bottom sections of the cushion on the cording line. Turn cover to right side, press, and insert cushion.

To Cover a Couch—Once you have made a slipcover for a chair, you are only a hop, skip, and a jump away from slipcovering the couch—the procedure is the same. Pin-fit all pieces to the couch, following the construction lines carefully. (Fig. 604) Allow 5-inch

Fig. 604

(12.5 cm) tuck-in across back seat and inside arm sections. Start to work at the top center of the couch, toward the sides and down. Leave an opening for the zipper on each side of the cover. (Fig. 605)

Fig. 605

To Sew the Cover   Complete each section as for a chair, inserting cording or decorative trim in the seams. Place the completed section on the couch for a try-on. Join all sections, apply skirt of your choice, and insert zippers.

The cushions are covered in the manner previously described. (Fig. 606)

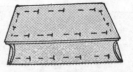

Fig. 606

Slipcovers for a New Look to an Old Piece—There may be a number of odds and ends of furniture in your house that you want to rejuvenate with slipcovers. If you have a small round table that is the worse for wear, you can make it useful and attractive by cutting a special cover for it of felt or linen and edging it with a wide fringe or other type of trimming. The cover should hang to the floor.

In a smaller house where there is no guest room, a folding bed will be less conspicuous if it is covered with an appropriate slipcover when not in use.

Even the ordinary kitchen chair can be made gay and more comfortable with a padded slipcover for the seat and back. You can make your own chair pads by cutting the padding to fit the seat and covering it with vinyl or leather-like fabric. An old dining room chair can also be given a second life by covering the faded upholstery on the seat and the back. Some chairs need little or no sewing: the fabric is stretched over the seat and held in place on the underside with staples.

You can make covers for so many things that the list is endless. The sewing procedures are the same for each type of cover. The slipcovers can be cut from a paper pattern or they can be fitted by pinning the material directly on the article you want to cover.

DECORATIVE PILLOWS

Decorative pillows are "at home" in every room of the house and with all decorating periods and furnishings. The fabric range is limitless—from rich antique taffetas and velvets in the formal room to cotton sailcloth or denim ticking in the family room or on the terrace. Pillows can add that spot of color to contrast or harmonize with or complement the décor of the room. Because you make your own pillows, you can choose fabrics and colors that are just right for your home.

Pillow forms can be purchased in various shapes and sizes. These forms come in molded foam rubber or muslin-covered pillows filled with kapok, shredded foam rubber, or polyester stuffing. If you prefer to design your own shape, fillings of polyester and shredded foam rubber are available in package form—or save all those old nylon stockings and cut them into small pieces. They make an excellent stuffing material. Experiment with the sizes and shapes of pillows you plan to design by cutting patterns in paper first. Then make the muslin covering and fill solidly. Foam rubber is also available by the yard in sheet form—widths vary from ½ to 2 inches (1.3 to 5 cm)—and this is excellent for making chair pads or bench seats.

Although the shapes and sizes of pillows may vary, there are only two basic types of pillows, the knife-edge and the box-edge. Once you know how to cover these pillows, let your imagination be your guide, but do plan for a zipper in the pillow cover. This makes it so much easier when laundering or dry-cleaning.

Knife-edge Pillow (Fig. 607)—This type of pillow is made with a

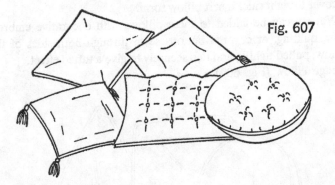

Fig. 607

cording, fringe, or other decorative trim around the edges. Make the pillow cover to fit the form snugly.

TO MAKE: Measure the pillow from edge to edge; add ½-inch (1.3 cm) seam allowance on each edge. (Fig. 608)

- Cut two pieces of fabric to this measurement.
- Pin and stitch cording or trim in place to the right side of one fabric section, with raw edge of cording even with raw edge of fabric.
- Pin pillow sections together along one edge, with wrong sides together.
- Machine-baste seam for length of zipper to be used.

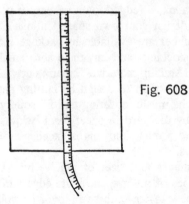

Fig. 608

- Insert zipper in seam according to a lapped-seam application; press zipper application and remove bastings.
- Open zipper; pin and stitch other edges of pillow cover; turn cover to right side. Insert pillow form.

Variety can be added to these pillows with decorative embroidery, quilting, or covered buttons sewn through both sides of the pillow, pulled tightly, and tied securely to give a tufted effect.

Box-edge Pillow (Fig. 609)

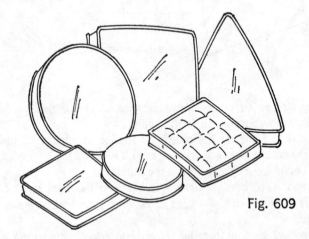

Fig. 609

This type of pillow has a boxing strip between the fabric pieces. Both edges of the pillow are usually corded or trimmed.

TO MAKE: Measure the pillow across the top from one edge to the other; add ½ inch (1.3 cm) for seams to each edge. Measure the depth of the boxing and the circumference of the pillow form. (Fig. 610)

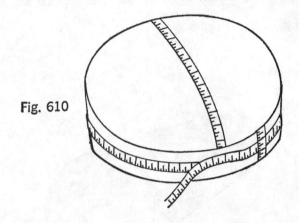

Fig. 610

- Cut two pieces of fabric to the pillow measurement.
- Cut one piece of the fabric for the boxing strip the depth of the boxing plus 1 inch (2.5 cm) for seams and half the circumference of the pillow form plus 1 inch (2.5 cm).
- Cut another piece of fabric for the boxing strip the depth of the boxing plus 2½ inches (6.5 cm) and half the circumference plus 1 inch (2.5 cm).
- Pin and stitch cording or trim to all edges of each pillow section; be sure raw edge of trim is even with raw edge of fabric section.
- Insert zipper in boxing strip according to directions given for slipcover cushions; complete boxing strip.
- Open zipper; pin and stitch strip to each pillow section. Insert pillow form.

BOLSTERS

Bolsters come in various shapes and sizes—round, square or rectangular, and wedge-shaped. They are used on couches or studio-type beds and with outdoor lounge furniture. Forms are available in foam rubber or kapok-filled muslin, but you can easily make your own muslin form to the size and shape you want.

Before making the cover, take all the measurements of the form accurately; add the necessary seam allowances. Make a paper pattern of the end pieces, particularly wedge-shaped ends, and add seam allowance—in this way those important corners will remain sharp.

Round Bolster (Fig. 611)

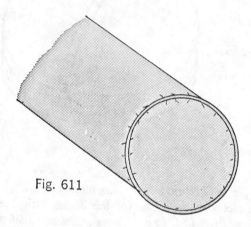

Fig. 611

TO MAKE: Measure the diameter of the end pieces, add ½ inch (1.3 cm) all around for seams.

- Cut two circles of fabric.
- Cut one fabric piece the length of the bolster plus 1-inch (2.5 cm) seam allowance and the width of the measured circumference of the end piece plus 1 inch (2.5 cm).
- Pin long edges of center section.
- Measure length of zipper opening—zipper should be long enough for bolster form to slip in and out easily.
- Machine-baste zipper opening and finish seam with regular stitch; insert zipper according to the lapped-seam application; press zipper application, remove bastings, and open zipper.
- Pin and stitch cording or trim to end pieces.
- Pin and stitch end pieces in place on center section. Insert bolster form in cover.

Square Bolster (Fig. 612)

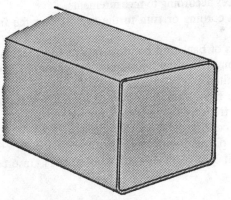

Fig. 612

TO MAKE: Measure the length and width of the bolster form; add 1 inch (2.5 cm) for seams. Cut one fabric section to this measurement.

- Cut two squares of fabric 1 inch (2.5 cm) larger than the measurement of the form for the end pieces.
- Pin long edges of center section.
- Measure length of zipper opening.
- Machine-baste zipper opening and finish seam with regular stitch; insert zipper according to the lapped-seam application; press zipper application, remove bastings, and open zipper.
- Pin and stitch cording or trim to end pieces.
- Pin and stitch end pieces in place on center section.
- Keep corners square by clipping seam allowance of center section. Insert bolster form in cover.

Wedge-type Bolster (Fig. 613)

Fig. 613

TO MAKE: Plan this cover in five sections: two end pieces and front, back, and bottom pieces; add ½-inch (1.3 cm) seam allowance to all edges.

- Cut fabric pieces according to measurements.
- Pin and stitch cording or trim to the top edge of the front section.
- Pin long edges of back and bottom sections together; insert zipper in this seam, using the lapped-seam application; finish seam with regular stitch.
- Pin and stitch front section to back section along corded edge.
- Pin and stitch front section to bottom section.
- Pin and stitch cording or trim to end pieces.
- Open zipper; pin and stitch end pieces in place on completed center section; clip seam allowance at corners. Insert form in cover.

Index

A

Accessories, 322–31
 bags, 323
 belts, 324–26
 collars, 328–29
 hats, 326
 miscellaneous (gifts), 330–31
 scarves, 328
 shawls (stoles), 326–27
 vests, 327–28
Accordion pleats, 127
Acetate, 18
 characteristics, care, and use of,
  18
 for linings, 87, 88, 89
Acrylics, 18
 characteristics, care, and use of,
  18
Airing of clothes, 341
Allover prints, 15
 cutting, 15
 for linings, 87
 See also Print designs
Alteration lines, 24
Alteration of patterns, 25–43
 bodice, 28
 bust, 28–31
 for a custom fit, 26–43
 neckline, 38–39
 pants, 39–43
 pleats in, 27
 shoulder, 31–33
 skirts, 28, 35
 sleeves, 35–38
 spreading, 26
 tapering, 27–28
 terms used in, 26–27
 tucks, 26
 waistline, 34–35
Alteration of ready-to-wear clothing, 337–39
 buying for size, 337–38
 lengthening skirt, 338
 letting out skirt, 338–39
 pants, 339
 shortening skirt, 338
 taking in skirt, 338
Animals, stuffed, 330
Anti-static fabric finish, 20
Applied band, 165
Applied casing, 168
Appliqué, 257–58
 decorative, 333
 hand, 257
 machine, 257–58
Arms
 and pattern alteration, 35–38
 See also Sleeves
Arrowhead, 266–67
Austrian fabric shades, 376–79

B

Babies, pattern sizes for, 293
Backstitch, 101
Back waist length, measuring, 5
Bags, 323
Ball buttons, fabric-covered, 183–84
  Chinese, 184
Ball-point needles, use of, 76
Band cuff, 154–55
Bandings (bands), 165–66
  applied, 165
  collar on, 309–12
  extended, 165–66
Bar fagoting, 252
Basting, 92, 97–100
  bias to straight edge, 100
  diagonal, 100
  edge marked "ease," 100
  even, 99
  hand, 99
  machine, 98–99
  methods, 97–98
  pin, 98
  plaids, 70
  slip (right-side), 99–100
  uneven, 99
Batwing sleeve, 146
Beading, 272–73
Beanbags, 330–31
Beds, folding, slipcovers for, 400
Bedspreads, 382–86
  coverlets, 383–84
  dust ruffles, 384–86
  patchwork, 260
  throw, 383
Belt loops, 224–26
  chain, 225
  fabric, 225
  fabric carrier, 224
  thread, 226
Belts, 222–24, 324–26
  with backing, 223–24

with interfacing, 223
without stiffening, 222–23
tie, 223
Bias binding, 234–39
  attaching collar with, 137–38
  corded piping, 239
  cutting strip, 235
  double, 73, 237
  French, 73, 237
  hand hemming, 237
  for inside corners, 239
  joining two strips, 235
  making continuous strip, 235–36
  making single fold, 236
  for outside corners, 238
  for scallops, 238
  stretching, 236
  topstitching, 236–37
  tubing, 240–41
Bias edge, basting to straight edge, 100–1
Bias facing, 157, 161
  cuff applied with, 152–53
  for V neckline, 131–32
Binding, bias, 234–39
  See also Bias binding
Binding, seam
  for hem finish, 175
  tight sleeve opening faced with, 153
Blanket stitch, 246
Bodices
  lining, 87
  in pattern alteration, 28
  in putting dress together, 92 ff.
  See also specific parts of garments
Bolsters, 403–6
  round, 404
  square, 405
  wedge-type, 405–6
Bonded fabrics, 76–77
  bonding process, 16

Border prints, 72
See also Print designs
Bound buttonholes, 188–94
corded, 194
facing, 194
patch method I, 188–90
patch method II, 190–92
two-piece (piped), 192–94
Bound seam, 111–12
Bows, tailored, 273
Box-edge pillow, 402–3
Box pleats, 126
draperies with, 359
slipcovers with, 394
Boys
measuring, 296, 302–3
and men, sewing for, 301–21
See also Men and boys, sewing
for
pattern sizes for, 294, 301
See also Children, sewing for
Braid
horsehair, for hem, 179
narrow, 179
wide, 179
passementeries, 265–66
Broad shoulders, altering pattern
for, 33
Bullion stitch, 248–49
Bust
altering pattern, 28–31
measuring, 5
and selecting patterns, 8
Buttonholes, 187–98
bound, 188–94
corded bound, 194
facing, 194
machine, 198
measuring for, 187
patch method, 188–92
spacing, 187–88
tailored, 197–98

two-piece bound (piped), 192–
94
worked, 195–98
Buttons, 181–86
ball, fabric-covered, 183, 184
Chinese ball, 184
covered, making, 182–83
crocheted, 184
fabric, 181–82, 183–84
frogs, 185
sewing on, 185–86

C

Cable stitch, 249
in smocking, 253–54
Café curtains, 362
Capes, 276
Cap sleeve, 144
Carbon paper, dressmaker's, 47,
59, 61
Caring for clothes, 340–46
fabric characteristics, 16–21
mending, darning, patching, 342
See also Mending
pointers for daily care, 340–41
pressing, 341
recycling (remodeling) and,
344–46
stain removal, 342–44
Cartridge pleats, draperies with,
359
Casings, 166–68
applied, 168
elastic, 167–68
Catch stitch, 244–45
hem, 176
Chain loops, 225
Chain stitch, 245
Chairs, slipcovers for, 386–98, 400
cushions, 396–99
cutting and pinning fabric,
389–92

Chairs, slipcovers for (*cont'd*)
  details for construction, 392–98
  kitchen, 400
  seams, 392–93
  skirts and skirt finishes, 393–95
  stitching, 393
  zippers, 395–96
Chalk, tailor's, 47, 59–60
Chemical finishes, fabrics and,
    20–21
Chewing gum, removing, 342–43
Children, sewing for, 293–300
  adjusting and understanding pat-
    terns, 295–96
  choosing fabric, 293
  fabrics, 293
  iron-on patches, 333
  make-overs for, 346
  measurements for, 294–95
  pattern sizes, 293–94
  sewing tips, 296–97
  toys, 330–31
  See also Boys; Girls
Chinese ball buttons, 184
Chubbie, patterns for, 294
Circular ruffles, 232
Classic shirt, men's, construction
    points for, 308–21
  See also under Shirts
Cleaning fluid, care in use of, 342
Coats
  attaching fur collars, 80–81
  buying patterns, 6
  elbow patches, 336
  tailoring, 274–92
    facing, 277, 284–85
    hemming, 288
    interfacing, 277, 280–81,
      282–83
    interlining, 277, 289–92
    lining, 276–77, 288–89
    materials, 274–77
    muslin reinforcement, 281–82
  pad-stitching, 279–80, 283–84
  patterns, 274–76, 279
  setting in sleeves, 285–87
  underarm shields, 292
  underlining, 277
Coffee stains, removing, 343
Collars, 131, 135–43, 328–29
  attaching with bias binding,
    137–38
  attaching with facing, 138–39
  convertible tailored, 141–42
  detachable, 142
  with edging, 142–43
  fur, 78–81
  men's classic shirt, 309–12
    on a band, 309–11
    and band in one, 312
  Peter Pan, 329
  shaped, faced and interfaced,
    135–37
  straight, 328–29
  straight, with slashed neckline,
    139–41
  for tailored garments
    interfacing, 282–83
    pad-stitching to shape roll,
      283–84
    stitching and facing, 284–85
  turning, 336–37
Colors
  in home decorating, 347, 386
  matching thread to fabric, 52
  selecting patterns and, 9
  for slipcovers, 386
Combination stitch, 102
Continuous lap placket, 154–56,
    312
Convertible tailored collar,
    141–42
Corded bound buttonhole, 194
Corded piping, 239
  covering, 239
  made into loops, 241

Corded seam, 108
Corded tubing, 240–41
Corduroy, 14, 71
  patches, 335–36
  for tailored garments, 276
Corners
  bias binding for, 238–39
  facing for, 162
Cornices, 369
Cottons, 17, 52
  characteristics, care, and uses of,
    17
  for linings, 88, 89
  mercerized, 20
  shrinking to cut, 56
Couches, slipcovers for, 398–400
Couching stitch, 248
Covered buttons, making, 182–83
Coverlets, 383–84
Crisscross fagoting, 251–52
Crocheted buttons, 184
Cross-stitch, 244
Cross tucking, 122
Crosswise grain, 53
Crotch, in altering pants pattern,
    39–41, 304–5
Cuffs
  applied with bias facing, 152–53
  band, 154–55
  men's shirt, classic, 313–14
  turnback, cut with sleeve,
    151–52
  turning, 336–37
Curtains, 351–64
  café, 362
  construction techniques, 352–61
  glass, 361–62
  headings, 355–61, 362–64
  hems, 353–56
  measuring for, 351–52
  ruffled, 362–64
  with ruffled valance, 364
  seams, 353

  shirred, 361–62
  tiebacks for, 364
  valances, 369–74
  weights, 354–55
Curved tucks, 122
Cushions, slipcovers for, 396–99
Cutting, 56–59
  following layout, 56–59
  preparing fabric for, 52–56
  in recycling (remodeling), 345
  slipcovers, 387–92
  supplies, 44–45
  understanding and using patterns
    and, 21–24
  See also specific garments, parts
    of garments
Cutting line, 24

D

Damask hem, 178–79
Darning, 333–34
  reinforcing, 334–35
Darts, 115–20
  altering bust line, 28–31
  decorative, 117–18
  finishing, 116
  in lace, 72
  most frequently used places,
    118–20
  for sheer fabrics, 73
  smooth, making, 116
Dart tucks, 120–21
Decorative appliqués and patches,
    333
Decorative darts, 117–18
Decorative pillows, 400–3
  box-edge, 402–3
  knife-edge, 400–1
Decorative stitches and techniques
  See Embroidery stitches;
    Stitches; specific kinds,
    techniques, uses

Decorative trimming tricks
  See Trimmings
Deep-pile fabrics, 81–82
Design, pattern buying and, 6–9
Detachable collar, 142
Diagonal basting, 100
Diagonal hemstitching, 250–51
Dolls, rag, 330
Dolman sleeve, 146
Double bias binding, 73, 237
Double hemstitching, 250, 251
Double kick pleats, 130
Double knits, 75
Double ruffles, 232
Double-stitched seam, 112
Draperies, 351–52, 365–69
  construction techniques, 352–61
  headings, 355–61, 362–64
  hems, 353–56
  lined and unlined, 365–69
  measuring for, 351–52
  seams, 353
  valances, 369–74
  weights, 354–55
Drawn work, 249–51
  diagonal hemstitching, 250–51
  double hemstitching, 250, 251
Dresses
  buying patterns, 6, 10–11
  methods of putting together,
      90–94
    custom method, 91
    factory method, 90–91
    fitting, 93–94
    general procedure, 92–93
  See also specific parts of
      garments
Dress form, 278
Dressmaker's carbon paper, 47, 59,
      61
Dressmaker shears, 45
Dry-cleaning fluid, care in use of,
      342

Durable-press fabrics, 20
  See also Permanent-press fabrics
Dust ruffles, 384–86

E

"Ease," basting edge marked,
      100–1
Ease, pattern, 6
Edges
  See Facings; specific garments,
      parts of garments; types of
      edgings
Edgestitched hem, 178
Edgestitched seam, 110
Egg stains, removing, 343
Elastic casing, 167–68
Elastic thread, for shirring, 229–
      30
Elbow, darts at, 119
Elbow patches, 333, 335–36
  iron-on, 333
Embroidered edgings, 269–70
Embroidery stitches, 243–62
  appliqué, 257–58
  blanket, 246
  bullion, 248–49
  cable, 249, 253–54
  catch, 244–45
  chain, 245
  couching, 248
  cross-, 244
  drawn work, 249–51
  fagoting, 251–52
  feather, 247–48
  French knots, 246
  hemstitching, 249–51
  herringbone, 244–45
  honeycomb, 254–55
  lazy daisy, 245–46
  machine, 259–60
  outline, 244, 253
  patchwork, 260–62

Embroidery stitches (*cont'd*)
quilting, 255–57
saddle, 249
satin, 243
scallops, 246–47
seed, 248
smocking, 252–55
Envelope, pattern, 9–15
Even basting, 99
Extended band, 165–66
Eyelets, 226
Eyes
See Hooks and eyes

F

Fabric belt carrier, 224
Fabric belt loops, 225
Fabric-covered buttons, 181–82,
183–84
Fabrics
buying (selecting) patterns
and, 6, 9, 10–21
for children, 293
choosing correct needle and
thread for, 45, 51–53
cutting, 44–45, 56–59
fibers and construction of, 16–21
handling special, 67–82
bonded, 76–77
border prints, 72
deep-pile, 81–82
double knits, 75
fur, 78–82
jersey, 75
lace, 72–73
leather, 77–78
leather-like, 77–78
metallic, 78
napped, 71
one-way, 71
permanent-press, 73–74
pile, 71, 81–82
plaids, 67–70

sequined, 78
sheer, 73
stretch, 74–75
suede, 77–78
wash-and-wear, 73–74
for home decorating, 347–48,
374–81, 386
preparing, 352–53
for interlinings, 83–84, 88
kinds, characteristics, care, and
uses of, 17–21
for linings, 87, 88
marking, 59–61
for men's wear, 306–7
preparing for cutting, 52–56
grain, 52–54
pressing, 56
shrinking, 56
straightening, 55–56
pressing, 56, 63–66
in recycling (remodeling),
344–45
for slipcovers, 386 ff.
special finishes, 20–21
for tailored garments, 274–77
for underlinings, 84–85, 88
what you should know about,
16–20
Fabric shades, 374–81
Faced hem, 176
Facings, 157–71
attaching collar with, 138–39
bandings, 165–66
bias, 157, 161
bound buttonhole, 194
casings, 166–68
corners, 162
cuffs, 152–53
fitted, 157, 170
front slashed, 132–33
hem, 176
neckline, 131–35
preparing, 158–59

Facings (*cont'd*)
  ribbon, 170–71
  saw-tooth edge, 164
  scalloped edge, 163–64
  shaped, 158
  shaped neck, 134–35
  slashed openings, 162–63
  stitching, 159–61
  tailored garments, 277, 284–85
  types of, 157 ff.
  waistline, 168–71
Factory-made dresses, 90–91
Fagoting, 251–52
  bar (spoke), 252
  crisscross, 251–52
Fake furs, 81–82
Fan pleats, 127
Fastenings, 181–211
  buttons and buttonholes, 181–98
  hammer-on snaps, 209
  hooks and eyes, 210–11
  nylon tape, 210
  snaps, 209
  zippers, 198–208
Fat stains, removing, 343, 344
Feather stitch, 247–48
Felting fabrics, 16
Fibers, and fabrics, 16–20
  man-made, 16, 17–20
  natural, 16, 17
Figure types
  altering patterns to suit, 25–43
    See also Alteration of patterns
  buying patterns and, 4–6, 7–9,
    10–11
  design and, 7–9
  figure faults and, 8–9
  sizing, 4–6
Finishes, chemical, fabrics and,
  20–21
Fitted facing, 157, 170
Fitting
  dresses, 93–94

pants, 94
Flame-resistant fabric finish, 20
Flat felled seam, 105
Fleece, 71
Fly-front zipper opening, 315–19
Folding beds, slipcovers for, 400
Fold line, 24
French binding, 73, 237
French knots, 246
French seam, 106–7
  mock, 107
Fringe, 267–68
  knotted, 268
  self, 267–68
Frogs, 185
Front slashed facing, 132–33
Fruit stains, removing, 343
Fur, 78–82
  fake, 81–82
Furniture, slipcovers for, 400
  See also Slipcovers, specific
    kinds
Fusible interfacings, 84

G

Gathered sleeve, 147–48
Gathered slipcover skirts, 393
Gathered valance, 370
Gathering (gathers), 227–28
  by hand, 227
  to hold fullness, 228
  by machine, 227–28
Getting ready to sew, 44–66
  cutting fabric, 44–45, 56–59
  marking fabric for cutting,
    59–61
  preparing fabric for cutting,
    52–59
  sewing machine, use and care of,
    48–51
  supplies, 44–48, 51–53, 59–61

Gifts, 322, 330–31, 346
 toys, 330–31
 See also Accessories
Girls
 pattern sizes for, 4, 5–6, 294–95
 See also Children, sewing for
Glass curtains, 361–62
Gloves, care of, 341
Grain, in preparing fabric for
  cutting, 52–54
Grain line, 24
Grease stains, removing, 343, 344
Gripper tape, 379
Group pleats, slipcovers with,
  394–95
Gum, chewing, removing, 343–44

H

Hair-canvas interfacing, 84
Half-size patterns, 4
Hammer-on snaps, 209
Hand sewing
 appliqué, 257–58
 basting, 99
 gathering, 227
 hemming bias binding, 237
 knot for, 95–96
 needles for, 51
 zipper application, 205
 See also Stitches; specific
  stitches, techniques
Hangers, use of, 340–41
Hats, 326
 care of, 341
Headings
 for curtains and draperies, 355–
  61, 362–64
  plain casing with, 355–56
  pleated, 356–60
  ruffled, 362–64
  scalloped, 360–61

 ruffles with, 232–33
Height
 measuring, 5
 and selecting patterns, 5, 7, 8
Hems, 157, 171–80
 catch-stitched, 176
 for curtains and draperies,
  353–56
  bottom, 354–55
  side, 353
  top, 355–56
 damask, 178–79
 edgestitched, 178
 faced, 176
 finishing, 173–80
 horsehair braid for, 179
 machine-stitched, 178
 marking, 172
 men's pants, adjusting width,
  305–6
 plain, as sleeve finish, 151
 in pleats, 180
 rolled, 176–77
 seam binding for, 175
 for tailored garments, 288
 tailor's, 175
 turned and stitched, 176
 whipped, 177
 See also Skirts
Hemstitching, 249–51
 diagonal, 250–51
 double, 250, 251
Herringbone stitch, 244–45
Hips
 measuring, 5–6
 and pattern alterations, 35
  for pants, 39, 41
 and selecting patterns, 8
Home, the, sewing for, 347–406
 bedspreads, 382–86
 bolsters, 403–6
 curtains, 351–64
 draperies, 351–52, 365–69

Home, the, sewing for (*cont'd*)
  fabrics for, 347–48, 374–81
    preparing, 352–53
  pillows, decorative, 400–3
  shades, 374–81
  slipcovers, 386–400
  valances, 369–74
  windows, 348–81
Honeycomb stitch, 254–55
Hong Kong finish, 112–13
Hooks and eyes, 210–11
Horsehair braid for hem, 179
  narrow, 179
  wide, 179

I

Imitation fur fabrics, 81–82
Imitation leather and suede fabrics, 77–78
Ink stains, removing, 343
Interfacing, 83–84, 88
  belt with, 223
  collars, 135–37, 309–10
  fusible, 84
  iron-on, 84
  tailored garments, 277, 280–81, 282–83
  waistband, 169–71
Interlining, 87–88
  tailored garments, 277
    coats, 277, 289–92
Inverted pleats, 126–27
  slipcovers with, 395
Invisible zipper application, 205–7
Ironing, 63
  man-made fabrics, 16
  See also Pressing
Ironing board, 44, 48
Iron-on interfacing, 84
Iron-on mending tape, 333
Irons, 48
Italian quilting, 256–57

J

Jackets
  buying patterns, 6
  elbow patches, 336
  men's, 303, 306
    adjusting, 306
  tailoring, 274–92
    facing, 277, 284–85
    hemming, 288
    interfacing, 277, 280–81, 282–83
    lining, 276–77, 288–89
    making, 278–89
    material, 274–77
    muslin reinforcement, 281–82
    pad-stitching, 279–80, 283–84
    patterns, 274–76, 279
    setting in sleeves, 285–87
    underarm shields, 292
    underlining, 277
Jersey, 75
Junior patterns, 4
Junior Petite patterns, 4

K

Kick pleats, 127–30
  double (set-in), 130
  single, 127–29
Kimono sleeves, 144–46
  with one-piece gusset, 145–46
  with two-piece gusset, 146
Knee patches, 333, 335
Knife-edge pillows, 400–1
Knit fabrics (knits), 75–76
  bonded, 76
  double, 75
  knitting process, 16
  shrinking to cut, 56
  stretch, 75
  tricot, 75
Knitted garments, care of, 341
Knotted fringe, 268

Knots
French, 246
for hand sewing, 95–96

L

Labels, reading, special fabric
finishes and, 20–21
Lace, 72–73
applying to a hemmed edge, 264
applying to a raw edge, 263–64
fabrics, 72–73
inserts (bands), 264
lining, 72, 88
Lapped seam, 105
Lap placket, continuous, 154–56,
312
Large circle, as pattern marking,
23
Lazy daisy stitch, 245–46
Leather and leather-like fabrics,
77–78
See also Suede
Length
See Hems; specific garments,
parts of garments
Linen, 17
characteristics, care, and uses of,
17
Lining, 85–87, 88
for coverlets, 384
for draperies, 365–69
for men's wear, 207
for tailored garments, 276–77,
288–89
Lipstick stains, removing, 343
Loops, belt
See Belt loops

M

Machine basting, 98–99
Machine buttonholes, 198

Machine overcast seam, 110
Machine-picoted seam, 108
Machine sewing
See Sewing machine; specific
garments, parts of gar-
ments, techniques
Machine-stitched hem, 178
Make-overs
See Recycling (remodeling)
clothes
Man-made fabrics, 16, 17–20
See also specific kinds
Marking
fabric for cutting, 59–61
hems, 172–73
supplies for, 47, 172
Materials
See Fabrics
Maternity patterns, 6
Measuring
buttonholes, 47
for curtains and draperies,
351–52
how to take measurements, 5–6
children, 294–95, 296
men and boys, 302–3
for slipcovers, 387
supplies for, 46
Men and boys, sewing for, 301–21
construction points for classic
shirt, 308–15
construction points for pants,
315–21
fabrics, 306–7
measurements for, 302–3
notions, 307
pattern adjustments, 303–6
pattern sizes, 301, 303
pressing pants, 301
seams and seam finishes, 307–8
Mending, 332–37
avoiding zipper trouble, 332–33
darning, 333–34

Mending (*cont'd*)
  with mending tape, 333
  patching, 335–36
  pockets, 337
  reinforcing, 334–35
  reweaving, 333
  rips and tears, 333
  turning collars and cuffs, 336–37
Mending tape, 333
Mercerization, 20
Metallic-fiber fabrics, 19–20, 78
  characteristics, care, and uses
    of, 19–20
Mildew stains, removing, 343
Misses patterns, 4, 10–11
Miss Petite patterns, 4
Mock French seam, 107
Modacrylics, 18
  characteristics, care, and uses of,
    18
Muslin lining, 89
Muslin reinforcement, for tailored
    garments, 281–82

N

Nail polish stains, removing, 344
Nap, fabric with, 14, 71–72
  cutting, 14–15, 71
  See also specific kinds
Natural fibers, 16, 17
Neckline
  darts at, 118
  finishes, 131–35
    bias-faced V, 131–32
    front-slashed facing, 132–33
    shaped neck facing, 134–35
    See also Collars
  in fitting dress, 93–94
  and pattern alteration, 38–39
  and pattern selection, 8
  See also Collars
Needle board, 66

Needles, 48
  choosing, kinds, 51, 52, 53, 76
Notches, 23
Notions, for men's wear, 307
Nylon, 18–19, 20
  characteristics, care, and uses
    of, 18–19, 20
  for linings, 88
  tape closure, 210

O

Oiling sewing machine, 48–49
Oil stains, removing, 343, 344
Olefins, 19
  characteristics, care, and uses
    of, 19
One-way fabrics, 14–15, 71
  cutting, 14, 15, 71
Organdy, 293
  for linings, 88
  sewing for children and, 293
Outline stitch, 244
  in smocking, 253
Outseam, adjusting in men's pants,
    305
Overcasting, 102
  quick, 103
Overcast seam, 110
  machine, 110
Overhanding, 103
Overhand tucks, 124

P

Pad stitching
  to shape roll of collar, 283–84
  for tailored garments, 279–80
Pants
  altering pattern, 39–43
    men and boys, 303 ff.
  altering ready-to-wear, 339
  buying patterns and, 10–11

Pants (cont'd)
  fitting, 94
  knee patches, 333, 335
  men's, 303 ff., 315–21
    adjusting crotch depth, 304–5
    adjusting outseam, 305
    pockets, 319
    pressing, 321
    waistband, 319–21
    zippers, 307, 315–19
  repairing pockets, 337
Passementeries, 265–66
Patch-bound buttonholes, 188–92
Patching, 335–36
  elbow and knee, 333, 335–36
  iron-on, 333
Patch pocket, 212–14
Patchwork, 260–62
Patterns, 3–24
  for accessories, 322
  altering, 25–43
    See also Alteration of patterns
  buying, 3–24
    ease in, 6
    how to take measurements,
      5–6
    sizing, 4–6
  for children, 293 ff.
  and cutting fabrics, 56–59
  envelope, 9–15
  fabrics and, 6, 9, 10–21
  meaning of markings, 23
  for men and boys, 301 ff.
  recycling (remodeling) and, 345
  selecting the most becoming, 6–9
  for tailored garments, 274–76,
    279
  understanding and using, 21–24
Permanent care fabric labels,
  20–21
Permanent-press fabrics, 20, 73–74
Peter Pan collar, 329
Pile fabrics, 14, 19, 71
  cutting, 14–15, 71
  deep, 81–82
  See also specific kinds
Pillows, decorative, 400–3
  box-edge, 402–3
  knife-edge, 400–1
Pin basting, 98
Pinch pleats, draperies with,
  358–59
Pincushion, 45
Pinked seam, 109–10
Pinking shears, 45
Pins, 45
Pin tucks, 121–22
Piped buttonhole, 192–94
Piped seam, 108
Piping, 239
  corded, 239
  covering, 239
Placket, continuous lap, 154–56,
  312
Plaids, 12, 14, 67–70
  basting, 70
  cutting, 14–15
  matching, 69
  types of, 67–68
Plain hem, as sleeve finish, 151
Plain seam, 104
Pleated headings, 356–60
  box, 359
  cartridge, 359
  pinch, 358–59
  tape for, 359
Pleated slipcovers, 394–95
  boxed, 394
  group, 394–95
  inverted, 395
Pleated valance, 371
Pleater tape, 359
Pleats, 124–30
  accordion, 127
  box, 126
  fan, 127

Pleats (*cont'd*)
  hem in, 180
  inverted, 126–27
  kick, 127–30
  in pattern alteration, 27
  side, 125–26
  sunburst, 127
Pockets, 212–21
  children's patterns and, 297
  men's pants, 319
  patch, 212–14
  side seam, 214–15
  slot, 215–18
  trouser, repairing, 337
  welt, 218–21
Point presser, 65–66
Polyesters, 19, 20
  characteristics, care, and uses of, 19, 20
  for linings, 87
  shrinking to cut, 56
Pounding block, 65
Preparation for sewing
  See Getting ready to sew
Press cloth, 48
Pressing, 63–66
  in care of clothes, 341
  men's pants, 321
  in preparation for cutting, 56
  supplies, 47, 64–66
  techniques and aids, 63–66
Pre-teen patterns, 4
Print designs (prints)
  allover, 15
    cutting, 15
    for linings, 87
  border, 72
  selecting patterns and, 9, 15
Puffed sleeve, short, 147–48

Q

Quick overcasting, 103

Quick rolled hem, 177
Quilting, 255–57
  trapunto (Italian), 256–57
Quilts, patchwork, 260, 261–62

R

Rag dolls, 330
Raglan sleeves, 147
Raincoats, 276
Rayons, 17–18
  characteristics, care, and uses of, 17–18
  for linings, 87
Ready-to-wear clothing, alterations in
  See Alteration of ready-to-wear clothing
Recycling (remodeling) clothes, 344–46
  cutting, 345
  piecing material, 345
  preparing material, 345
  selecting patterns, 345
  suggestions for, 346
Reinforcing, 334–35
Reweaving, 333
Ribbon facing, 170–71
Rickrack, 271–72
Right-side basting, 99–100
Rips and tears, mending, 333–34
  See also Mending
Rolled hems, 176–77
Rolled seam, 111
Roman fabric shades, 379–81
Round shoulders, altering pattern for, 33
Ruffling (ruffles), 230–33
  circular, 232
  curtains with, 362–64
  double, 232
  dust, 384–86
  with heading, 232–33

Ruler, use of, 46
Running stitch, 101
Rust stains, removing, 344

S

Saddle stitch, 249
Satin stitches, 243
Saw-tooth edge, facing for, 164
Scalloped edge, facing for, 163–64
Scalloped headings, for curtains
        and draperies, 360–61
Scallops, 246–47
    to bind, 238
Scarves, 328
Scissors, use of, 45
Seam binding
    for hem finish, 175
    tight sleeve opening faced with,
        153
Seam line, 24
Seam roll, 65
Seams and seam finishes, 103–14
    bound, 111–12
    corded, 108
    for curtains and draperies, 353
    double-stitched, 112
    edgestitched, 110–11
    flat felled, 105
    French, 106–7
    Hong Kong, 112–13
    knit fabrics, 76
    lace fabrics, 72
    lapped, 105
    leather and suede, 77–78
    machine overcast, 110
    machine-picoted, 108
    men's wear, 303, 305, 307–8
    mock French, 107
    overcast, 110
    pinked, 109–10
    piped, 108
    plain, 104

    in recycling clothes, 345
    rolled, 111
    sheer fabrics, 73
    slipcovers, 392–93
    slot, 106
    stitched and pinked, 110
    strap, 106
    taped, 109
    topstitched, 104
    tricks with, 113
    types of, 109–14
    upholsterer's, 108–9
    ways of finishing seams, 104–14
    welt, 105
Seed stitch, 248
Self fringe, 267–68
Sequined fabrics, 78
Sequins, 272
Set-in kick pleats, 130
Set-in sleeves, 148–49
Sewing machine, 45, 48–51
    cleaning, 48
    knowing possibilities of, 49–51
    needles, 51–53
    oiling, 48–49
    use and care of, 48–51
    See also specific garments, parts
        of garments, stitches,
        techniques
Shades, fabric, 374–81
    Austrian, 376–79
    Roman, 379–81
Shaped collar, faced and inter-
        faced, 135–36
Shaped facing, 158
    neck, 134–35
Shawls, 326–27
Shears
    dressmaker, 45
    pinking, 45
    See also Scissors
Sheer fabrics, 73, 88
    cutting, 73

Sheer fabrics (cont'd)
  darts, 73
  double bias binding, 73
  hems, 73
  seams, 73
Shell tucks, 123
Shirring, 228–30
  curtains with, 361–62
  elastic thread for, 229–30
  by machine, 229
  using stay under, 229
Shirts
  classic, men's, 308–15
    adjusting sleeve length, 306
    collar, 309–12
    cuffs, 313–14
    stitching sleeve to, 314–15
    yoke, 308
    turning collars and cuffs of,
        336–37
Shoes, care of, 341
Shoulders
  altering patterns for, 31–33
  darts at, 118
  and selecting patterns, 9
Shrinking fabrics, 56
Shrink-resistant fabrics, 20
Side pleats, 125–26
Side seam pocket, 214–15
Silks, 17
  characteristics, care, and uses
      of, 17
  lining, 87
  underlining, 85
Single kick pleat, 127–29
Size
  buying ready-to-wear clothes,
      337–38
  figure type and, 4
  patterns and, 4–6
    children, 293–94
    men and boys, 301
  taking measurements and, 5–6

See also Measuring
Skirt marker, 46, 172
Skirts
  darts, 119, 120
  lengthening ready-to-wear, 338
  letting out ready-to-wear,
      338–39
  lining, 85–87
  pattern alterations, 28, 35
  pattern buying and, 6
  pleated
    See Pleats
  in putting dress together, 92 ff.
  shortening ready-to-wear, 338
  slipcover, 393–95
  taking in ready-to-wear, 338
  underlining, 85
  See also Dresses; Hems; Waist-
      line
Slashed neckline, straight collar
      with, 139–41
Slashed opening, facing for,
      162–63
Slashed placket, zipper in, 203–4
Sleeve board, 48, 64
Sleeve finishes, 151–56
  band cuff, 154–55
  cuff applied with bias facing,
      152–53
  plain hem, 151
  tight opening faced with seam
      binding, 153
  turnback cuffs, 151–52
  See also Cuffs
Sleeves, 144–51
  adjusting in men's shirt, 306
  altering pattern, 35–38
  batwing, 146
  cap, 144
  darts at, 119
  dolman, 146
  elbow patches, 333, 335–36
  finishes, 151–56

Sleeves (*cont'd*)
See also Sleeve finishes
gathered (short, puffed), 147–48
how to set in, 149–51
kimono, 144–46
men's shirt, classic, 312–15
in putting dress together, 92 ff.
raglan, 147
set-in, 148–49
setting in tailored garments,
285–87
styles, 144–49
See also Cuffs; Shoulders
Slip basting, 99–100
Slipcovers, 386–400
for couches, 398–400
for cushions, 396–97
cutting and pinning fabric,
387–92
details for construction, 392–99
fabrics for, 386 ff.
for furniture odds and ends, 400
seams, 392–93
skirts and skirt finishes, 393–95
stitching, 393
zippers, 395–96
Sloping shoulders, altering pattern
for, 33
Slot pocket, 215–18
for tailored garments, 217–18
Slot seam, 106
Small circle, as pattern marking,
23
Smocking, 252–55
cable stitch, 253–54
honeycomb stitch, 254–55
outline stitch, 253
quilting, 255–57
trapunto (Italian) quilting,
256–57
Snaps, 209
hammer-on, 209
Sofas, slipcovers for, 386 ff.

Spanda fabric, 19
characteristics, care, and uses of,
19
Spoke fagoting, 252
Spot-resistant fabrics, 20
Spreading, to alter patterns, 26
Square, as pattern marking, 23
Square shoulders, altering pattern
for, 33
Stain-resistant fabrics, 20
Stains, removing, 342–44
chewing gum, 342–43
coffee, 343
egg, 343
fat, 343
fruit, 343
general directions, 342
grease, 343
ink, 343
lipstick, 343
mildew, 343
nail polish, 344
oil, 344
rust, 344
tar, 344
water spots, 344
Stay stitching, 62
Stitched and pinked seam, 110
Stitches, 95–103
basic, 101–3
backstitch, 101–2
combination, 102
overcasting, 102
overhanding, 103
quick overcasting, 103
running, 101
decorative (embroidery),
242–62
appliqué, 257–58
blanket, 246
bullion, 248–49
cable, 249, 253–54
catch, 244–45

Stitches (*cont'd*)
   chain, 245
   couching, 248
   cross-, 244
   drawn work, 249–51
   embroidery, machine, 259–60
   fagoting, 251–52
   feather, 247–48
   French knots, 246
   hemstitching, 249–51
   herringbone, 244–45
   honeycomb, 254–55
   lazy daisy, 245–46
   outline, 244, 253
   patchwork, 260–62
   quilting, 255–57
   saddle, 249
   satin, 243
   scallops, 246–47
   seed, 248
   smocking, 252–55
Stockings, care of, 341
Stoles, 326–27
Straight collar, 328–29
   with slashed neckline, 139–41
Straightening fabrics, 55–56
Strap seam, 106
Stretch fabrics, 74–75
Striped fabrics, 12, 14, 70–71
   cutting, 14, 15
   for linings, 87
Stuffed toys, 330–31
Suede, 77–78
   accessories, 323
   patches, 335–36
Suits
   buying patterns, 6, 274–76
   tailoring, 274–92
      facing, 277, 284–85
      hemming, 288
      interfacing, 277, 280–81,
         282–83
      lining, 276–77, 288–89

   making, 278–92
   material, 274–77
   muslin reinforcement, 281–82
   pad-stitching, 279–80, 283–84
   patterns, 274–76, 279
   setting in sleeves, 285–87
   underarm shields, 292
   underlining, 277
   See also specific parts of
      garments
Sunburst pleats, 127
Swags, 369, 372–74
Sweaters, care of, 341

T

Tables, slipcovers for, 400
Tailored bow, 273
Tailored buttonhole, 197–98
Tailored collar, convertible, 141–
   42
Tailoring (tailored garments),
   274–92
   facing, 277, 284–85
   interfacing, 277, 280–81,
      282–83
   interlining, 277, 289–92
   lining, 276–77, 288–89
   making coat or jacket, 278–92
   materials, 274–77
   muslin reinforcement, 281–82
   pad-stitching, 279–80
   patterns, 274–76, 279
   setting in sleeves, 285–87
   slot pocket for, 217–18
   supplies, 278
   underarm shields, 292
   underlining, 277
   See also specific garments, parts
      of garments, sewing
      techniques
Tailor's chalk, 47, 59–60
Tailor's ham, 64

Tailor's hem, 175
Tailor's tacks, 59
Taking care of clothing
    See Caring for clothes
Tape
    gripper, 379
    pleater, 359
Tape closures, 210
Taped seam, 109
Tape measure, 46
Tapering, in pattern alteration, 27–28
Tar stains, removing, 344
Tassels, 268–69
Tears and rips, mending, 333–34
    See also Mending
Teddy bears, 330
Teen-Boys patterns, 301
Thigh, in altering pants pattern, 39, 41–42
Thimble, 45
Thread, 45
    belt loops, 226
    choosing, 51, 52, 53
    elastic, for shirring, 229–30
Throw bedspreads, 383
Tiebacks, curtain, 364
Tie belt, 223
Toddlers, pattern sizes for, 293
Top and pants, pattern envelope and, 10–11
Topstitched seam, 104
Toys, 330–31
Tracing wheel, 47, 59, 61
Trapunto quilting, 256–57
Triacetate, 18
    characteristics, care, and uses of, 18
Triangle, as pattern marking, 23
Tricot knits, 75
Trimmings (trimming tricks), 263–73

arrowhead, 266–67
beading, 272–73
braid, 265–66
embroidered edgings, 268–70
knotted fringe, 268
lace, 263–65
passementeries, 265–66
rickrack, 271–72
self fringe, 267–68
sequins, 272
tailored bow, 273
tassels, 268–69
Trousers
    See Pants
True bias, 53
Tubing, 240–41
    bias cord loops, 241
    corded, 240–41
Tucks, 120–24
    cross tucking, 122
    curved, 122
    dart, 120–21
    overhand, 124
    in pattern alteration, 26
    pin, 121–22
    shell, 123
Turnback cuffs, 151–52
    cut separately, 152
    cut with sleeve, 151
Turned and stitched hem, 176
Tweeds, underlining, 85

U

Underarm seam, darts at, 118
Underarm shields, 292
Underlining, 84–85, 88
    tailored garments, 277
Understitching, facing, 161
Uneven basting, 99
Upholsterer's seam, 108–9

V

Valances, 369–74
  gathered, 370
  pleated, 270
  ruffled curtain with, 364
  swags, 372–74
Velcro tape closure, 210
Velvet, 14, 71
Velvet board, 66, 71
Velveteen, 293
  for tailored garments, 276
Vests, 327–28
V neckline, bias-faced, 131–32

W

Waistband, 168–71
  men's pants, 319–21
  pattern pieces, 22
Waistline
  altering patterns, 34–35, 305,
    319–21
    pants, 39, 41, 305
  dart at, 119
  finishes, 168–71
  measuring, 5
  men's pants, 305, 319–21
  and selecting patterns, 8
  See also Waistband
Wash-and-wear fabrics, 20, 73–74
Waterproofing, 20
Water-repellent fabrics, 20
Water-spot stains, removing, 344
Weaving fabrics, 16
Weight, and selecting fabrics, 8, 9
Weights, for curtains and draperies,
    354–55
Welt pocket, 218–21
Welt seam, 105–6
Whipped hem, 177
Windows, decorating, 348–81
  curtains and draperies, 351–69

  hardware for, 349–50
  shades, fabric, 374–81
  valances, 369–74
Women's patterns, 4
Woolen fabrics (woolens)
  characteristics, care, and uses
    of, 17
  linings, 88, 89
  recycling (remodeling), 344–45
  shrinking to cut, 56
  for tailored garments, 274–76
Worked buttonhole, 195–98
  tailored, 197–98
Wrinkle-resistant fabrics, 20
  See also Permanent-press
    fabrics

Y

Yardstick, use of, 46
Yoke, for men's classic shirt,
    308–9
Young Junior/Teen patterns, 4

Z

Zigzag sewing machine, 48, 51
Zippers, 198–208
  avoiding trouble with, 332–33
  care of, 207–8
  center seam application, 203
  fly-front opening, 315–19
  hand application, 205
  invisible application, 205–7
  lapped application, 199
  length of opening for, 199
  men's pants, 307, 315–19
  preparing placket, 199–201
  replacing, 207
  in a slashed placket, 203–4
  in slipcovers, 395–96